M000289385

David Harvey

David Harvey is among the most influential Marxist thinkers of the last half century. This book offers a lucid and authoritative introduction to his work, with a structure designed to reflect the enduring topics and insights that serve to unify Harvey's writings over a long period of time.

Harvey's writings have exerted huge influence within the social sciences and the humanities. In addition, his work now commands a global readership among Left political activists and those interested in current world affairs. Harvey's central preoccupation is capitalism and the impacts of its growth-obsessed, contradictory dynamics. His name is synonymous with key analytical concepts like 'the spatial fix' and 'accumulation by dispossession'. This critical introduction to his thought is an essential companion for both new and more experienced readers. The critique of capitalism is one of the most important undertakings of our time, and Harvey's work offers powerful tools to help us see why a 'softer' capitalism is insufficient and a post-capitalist future is necessary.

This book is an important resource for scholars and graduate students in geography, politics and many other disciplines across the social sciences and humanities.

Noel Castree is Professor of Geography at the University of Manchester and Professor of Society and Environment at the University of Technology, Sydney. He has published numerous articles and chapters about Harvey's Marxism and co-edited *David Harvey: A Critical Reader* (2006).

Greig Charnock is Senior Lecturer in International Politics at the University of Manchester, where he teaches the politics of globalisation and Marxist critical theory. He has published several articles that engage directly with Harvey's writings about dialectics, crisis and urbanisation. He is the co-author of *The Limits to Capital in Spain* (2014), which draws upon Harvey's work to explain the roots and fall-out of crisis in Southern Europe.

Brett Christophers is Professor of Human Geography, Uppsala University. He is the author or co-author of seven books including, most recently, *Rentier Capitalism* (2020), *Economic Geography: A Critical Introduction* (2018, with Trevor Barnes) and *The New Enclosure: The Appropriation of Public Land in Neoliberal Britain* (2018).

'An indispensable guide to the life and work of one of the greatest Marxist intellectuals of his generation. The authors provide a far-reaching overview of Harvey's intellectual project and the way it has developed over time, which allows the reader to build a much deeper relationship with Harvey's oeuvre than that they might gain by reading a few key texts from within a specific discipline – much in the same way that Harvey's familiarity with Marx has made his *Introduction to Capital* the most popular accompaniment to Marx's work.'

Grace Blakeley, *author of* Stolen: How to Save the World from Financialisation

'I arrived at the Johns Hopkins University in 1997. By 1999 I was co-teaching a graduate seminar with David Harvey on Gramsci and Keynes. I went in there as a recovered Marxist. I came out having recovered my Marxism. That's what Harvey will do to you.'

Mark Blyth, *Brown University, USA, author of* Austerity: The History of a Dangerous Idea *and co-author of* Angrynomics

'No living intellectual has done more to reinvigorate Marxism than David Harvey. True to its spirit, he has insisted on the unbreakable link between scientific research and political practice. Here, for the first time, we have a survey of Harvey's entire oeuvre – but not a mere summary or for-dummies: Castree, Charnock and Christophers engage critically with all the issues swirling through his work, down to the question of how to change the world. In wonderfully accessible prose, they catch a genius in motion, always attuned to the latest developments in capitalism. This will be a book to chew on, for Harvey aficionados and newcomers alike, and for everyone grappling with the unbearable contradictions of this world order.'

Andreas Malm, *Lund University, Sweden, author of* Fossil Capital, The Progress of This Storm, *and* How to Blow Up a Pipeline

David Harvey

A Critical Introduction to His Thought

NOEL CASTREE, GREIG CHARNOCK AND
BRETT CHRISTOPHERS

Routledge
Taylor & Francis Group
LONDON AND NEW YORK

First published 2023
by Routledge
4 Park Square, Milton Park, Abingdon, Oxon, OX14 4RN

and by Routledge
605 Third Avenue, New York, NY 10158

Routledge is an imprint of the Taylor & Francis Group, an informa business

© 2023 Noel Castree, Greig Charnock and Brett Christophers

The right of Noel Castree, Greig Charnock and Brett Christophers to be identified as authors of this work has been asserted in accordance with sections 77 and 78 of the Copyright, Designs and Patents Act 1988.

All rights reserved. No part of this book may be reprinted or reproduced or utilised in any form or by any electronic, mechanical, or other means, now known or hereafter invented, including photocopying and recording, or in any information storage or retrieval system, without permission in writing from the publishers.

Trademark notice: Product or corporate names may be trademarks or registered trademarks, and are used only for identification and explanation without intent to infringe.

British Library Cataloguing-in-Publication Data
A catalogue record for this book is available from the British Library

Library of Congress Cataloging-in-Publication Data
Names: Castree, Noel, 1968- author. | Charnock, Greig, author. |
Christophers, Brett, 1971- author.
Title: David Harvey : a critical introduction to his thought /
Noel Castree, Greig Charnock and Brett Christophers.
Description: Milton Park, Abingdon, Oxon ; New York, NY : Routledge, 2023. |
Includes bibliographical references and index.
Identifiers: LCCN 2022026570 (print) | LCCN 2022026571 (ebook) |
ISBN 9780367136970 (hardback) | ISBN 9780367136987 (paperback) |
ISBN 9780429028120 (ebook)
Subjects: LCSH: Harvey, David, 1935- | Economic geography. |
Geography--Philosophy. | Capitalism.
Classification: LCC HF1025 .C338 2023 (print) | LCC HF1025 (ebook) |
DDC 330.9--dc23/eng/20220628
LC record available at https://lccn.loc.gov/2022026570
LC ebook record available at https://lccn.loc.gov/2022026571

ISBN: 978-0-367-13697-0 (hbk)
ISBN: 978-0-367-13698-7 (pbk)
ISBN: 978-0-429-02812-0 (ebk)

DOI: 10.4324/9780429028120

Typeset in Dante and Avenir
by KnowledgeWorks Global Ltd.

David Harvey (1935–).
Drawn by Tone Bjordam.

All that is solid melts into air, all that is holy is profaned ... The bourgeoisie has through its exploitation of the world market given a cosmopolitan character to production and consumption in every country ... In place of the old wants ... we find new wants, requiring for their satisfaction the products of distant lands ... In place of the old ... seclusion and self-sufficiency, we have intercourse in every direction.

Karl Marx and Friedrich Engels (1848). *The Communist Manifesto.*

In its hunt for profit, [capitalism] will travel any distance, endure any hardship, shack-up with the most obnoxious of companions, suffer the most abominable humiliations ... and cheerfully betray its next of kin ... It thrives on bursting bounds and slaying sacred cows ... Its law is the flouting of all limits ... In its sublime ambition and extravagant transgressions, it makes its most shaggily anarchic critics look staid and suburban.

Terry Eagleton (2003). *After Theory*, p. 19.

Changes in ideas and values ... result from the work done by writers, scholars, public intellectuals, social activists, and participants in social media. It seems insignificant or peripheral until very different outcomes emerge from transformed assumptions about who and what matters, who should be heard and believed, who has rights.

Rebecca Solnit (2016). *Hope in the Dark*, pp. xiii–xiv.

In order to change the world ... we have to understand it ... Active reflection on our understandings ... [and] the struggle to make Marxian concepts both plain and hegemonic ... are as important activities as active engagement on the barricades. That is why Marx wrote *Capital*. And that is why I can write these words.

David Harvey (1985a). *The Urbanization of Capital*, p. x.

Contents

List of Figures

List of Tables

Acknowledgements

We would like to thank Andrew Mould, our editor at Routledge, for inviting us to write this book. Egle Zigaite usefully badgered us to put fingers to keyboards when there was a risk this book would never get started, let alone be finished. The four anonymous reviewers of the original prospectus offered us nutritious food for thought. We thank the readers of the first draft – Eric Sheppard and Melissa W. Wright – for their helpful comments and criticisms. Max Gustafson kindly granted us permission to reproduce his 'Hard Times' cartoon. Nick Scarle did his usual expert job in ensuring the visual aids look good. We are also lucky to have crossed paths with visual artist Tone Bjordam, whose wonderful drawing of David Harvey appears after the title page.

This book was written in three countries in rather different circumstances as the global pandemic unfolded. Noel spent 2021 and early 2022 writing in relative isolation, except for virtual interactions with colleagues in Sydney, Manchester and elsewhere. He thanks Jamie Woodward, Gordon Waitt, Sarah Hall, Nick Fowler and David Demeritt, in particular, for good conversations that punctuated solitary home working. His interactions with Ana Lambert Grossi and Candice Delaney also proved to be mentally stimulating. He dedicates this book to Felicity and Tom, whose adult lives will be shaped profoundly by the relentless, omnivorous dynamics of capitalism near and far. Greig dedicates this book to Cath, Ben and Alex; also, to Ramon Ribera-Fumaz, who encouraged him to enrol on Noel's inaugural graduate seminar on David Harvey's work back in 2001. He is grateful to Tom Purcell, Stuart Shields, Guido Starosta and Japhy Wilson, who have all been willing participants in regular and long conversations about Harvey's work over the years. Finally, Brett dedicates this book to his family, Agneta, Elliot, Oliver and Emilia.

Introduction

1

This book introduces readers to the thought of David Harvey (born 1935). Harvey is a world-famous intellectual and among the few Marxist thinkers known widely in academia (where he continues to work), in activist circles and among sections of the public seriously interested in current affairs. A geographer by training, and revered by many in his chosen discipline, his name is synonymous with key analytical concepts such as the 'spatial fix', 'time-space compression', 'accumulation by dispossession' and 'the right to the city'. Now in his ninth decade, Harvey remains an indefatigable critic of contemporary capitalism. This is doubly remarkable: not only is Harvey vigorous at an age when most people would opt for a quiet life, but he has kept the flame of Marxist thought alive during decades when Marxism was frequently declared dead and buried. This involves uncommon tenacity and a willingness to be unfashionable (even disliked).

The author of over twenty books and a very large number of other published pieces (e.g. book chapters, peer-reviewed articles, commentaries and book reviews), Harvey's *oeuvre* is formidable. He also has a website and is a frequent podcaster. Only the most dedicated reader would be able to survey his works across a sixty-year career that comprises a relatively short pre-Marxist phase and a very long Marxist one. While few people have the time or energy to make sense of the entire body of his writings, many of his readers nonetheless want to know more. As we can attest, reading a single book or article by Harvey tends to leave a lasting impression. The present text is not intended as a substitute for reading (more of) David Harvey's work first-hand. But it is intended to help new readers, and even

DOI: 10.4324/9780429028120-1

more experienced ones, make sense of the larger body of writing Harvey has authored during his long career.

This book seeks to present Harvey's written corpus faithfully on the basis of our long familiarity with it. While some mention is made of Harvey's pre-Marxist years, we focus squarely on his work as an 'historical-geographical materialist'. After all, it's as a Marxist that Harvey has made his name outside Geography, the discipline he still calls his own (despite not working in a geography department for many years now). This book is a *critical* introduction in that we seek to acknowledge and assess various claims made about the shortcomings of Harvey's work. These critical claims have issued from several quarters over the years, and Harvey has engaged directly with the majority of them.[1] We consider the critiques at various points in the book, but especially in the second half, and venture a few of our own. As readers will see, we're not only fans of Harvey's major writings but are also persuaded by many – though certainly not all – of his ripostes to his critics. Even when venturing his least secure formulations, we believe that Harvey is largely 'good to think with'. In other words, while we avoid hagiography, in the end we offer a sympathetic assessment of his contributions to human understanding.

Despite his high profile in the social sciences and humanities and his global reputation outside academia, there's currently no advanced introduction to Harvey's thought. If one compares this to the likes of Noam Chomsky, Judith Butler, Jacques Derrida, Michel Foucault, Anthony Giddens or Jürgen Habermas, it's a glaring absence. True, there's one edited collection that offers a deep dive into Harvey's work (Castree and Gregory, 2006). But it's now dated in crucial respects and lacks the coherence of an authored assessment of Harvey's complete body of published writing. Likewise, though he's published a number of 'greatest hits' collections (e.g. *The Ways of the World* [2016]), these books lack the sort of integrity possessed by an authored work. Finally, it is the case that Harvey's published a few insightful autobiographical essays over the years. Yet these career sketches, while very interesting, do not delve into the substance of his books and other major texts. In *David Harvey: A Critical Introduction to His Thought* by contrast, we attend to both the context *and* content of his writings. The result, we hope, is a fairly complete picture that allows readers to understand how and why Harvey's thought has unfolded in the ways it has.

Given the enormous number of things Harvey has published, it's important to ensure coverage of major publications while avoiding a linear narrative organised according to decades (the 1970s, 1980s, 1990s etc.) that takes each major published work in turn. Such a narrative would lead to undue repetition. A better approach is thematic rather than temporal. It's the approach we favour here. To use one of Harvey's favoured metaphors, we make 'cuts' into his work taken as a whole so as to reveal the bone and marrow. The book's structure is designed to reflect the *enduring* topics and insights that serve to unify Harvey's writings over a long period of time. And make no mistake: Harvey is a massively consistent thinker whose work is deeply anchored in the later writings of Karl Marx. This is not to say his worldview hasn't evolved, and the chapters to come will ensure innovations and modifications in his work are described, contextualised and assessed. But it is to say that the core concepts animating Harvey's *oeuvre* have stood the test of time very well (which is why he refuses to relinquish them).

The novelty of this book is to elucidate these patterns of consistency, and change, across a huge body of published writing. This has been no small task. Much of Harvey's work is very complex – as with books such as *Social Justice and the City*, *The Limits to Capital* and *Cosmopolitanism and the Geographies of Freedom*, to take three examples. This being so, an additional contribution of this book is to simplify things just enough to make this complexity intelligible to a variety of readers. Throughout, while we quote liberally from Harvey's many writings, we also inevitably gloss and summarise time and again and ask readers to trust that our interpretations are faithful not fanciful. We hope readers with some expertise in Harvey's work will appreciate how we have distilled the essentials of his work, while 'adding value' here and there through some of our independent insights (e.g. in Chapter 8).

A note here for younger readers of this book: while works published by Harvey in the 1980s, 1990s and early 2000s might seem like 'history', we maintain (as, of course, does Harvey himself) that their central insights remain relevant in 2023 and beyond. A note to all readers: the fullness of Harvey's approach to capitalism is only fully evident at the end of this book, so it's worth re-visiting the early chapters after a first reading of the book in its entirety. That way a better – that is, holistic and dialectical – understanding can be achieved. We have included numerous forward and backward references in the chapters so as to knit things together as tightly as we can.

We've sought to write this text in an accessible manner. To that end, we largely avoid jargon. Throughout, when we use the terms 'capital' and 'capitalism', we're describing a hyper-complex, evolving mode of production that no one – not even the wealthiest people on Earth – is in control of. 'The system' is a driverless juggernaut of shifting size and shape: a macro-phenomenon powered by billions of everyday micro-decisions and actions. We hope this book can be read by degree students studying for social science and humanities degrees where Harvey's work features in various modules. We also hope that people interested in world affairs, and who are curious to know more about Harvey's work and the enduring value of Marxism, might wish to read this book. While many would regard Harvey as a 'radical' thinker, what strikes us is how radical it is to *deny* the key messages that Harvey's Marxism seeks to teach us. As another leading Marxist, Terry Eagleton, once noted: 'It's the hard-nosed pragmatists who behave as though the World Bank and café latte will be with us for the next two millennia who are the real dreamers, and those who are open to the as yet unfigurable future who are the true realists' (2005: np).

We live in a twenty-first-century world that's at once wondrous and deeply troubling. At the time of writing, the COVID-19 pandemic is still dominating the daily news. In geopolitical and geoeconomic terms, the United States' power continues to wane, the Russian military has invaded Ukraine, while China's rise seems inexorable (albeit hardly problem-free). Right-wing populism is evident in a great many countries, so too persistent racism, sexism and economic poverty. Civil wars abound, as do struggles for human rights, social justice and environmental protection. Every single day, refugees across the globe take huge (and often fatal) risks to escape their home-places. In a world of enormous food abundance, we still witness starving people and chronic malnourishment. Millions of humans receive nothing like a living wage each week. Biblical floods, wildfires and heatwaves are afflicting several continents as we type these words. Species extinctions proceed apace, while the polar ice caps shrink, and coral reefs suffer huge bleaching events. For all our cleverness and capacity for care, we humans are hugely destructive – so much so that we're poised to take the Earth into a new geological epoch that may make life inhospitable for the majority of people and countless non-human species and ecosystems.

But, as Harvey rightly argues (following Marx), this is not an inevitable outcome of some universal drive embedded in our genes. Instead, many of the problems in our world are caused by an economic system that's anything but natural. Capitalism is a particular way of defining, creating and distributing wealth that first emerged in the eighteenth-century. It long ago outgrew its regional origins and today permeates all aspects of life at all points of the compass. While a human creation, capitalism confronts us a system whose rules and impacts most of us feel compelled to obey. To study it requires political economy, not mainstream economics: questions of power, social relations and inequality are central, and so too is a broader appreciation of how economic affairs bleed into pretty much everything else in life.

David Harvey's writings help us understand why capitalism is so promiscuous, how it structures people's thought and practice, what impacts it has on the world and what's required to move beyond the 'iron law' of growth for growth's sake. If we're to change the world for the better, we must first comprehend it. David Harvey's many publications reveal the forces inhibiting and enabling a progressive politics in our time (though as we note in Chapter 8, he says too little about the precise *content* of such politics). To live well on this Earth, we have to reckon with these forces rather than settle for business-as-usual or else fret about our own seeming impotence. In practical terms, that reckoning will involve extraordinary efforts of political tenacity, global coordination and mutual understanding among very different people. For Marxists, the tragedy of our age may be that we know broadly what we need to do but lack the wherewithal to seriously reform, let alone end, the rule of capital.

Note

1. Though he has rarely engaged in debates about the late Marx's work, which remain lively in some academic circles, as the recent exchange between Moseley (2021) and Hahnel (2021) demonstrates.

2 David Harvey

Geographer, Marxist and public intellectual

The early decades: the making and unmaking of a 'spatial scientist'; From 'a Marxist of sorts' to a Marxist geographer; A geographical Marxist; Back to the United States of America; Promoting Marxism beyond the university; Making sense of David Harvey's Marxism; Conclusion

This chapter presents an overview of David Harvey's life and work. It sets the scene for all the chapters to follow. It offers insight into the why, what, when and where of Harvey's decisions to research, write and communicate in the ways that he has. It places a particular emphasis on his books. As you will discover, during his long career Harvey has been shaped by – and sought to shape – three things above all else. The first is the discipline of university-level Geography, in which he was trained in the 1950s before going on to be an agenda-setting practitioner. Remarkably, Harvey had a formative influence on Geography not once but twice: first as a 'spatial scientist', then later (from 1972 onwards) as among the very first Marxist geographers. The second reference point for Harvey's work is academic Marxism in the wider social sciences and humanities. After 1945, Marxist thinkers in the West became concentrated in universities. They used their academic freedom to significantly develop Marxist analysis of a fast-changing world. However, with the notable exception of the writings of French Marxist Henri Lefebvre, virtually none of the leading Marxists after Marx was able to understand how pivotal 'space' is to capital accumulation. Harvey has furnished this understanding, thereby adding a key analytical and normative pillar to Marxist political economy. The third key reference point for Harvey has been the turbulent career of socialist politics in the twentieth- and twenty-first centuries. Socialism, with its focus

DOI: 10.4324/9780429028120-2

on shared wealth and the collective control of human affairs, is a political programme rarely found anywhere these days. As we will see, in the later stages of his career Harvey has sought a more public (and less academic) profile for his critique of capitalism in order to keep alive the idea of a socialist (anti-capitalist) alternative.

In sum, this chapter will show that Harvey is a Marxist *geographer*, a geographical *Marxist* and a *public advocate* for Marxist analysis and politics in equal measure. It's based on a set of biographical pieces by or about Harvey.[1] Let's begin at the beginning, nearly ninety years ago in between the two great wars of the twentieth century.

The early decades: the making and unmaking of a 'spatial scientist'

David Harvey was born in late 1935 in the small town of Gillingham in Kent. He was the second child of aspirational working-class parents seeking to make ends meet in the decade of the Great Depression.[2] The main source of local employment was Chatham docks, a major shipbuilding and ship-maintenance facility. Harvey came of age during the Second World War (1939–1945). While Britain and its allies won that conflagration, the austerity of the 1930s continued well into the 1950s. In Harvey's own estimation, as a child he inherited his father's self-discipline, his mother's commitment to education as a means to self-improvement and his maternal grandmother's independence of mind (as well as her socialist sensibilities). State school-educated, Harvey was offered a place at Cambridge University in the mid-1950s to read Geography. It was a subject he enjoyed. His being able to attend an elite university occurred during a period when British governments were fostering social mobility by giving working-class children more opportunities for advancement. But, as with many Oxbridge students from humble backgrounds, the experience of entering an elite arena was not entirely happy. As Harvey later recalled: 'Call it class envy, prejudice or war, but Cambridge taught me about class in a way I had not earlier experienced' (Harvey, 2002a: 162).

In the 1950s, geography at Cambridge was typical of geography departments in most other British universities. It placed great emphasis on recording regional and national difference, both biophysical and human – what geographer Derek Gregory (2006: 4) has called 'unique or singular constellations in space and time'. Working within this 'exceptionalist' (or idiographic) tradition, Harvey did his undergraduate dissertation on fruit cultivation in mid-Kent (his home county) and his PhD thesis on hop cultivation in the same area. Both involved archival work and careful empirical analysis of land-use change over time.

Bristol

If these earnest studies in historical geography seem unlikely origins for one of today's leading Marxist theorists, the 1960s saw him apparently move no nearer his eventual intellectual destination. Having completed his doctorate in 1962, Harvey became a lecturer in Geography at Bristol University. There, he underwent something of a Damascene conversion. At Cambridge (and Oxford too), geography was taught as a largely descriptive and synthetic discipline distinct from the 'nomothetic' (or law seeking) sciences. Students would learn to understand unique combinations of factors locally and regionally. However, during the 1960s it was ambitious Oxbridge graduates like Richard Chorley, Peter Haggett and Harvey himself who sought – very successfully – to make geography a 'spatial science'. They were thinking outside the proverbial box because they were dissatisfied with the existing paradigm. For this trio of pioneers and for fellow travellers elsewhere (e.g. at the University of Washington), the ontological presumption was that the world had a good deal of hitherto undiscovered, intrinsic spatial order to it; the epistemological and methodological assumption was that this order could be revealed following the protocols of 'science'; and the disciplinary assumption was that a 'new Geography' could describe, explain and even predict spatial patterns at a variety of scales.

Harvey's signal contribution to the demise of 'idiography' as academic geography's central preoccupation was the landmark book *Explanation in Geography* (1969a). It was the first attempt to specify comprehensively the methodological procedures necessary for human and physical geographers to interrogate spatial order 'objectively'. The book (a tome of over 500 pages) became something of a bible among a new generation of geographers seeking to make their discipline more respected and useful in society. As Harvey put it in an interview many years later (with the editors of *New Left Review*),

> The established doctrine was that the knowledge yielded by geographical inquiry was different from any other kind. You can't generalise about it; you can't be systematic about it. There are no geographical laws; there are no general principles to which you can appeal ... I wanted to do battle with this conception of geography.
>
> (Harvey, 2002a: 76)

In this same interview, *New Left Review* editor Perry Anderson rightly opined that 'One would never guess from [*Explanation in Geography*] ... that the author might become a committed radical' (2002a: 77). Harvey conceded the point, noting that in the 1960s he was a 'Fabian progressivist' much taken with the idea of rational government planning as a means to improve the lot of the least fortunate in society. This was very much in keeping with the political optimism of 1960s Britain. Led by charismatic Prime Minister Harold Wilson, at that time the Labour Party promised to modernise a de-industrialising, post-imperial Britain and its iniquitous class system.

Yet the cool rationality of *Explanation in Geography* was a far cry from the social commotions coincident with its publication. By the late 1960s, a younger generation of people were protesting against many of the values and decisions favoured by those in positions of authority. Liberty and equality were watchwords of the period. The year 1968 was an especially febrile year that witnessed everything from the Prague Spring to student revolts in Paris to the assassination of US civil rights leader Martin Luther King Jr. As Harvey recalled, 'I was so absorbed in writing the book that I didn't notice how much was collapsing around me. I turned in my *magnum opus* to the publishers in May 1968, only to find myself acutely embarrassed by the change of political temperature at large' (Harvey, 2002a: 78). By that time married to an American, and juggling a trans-Atlantic life, in 1969 Harvey left England and emigrated to Baltimore in the United States. There he joined a multidisciplinary Department of Environmental Engineering at the prestigious and private Johns Hopkins University.

Baltimore

Upon completing *Explanation in Geography* in the UK, Harvey had resolved to explore normative questions not covered in that book (concerning ethics and values). Aiming to place the evidence revealed by the use of scientific methods in some sort of meaningful context, such questions suddenly assumed a local as well as national importance upon leaving England. Like Bristol, Baltimore was a port city. It also had a significant black population and levels of concentrated poverty rarely seen in British cities. The year before he arrived there, the killing of Martin Luther King Jr. in Memphis triggered a week of often violent protests among largely black Baltimore residents (similar protests occurred all over the United States of America, see Figure 2.1). The National Guard was called in and mass arrests occurred.

Though he had joined an elite university, Harvey quickly became keen to connect his academic work to the very real problems that were evident

Figure 2.1. The aftermath of a riot in Washington DC, April 1968 (Library of Congress via pingnews, Public Domain). Harvey moved to Baltimore a year after serious inner-city protests erupted there and in cities across the United States, contributing to his newfound interest in cities and social inequality.

both near and far. His move to Baltimore and the United States saw him not only shift his focus to cities; it also saw him encounter the writings of Karl Marx for the first time (Figure 2.2). A famous and furious critic of the ills caused by late-nineteenth-century capitalism, Marx's work (along with that of Friedrich Engels) attracted Harvey as he searched for ways to explain and evaluate what was happening in inner-city Baltimore. One outcome of this local interest was a research project about access to rented and owned accommodation among low-income Baltimoreans (conducted with Lata Chatterjee and published in 1974 in the still young radical journal of Geography called *Antipode*). It utilised the Marxian concepts of use value and exchange value to show that an emphasis on the latter among landlords and mortgage lenders meant that residents were often denied use of suitable quality accommodation. The right to decent housing was trumped by the right of owners to make a profit.[3]

Within four years of arriving in Baltimore, Harvey had virtually revolutionised his own thinking and switched his intellectual focus to urban geography. In 1973 he published *Social Justice and the City*. It was, in almost all respects, a very different book to Harvey's first – but it was equally profound

Figure 2.2. Karl Marx (1818–1883).

in its impact on human geographers (and others who researched cities). As its title announced, the book focussed on the causes of, and possible solutions to, urban social injustice (e.g. low-income black Americans living in cramped, dark, relatively over-priced inner-city rental accommodation in Baltimore). Where *Explanation* was an austere text about scientific method, *Social Justice* ventured a theory to both explain the origins and internal geography of modern cities *and* to criticise this unjust spatial arrangement. This theory, largely Marxist, shone through in the second half of the book. For instance, the final chapter ventured that the capitalist mode of production creates cities in its own image across the world. Their spatial form and overall function meet the needs of capitalism, Harvey showed. The first half of the book, by contrast, Harvey labelled as 'liberal' in its approach since it focussed on the spatial redistribution of income and assets while taking the capitalist character of urban life as a given. For him, these 'liberal formulations' addressed the symptoms of socio-spatial injustice but not the root causes. Read as a whole, *Social Justice* is a somewhat schizophrenic book: it records Harvey's journey from Fabian progressivism to being what he called 'a "Marxist" of sorts' (1973: 17) – of sorts because he'd only engaged with Marxist thought for three years at that point.

Even so, the book was Marxist enough to capture the attention of geographers who had regarded Harvey as a positivist to that point (i.e. someone committed to 'objective' analysis of a mind-independent, material world presumed to yield a single truth upon investigation utilising the 'right' methods). Suddenly, Harvey was at the forefront of a nascent Marxist geography. It was a sophisticated first venture, replete with significant analytical and normative complexity. The transition was variously thrilling and alarming for his assorted peers in academic Geography. But the major shifts to his thinking notwithstanding, there were two key elements of continuity between the 'old' and the 'new' Harvey.

One was a commitment to developing theory. Harvey had concluded *Explanation* with the injunction 'By our theories you shall know us' (1969a: 486). He later defined theory an 'an elaborated conceptual apparatus with which to grasp the most significant relationships at work within the intricate dynamics of social transformation' (1982a: 450–451). *Social Justice* was a first attempt to depict the relationships that govern the creation and internal patterning of capitalist cities. As we will see, thereafter theory has been central to everything Harvey has written. A second element of continuity was ontological (i.e. concerned with Harvey's outlook on the building blocks of reality). As noted above, the 'spatial scientists' of the 1960s challenged the idiographic view and maintained that there was approximate geographical order in the world awaiting scientific discovery. In *Social Justice* Harvey held fast to this notion of order, only now seen as generated by ongoing processes of capital accumulation. Harvey began to advance the idea that these processes did not merely unfold *across* the surface of the Earth, within and between nations. More than this, he suggested that capitalism actively *creates* built environments of production, transportation, consumption and social reproduction in order to sustain itself. Social systems and spatial structures were thus, in Harvey's emerging view, two sides of one coin.

From 'a Marxist of sorts' to a Marxist geographer

Getting to grips with Marx and Engels

During the 1970s Harvey immersed himself in the mid-to-late nineteenth century writings of Marx, and to a lesser extent Engels. In one sense, this intense focus on just one body of thought was odd. This is because a large and growing number of twentieth-century Marxists had sought to extend, modify and adapt Marxist thinking to an ever-changing world. By the 1970s, Marxism was a large and complex body of analysis and political practice. Yet Harvey largely ignored this larger terrain, and the contributions of most of Marx's subsequent interlocutors, and returned to the source. Why the selective – seemingly narrow – focus?

First, writing *Social Justice* had already shown Harvey that Marx's fundamental propositions about capitalism were still relevant nearly a century after his death. In other words, Harvey realised that while the forms taken by capitalism change over time and geographically, the essential relations and processes underlying these forms do not. Second, Marx's writings were voluminous, extending far beyond the famous and influential volume one of *Capital* (published in 1867). This meant that a serious investment of time was required to understand 'classical Marxism' properly, never mind the many post-classical modalities of Marxism. Third, it was already clear to Harvey three years into his reading of Marx (and Engels) – that is, by 1973, when *Social Justice* was published – that classical Marxism contained a largely hidden geographical element awaiting careful excavation. Disclosing this element as part of a more complete Marxist theory of capitalism became a central preoccupation for Harvey. Were there some fairly invariant geographical facets of capitalism amidst the shifting geographical details of its operation through time? This became a key question for Harvey. Having a secure university job, he was in a position to arrive at a very well-researched answer in the years after *Social Justice* was published.

Harvey's immediate intention after *Social Justice* was to fashion a more complete Marxist theory of capitalist urbanisation, with a focus on North American cities like New York and Baltimore. He began to teach volume one of *Capital* to students at Johns Hopkins, among other venues. This enriched his understanding of that text (and he's not stopped teaching *Capital* since the early 1970s). He also read Marx's other translated works carefully, such as the *Grundrisse* (1973). Between 1975 and 1976 he took a research sabbatical in Paris, the intention being to discover more about Marx's theory by learning from world-famous Marxist intellectuals concentrated in that city (e.g. Louis Althusser). While the learning largely did not occur (in part because Harvey's French was not, by his own admission, good enough), his time there inspired a deep interest in France's capital city. He began to connect his reading of Marx's theoretical works to the remarkable transformation of Paris that occurred during Marx's lifetime (roughly 1850–1870). That transformation involved conflicting visions of urban form and urban social relations. Immersion in the city archives ensued.

A geographical theory of capitalist accumulation

However, Harvey had already realised that Marx's implicitly geographical theory of capital accumulation required further work before a proper account of capitalist urbanisation in general, and Parisian urbanisation in particular, could be written. Through the 1970s he published a set of agenda-setting papers that began to make Marxist geography a real proposition. An early example was 'The geography of capitalist accumulation: a reconstruction of the Marxian theory', published in *Antipode* (Harvey, 1975a). The culmination of this several years of work, which included but extended beyond the urban question, was the magisterial book *The Limits to Capital* (1982a). It was based on a wide and deep interpretation of Marx's writings (especially the later ones).

The book's title had a double meaning. On the one side, Harvey sought to systematically add-in the 'missing' geographical elements of Marx's theory and thereby overcome existing conceptual limits. On the other hand, the book explored the contradictory and destructive dynamics of capitalism, pointing to the intrinsic real-world limitations of this particular mode of producing goods and services, including the necessity of crisis in capitalism. The first seven chapters reconstructed Marx's basic (largely ageographical) theory. The rest of the book then explained systematically how built environments are a fundamental component of capitalism, Harvey having first clarified its temporal aspects. Among other things, this explanation covered questions of rent (of land and property), the financing of infrastructure and buildings, and the geographical movement of different forms of capital (e.g. money and commodities). *The Limits to Capital* showed how capitalist growth – typically a punctuated story of boom periods followed by crises (like that of the 1930s) – requires an elaborate geographical landscape of nodes and networks. This landscape, Harvey demonstrated, is not an 'add on' to a fundamentally ageographical process of accumulation over time. Instead, it is *constitutive*. One way in which Harvey captured this was the concept of a 'spatial fix' (to be explained in Chapter 5).

As Harvey has since observed of many occasions, *The Limits* is his most important book (and has been reissued by the leading Left-wing publisher Verso more than once). It presented 'an elaborated conceptual framework' that's underpinned all of his subsequent monographs, chapters and articles. But it's a very difficult book to understand. This no doubt explains why many geographers didn't read it upon publication, even as they recognised how formidable a contribution to understanding it was. Meanwhile, though the book should have caught the attention of the many Marxist academics working in other disciplines (e.g. Sociology and Philosophy), it did not. This almost certainly reflected the fact that Harvey was a geographer. Geography's reputation in Western academia was, despite the turn to 'spatial science', still somewhat questionable in the 1970s and 1980s. Many academics (rather ignorantly) regarded the discipline as about fact-gathering and cartographing, thus lacking the prestige of 'real disciplines' like economics. It's likely, then, that *The Limits* – being authored by a professor of Geography – did not 'compute' outside Harvey's home discipline. Within Geography, however, it added huge weight to Marxist geography, whose momentum was also being built by the likes of Dick Peet (at Clark University in the United States of America) and Harvey's PhD students (such as Richard Walker and Neil Smith).[4]

By the mid-1980s, Marxist geography was thriving. It was applying Marxist ideas to geographical issues such as uneven spatial development. Harvey added further heft to the field by publishing not one but two books simultaneously about capitalist urbanisation – and thus realising his initial intentions after *Social Justice* appeared twelve years earlier. The books were *The Urbanization of Capital* (1985a) and *Consciousness and the Urban Experience* (1985b). The brace comprised a mixture of previously published articles and new material. The first book took a 'system level' perspective and explained why and how capitalism creates particular urban forms that, in turn, deeply influence the actions of governments, businesses, workers and local communities. A key message was that cities are not 'things' – that is, an assemblage of material artefacts like buildings and roads – but should be seen in processual terms. They are, as it were, more-or-less large nodes in a capital circulation process whose goal is to expand over time (since capitalism is focussed on growth).

The second book, however, took a less lofty view and homed-in on how various actors respond to capitalist urbanisation. At the heart of this book was the historical research about Paris that Harvey had begun in the mid-1970s. The brilliant, long chapter 'Paris, 1850-70' – coming in at 160 pages – in effect puts *The Limits to Capital* to work analytically to make sense of the conflict-ridden process of modernising the physical fabric of Paris in the mid-nineteenth century. Another chapter about the revolutionary Paris Commune of 1871 focussed on class struggles over symbolism in the built environment and the 'control of space'. *Consciousness and the Urban Experience* showed that people – workers, local communities, business owners, government leaders and others – make history and geography, but not under conditions that they can entirely control. This lack of control is particularly true for those who do not own the means of production and who otherwise have limited amounts of capital (e.g. money and property) at their disposal.

A geographical Marxist

By the mid-1980s, Harvey was a towering presence in Anglophone academic geography, and in urban studies more widely. By then, he was enormously influential, both via his many path-breaking publications and his talented doctoral students (like Neil Smith, who went on to have a distinguished career before his untimely death in 2012). However, by his own admission things were not so good for Harvey personally as his fiftieth birthday came and went. In 1987 he decided to make two life changes. One was to move back to his native Britain. The other was to re-join a department of Geography after nearly twenty years in an interdisciplinary milieu at Johns Hopkins. Harvey became the Halford Mackinder Professor in one of the oldest UK Geography departments, at Oxford University. The move was inspired by a personal desire for new experiences, though he retained a formal link with Johns Hopkins University.[5]

Oxford

It may seem ironic for a self-styled radical to become, by choice, part of such an elite institution (at least half of Oxford's undergraduates at that time had attended private schools such as Eton and Harrow). However, as Harvey opined in an interview conducted upon his arrival in the UK, 'I've never felt particularly that Marxists shouldn't work in institutions like that. I mean if you view academia as a place where you're engaging in the production and reproduction of ideology of some sort, then it seems to me that to try to occupy some of the more powerful positions within academia is a very important thing to do' (in Peake and Jackson, 1988: 7).

At Oxford, he continued to teach Marx's *Capital* every year, as he'd done at Hopkins (attracting students from several disciplines). He was also instrumental in adding Marxist Erik Swyngedouw to the Geography staff – Swyngedouw had been one of Harvey's Johns Hopkins doctoral students (and would go on to have a major influence on Human Geography in the United Kingdom and internationally). Oxford was (is) obviously very different to Baltimore. But it was not just a university town. It also had a history of big industry, notably car manufacture in nearby Cowley. As he had done in Baltimore, Harvey sought to connect his academic life to local issues. There was a trade-union-led campaign to protect jobs at the Rover car factory (under threat of partial closure from 1988 onwards). Harvey became involved as the campaign unfolded over several years.

The British car industry had undergone profound changes in the previous thirty years. What was happening in Cowley in the late 1980s was in some sense reflective of larger changes to the British economy during a period of Conservative political dominance (with Margaret Thatcher at the helm). After Jim Callaghan's Labour government had lost power in 1979, Britain's big industries (coal mining, metals production, ship building and other heavy manufacturing) faced intense overseas competition. Linked to this, Thatcher's governments sought to privatise many previously publicly owned goods, services, assets and industries. The 1980s were, in hindsight, the start of what we now recognise as 'neoliberalism', as well as 'globalisation' (one of the buzzwords of the 1990s), with similar things happening in both the United Kingdom and the United States of America (under Ronald Reagan's political leadership).[6] Harvey had, it seems, moved from one society undergoing significant change to another (see Figures 2.3 and 2.4). But the worst effects of change were geographically concentrated: the former centres of primary and secondary production, like Manchester and Detroit, bore the brunt. Though Oxford was generally wealthy, Cowley was one of the many casualties in central and south England after prior decades of prosperity before the likes of

Figure 2.3. Post-war Anglo-European capitalism unraveling? Harvey returned to the United Kingdom just after highly turbulent years that included the 1978 'winter of discontent', when lengthy strikes by public sector workers caused piles of uncollected refuse to accumulate on city streets.

Figure 2.4. The end of the Fordist-Keynesian era. This turbulent period in the United Kingdom also witnessed the protracted and often violent national miners' strike of the early 1980s.

Japan and South Korea began to make excellent, affordable cars, vans and trucks using 'leaner' production techniques and forms of organisation.

At the time, many analysts in disciplines like geography and sociology understood the economic sea-change of the 1970s and 1980s in the following terms. A relatively stable post-1945 'regime of capital accumulation' centred on Western Europe and North America was being eclipsed. This regime was Fordist-Keynesian: it was built on a set of big industries employing millions of relatively well-paid workers and with 'interventionist' governments determined to protect their citizens' well-being. The regime began dissolving in the context of a worldwide economic recession in the mid-1970s and was gradually replaced by a regime of so-called flexible accumulation. This emerging regime, it was said at the time, favoured smaller industries, innovation in process and product, far more differentiation among producers (with new sectors emerging like mobile phones), and more choice for consumers via intensified product differentiation within sectors. The big Fordist industries were forced to compete with new overseas rivals, while new firms were springing-up in 'clean' and creative manufacturing, in a growing services sector, in the growing 'knowledge industry', and so on. New kinds, and new geographies, of production and consumption were emerging (facilitated by sub-national and national government policies). The ongoing evolution of globalising capitalism was eroding the post-war social contract between workers, big capitalists and governments within somewhat closed national economies.

Making an impression outside Geography

It was in the context of this regime shift that Harvey wrote a book that had a major impact on thinking across the social sciences and humanities. It was called *The Condition of Postmodernity* (1989a). Within months of publication, it garnered wide attention in fields like architecture, sociology and cultural studies. It also served to elevate his profile in the wider community of Marxist academics – a community that had largely ignored his previous work. We will say more about this important text in Chapter 6. The book sought to explain a notable shift away from 'modern' ways of thinking in everything from novels to painting to philosophy to the interior design and exterior appearance of commercial and public buildings. 'Post-modernism' broadly marked a celebration of variety, difference and multi-perspectivalism. This shift was generally welcomed, with some in Harvey's own discipline (notably Michael Dear) advocating for it. While not entirely dismissing so-called post-modernism, Harvey questioned its perceived playful and putatively liberating qualities. More than this, he suggested that the sudden appearance of post-modernism across a seemingly disparate range of artistic, creative and intellectual arenas was symptomatic of the regime shift in capitalism summarised above. Post-modernism, for Harvey, was a reflex of the capitalist restructuring and internationalisation after 1973. Whatever its positive facets, he argued forcefully that postmodernism in the broad realm of 'culture' was part of a new historical condition – what he called 'post-modernity' – that was created by the crisis of Fordism-Keynesianism. It was thus, despite appearances, implicated in ongoing harms inflicted by the capitalist way of life.

The Condition was partly a polemic, partly a piece of serious analysis that showcased Harvey's breadth of learning. It was written with verve and enjoyed wide appeal across many academic disciplines.[7] The book discussed the changing dynamics of capitalism between around 1850 and 1985, building on his previous books; but it also discussed urban planning, architecture and design, cinema, literature, fashion, painting and much more besides. Though it had its detractors, the book was a *tour de force*. It offered a coherent and plausible account of coincident shifts in ostensibly different domains of contemporary life. It was the first wide-ranging critique of postmodern thought and practice. It popularised the concept of 'time-space compression' as a useful shorthand to capture the logics and tendencies of fast-globalising capitalism. It sold many more copies than all of Harvey's previous books combined. Insofar as any academic can claim to be 'famous', the book made him a thinker to be reckoned with well beyond his chosen discipline.

The year 1989 would also be a significant year for Harvey for other reasons. Reflecting his established reputation in Geography and urban studies, his first 'greatest hits' book was published (*The Urban Experience*, 1989b), coming on the heels of a reissue of *Social Justice* (in 1988). That same year, he also published an academic paper that would, in time, be his most highly cited by some margin. 'From managerialism to entrepreneurialism' (Harvey, 1989c), which appeared in the journal *Geografiska Annaler*, identified a new more competitive approach to governing cities across the globe, once again linking it to the emerging 'flexible' regime of accumulation. To cap the year, Harvey received the Anders Retzius Gold Medal from the Swedish Society for Anthropology and Geography. This was one of several prestigious academic honours to be conferred on him in the years to come.

Back to the United States of America

Connecting his interest in the 'big picture' back to local concerns, in 1993 an analysis of the fight for jobs at the Cowley car factory was published by Harvey and another Oxford researcher, Teresa Hayter. An edited book, it was called *The Factory and the City* (Hayter and Harvey, 1993). But that year Harvey returned to Johns Hopkins and Baltimore for personal and professional reasons. The forty-eight months since *The Condition* was published had been eventful in the United Kingdom and beyond. Though Margaret Thatcher lost power, the Conservative Party did not, and her political agenda lived on. In the United States, George Bush Snr. likewise continued the Reaganite pro-business programme; dramatically, the 'iron curtain' fell in 1989–1990 meaning that the Marx-inspired experiment in communist living largely ended; the first Gulf War began, with the United States and its allies seeking to topple Iraqi leader Saddam Hussein; the European Union officially came into being; and, after years of negotiation, the General Agreement on Trade and Tariffs (the world's first comprehensive 'free trade' framework) was signed by dozens of countries.

These were challenging times to be identified as a Marxist. The unexpected and rapid end of communism in the USSR and adjoining states was widely perceived as a sign that Marxism was dead as a political force. It was, as Eagleton (2003: 43) later noted, 'a solution to a set of questions that were no longer even on the agenda'. Meanwhile, in the Anglophone and West European social sciences and humanities, academic Marxism – such a magnet for bright minds in the 1960s and 1970s – was waning. A new generation of radical thinkers was drawn not to Marx but the likes of Jean Baudrillard, Jacques Derrida, Michel Foucault, Betty Friedan and Julia Kristeva. The environmental movement had also sprung into life from the late 1960s, but Marxists didn't seem to have much to say to it (despite the now obvious links between environmental destruction and the capitalist devaluing of the non-human world). To Harvey, and many other committed Marxists (see Figure 2.5), it seemed as if Marxism was being abandoned at precisely the wrong time. To add to the stresses and strains of the time, Harvey found Johns Hopkins distinctly less hospitable than during his first period there. Serious heart problems made things worse and required major surgery.

It was in this context that Harvey wrote his least cohesive, most ambitious, most interesting and in some ways most abstract book: *Justice, Nature, and the Geography of Difference* (1996a). It's a text of many parts and has several aims. Among those aims was a desire to defend Marxism from its detractors on the 'new Left' who had steadily gained strength since the 1970s. In essence, the book provided philosophical and theoretical arguments, leavened with evidence, about how to make sense of a

Figure 2.5. Leading Anglophone academic Marxists in post-Marxist times. In the 1990s, Harvey joined (from left to right) the likes of Terry Eagleton, Frederic Jameson and Erik Olin Wright as an internationally recognised advocate of Marxist thought.

'more than capitalist world'. It highlighted the central role of capitalism and the ongoing need for Marxist analysis; but it fully acknowledged the many important and legitimate issues that are irreducible to the critique of capitalism and which classic Marxist ideas about socialism and communism could not address without serious and careful modification. Where *The Condition* was a confident critique and demonstration of Marxism's relevance, *Justice* was rather more defensive yet also generous in both analytical and political terms. It explored the many points of connection and tension between various forms of analysis across the 'social' (e.g. Marxist, feminist and post-colonial) and 'green' (e.g. deep ecological) branches of Left-wing thinking. It considered the intersections between class politics, identity politics and environmental politics, with an eye on how geography affects all of them. It was not so much post-Marxist as 'Marxism-plus' and reflected Harvey's adaptiveness to the influence of new currents of Left thinking. A key point of connectivity was the concept of justice. Harvey, returning to this theme for the first time since his second book, explored how Left politics can productively focus on the critique of multiple, but connected, forms of injustice existing in a more-than-capitalist world that's highly integrated but also much differentiated.

For all its focus on elemental things like ontology and epistemology, *Justice* was very much a book about how to comprehend the real world. By the late 1990s, the globalisation of investment, trade, consumption and travel was well advanced. On Harvey's doorstep, the North American Free Trade Agreement (NAFTA) came into effect in 1994. The year after, the World Trade Organization (WTO) was launched and oversaw notionally 'free' commodity flows across the full range of economic sectors. For some years, the International Monetary Fund (IMF) and the World Bank had favoured policies that encouraged foreign direct investment, secure investor rights (e.g. through strict property laws), balanced public budgets and the removal of government subsidies to producers (the 'Washington Consensus'). So-called developing countries became more numerous and prosperous as capitalism extended its tentacles. Even China, ostensibly communist not capitalist, began to open-up to the world economically. The global working class expanded enormously, though levels of trade union membership did not. But there were losers, crises and plenty of dissent about what critics began to call 'neoliberal globalisation'. Most notably, a peasant revolt by the Zapatistas occurred in southern Mexico when NAFTA took hold in 1994; and then, five years later, thousands of protestors assembled in Seattle to protest the WTO. In between, a serious financial crisis gripped east and southeast Asia. The late 1990s saw the rise of international, grass-roots opposition to the new economic order, encapsulated in the terms 'anti-capitalism' and 'alter-globalisation' (which circulated far and wide). Meanwhile, in the United States – whose elites had promoted neoliberalism for years – socio-spatial inequality deepened. Baltimore exemplified the trend, as later depicted in the remarkable real-life drama series *The Wire* (2002–2008).

Harvey wrote a series of articles and chapters during this period. The year 1998 was the 150th anniversary of the publication of Marx and Engels' famous call to arms, *The Communist Manifesto*. Harvey marked the occasion by noting that 'The material conditions that sparked the moral outrage in the *Manifesto* have not gone away' (1998a: 384).[8] In 1999 Verso reissued *The Limits to Capital*. The timing was auspicious: while a work of abstract theory, it seemed very relevant to a world experiencing uneven capitalist neoliberalisation. Then, in 2000, Harvey published a collection of recent writings as a book. It was entitled *Spaces of Hope* (Harvey, 2000b). Comprising twelve chapters and a short work of imaginative fiction (called 'Edilia'), the book did two things. First, half of the text reaffirmed the value of Marx's critique of political economy to working people worldwide seeking to make sense of their own lives. Second, the remainder of the book focussed on political alternatives to capitalist globalisation, paying especial attention to the right to geographical difference. *Spaces of Hope* contains a long chapter about Baltimore, and also a story about an imagined post-capitalist world. The book was, to use Harvey words (borrowed from Antonio Gramsci), an exercise in 'optimism of the intellect' (2002a: 17) written in the belief that 'another world is possible' (the slogan promoted from 2001 onwards by the World Social Forum).

In 2001 Harvey published a second 'greatest hits' collection, *Spaces of Capital* (Harvey, 2001a). It assembled essays written across his thirty years as a Marxist; it was broader in focus than the earlier collection *The Urban Experience*. This same year he left Johns Hopkins for a second time. He moved north to join the Graduate Center of the City University of New York (CUNY) as a distinguished professor. There he reunited with long-term friends and intellectual soul mates Neil Smith and Cindi Katz. As Harvey arrived in New York, one of those rare events occurred that change the course of world history. The World Trade Center was attacked by radical Islamicists on 11th September (so too the Pentagon in Washington). The US-led 'war on terror' ensued, with major implications for Iraq and Afghanistan in particular. The twin towers attack – a globally significant local event – would soon shape Harvey's next major writing venture. That venture, as we will now see, initiated an enduring shift in his *modus operandi*.

Promoting Marxism beyond the university

Two transitional texts

In early 2003, Harvey returned to the University of Oxford (by invitation) to give a set of talks open to staff and students from all disciplines. He chose to focus these Clarendon Lectures on the global developments that eventually triggered the so-called second Gulf War, led by the United States and its allies. The lectures were rapidly published as a book called *The New Imperialism* (2003a). Its pointed title made clear Harvey's intention that the monograph be a major statement about the current direction of travel in world affairs. The text was written in narrative form and was highly readable. Though it used abstract Marxian concepts like 'the spatial fix', it was chock full of detail about *fin de millennium* geoeconomic and geopolitical shifts. Analytically, Harvey supplemented Marx's ideas with concepts drawn from the influential work of Italian Marxist Antonio Gramsci (1891–1937) and German-American political theorist Hannah Arendt (1906–1975). Empirically, Harvey synthesised material drawn from current affairs publications (e.g. *The New York Times*) and academic research (e.g. by his former Johns Hopkins colleague, the Marxist Giovanni Arrighi).

Harvey painted – seemingly effortlessly – on a very grand canvas. The book adopted a very didactic tone. Harvey cut through the confusing detail of the post-1970 era. America's early twenty-first century venture in the Middle East was shown not to be about the defence of freedom against radical Islamic 'terror' (the rhetoric used by President George Bush Jnr). Instead, it was shown to be part of a 'new imperialism' wherein the 'hard power' of the US military was used to bolster America's waning economic dominance. The book deployed the concepts of 'territorial power' (spatially delimited), 'economic power' (geographically expansive), hegemony (consent-based rule) and 'accumulation by dispossession' (legally sanctioned wealth appropriation) to great effect. In just over 200 pages, Harvey offered a plausible explanation of the great forces remaking people's collective history and geography. His new book quickly garnered wide academic attention and also achieved visibility beyond the university world.

As noted above, around this time a few activists and Left-wing academics began to use the term 'neoliberalism' – instead of the rather bland term 'globalisation' – to depict the new economic and political era. Broadly, this word describes a worldview that prioritises individual liberty, especially in the economic realm. Encouraged by the success of *The New Imperialism*, Harvey quickly wrote another book in an identical style. *A Brief History of Neoliberalism* (2005a) reframed what in *The Condition* he'd depicted as the emergence of a regime of 'flexible accumulation'. The book tracked the rise and global spread of neoliberal ideas first advanced in the 1930s during the Great Depression (when Harvey was born). Using a mix of theory and abundant secondary evidence, the uneven process of 'neoliberalisation' from the mid-1970s was shown to be an attempted solution to capitalism's inevitable crisis tendencies. As with *The New Imperialism*, the book punctured the rhetoric of those benefitting from the new world order. Far from advancing people's liberty, Harvey insisted that neoliberalism involved a restoration of class power by the owners and financiers of the means of economic production.[9]

The New Imperialism and *A Brief History* were published at a time when there was a large appetite among non-academic readers for analysis of a febrile period in human history (that appetite, of course, remains undiminished in our own troubling times). Economists like Jeffrey Sachs and Joseph E. Stiglitz were writing popular books about current world affairs, as were journalist-commentators such as Thomas L. Friedman and Christopher Hitchens, and also activists like Naomi Klein, George Monbiot and Jeremy Rifkin. But few, if any, were overtly Marxist. In this context, Harvey deliberately transitioned to writing accessible works that ordinary people could read as easily as the university students he taught at CUNY. At the same time, Harvey also made a move into the online world in order to broadcast Marxist thinking more easily, more regularly and more widely. Both things were a gamble, but Harvey had a secure university position and a formidable academic reputation. This allowed certain risks to be taken.

A new modus operandi

Since 2005, Harvey has been extraordinarily productive as a writer. Aside from a stream of articles, he's published the following books: *The Enigma of Capital* (2010a), *A Companion to Marx's* Capital, volume I (2010b), *A Companion to Marx's* Capital, volume II (2013), *Rebel Cities: From the Right to the City to the Urban Revolution* (2012a), *Seventeen Contradictions and the End of Capitalism* (2014a), *The Ways of the World* (2016a), *Marx, Capital and the Madness of Economic Reason* (2017a), A *Companion to Marx's* Capital, *The Complete Edition* (2018a, and a whopping 760 pages) and *The Anti-Capitalist Chronicles* (2020a). He has also prepared a companion to Marx's *Grundrisse* (Harvey, forthcoming). In rather different ways, all are intended to demonstrate the enduring value of Marx's critique of capitalist political economy. All are written in plain English and the usual academic conventions (e.g. citations in brackets) are largely avoided.

In brief, *The Enigma* sought to explain the global financial crisis (GFC) of 2008–2009 by situating it in the long-run problem of capital over-accumulation. This was a crisis of the neoliberalism instituted after the unravelling of Fordism-Keynesianism forty years earlier. We're still living with the consequences after elites doubled down on 'free market' capitalism rather than push for a new regime of accumulation. *Rebel Cities* built on Harvey's urban expertise and analysed the largely urban location of early twenty-first century anti-capitalist protest (e.g. the Occupy Wall Street movement that began in Manhattan's Zuccotti Park in 2011). The book asked how and why urban struggles are central to reforming and, ideally, moving beyond the rule of capital. *Seventeen Contradictions* is, in a sense, a lay person's representation of *The Limits to Capital* (which was reissued again by Verso in 2016). It anatomised the totality of capitalism through the lens of systemic contradictions, identifying the whole ensemble of elemental tensions that define capitalism past and present. *The Ways of the World* is yet another collection of Harvey's 'best' articles and chapters, but with present-day commentaries about their context, content and relevance. *The Madness of Economic Reason* applied Marx's *Capital* to reveal, brilliantly, the multiple irrationalities that are normalised in mainstream economics and everyday life. Most recently, *The Anti-Capitalist Chronicles* examines how neoliberalism has survived in the post-GFC period and what the forces of the Left need to do to overthrow it.

All these books grapple with present-day global capitalism in its 'zombie neoliberal' form (discredited and half-dead, yet somehow staggering on), set in a longer historical context. All are based on the foundational thinking Harvey did in the 1970s that led him to publish *The Limits*. In an effort to share this thinking, Harvey has also made Marx's three volumes of *Capital* (only one of which was published during his lifetime) accessible to general readers (with the support of the publisher Verso). A guide to *The Grundrisse* – Marx's extensive notes of 'self-clarification' from 1857–1858 – is being prepared for release by Harvey at the time of writing. In particular, these 'companion' books are targeted at a younger generation of readers which, because of the tenor of our neoliberal times, 'has grown up bereft of familiarity with … Marxian political economy' (2010b: viii). Without doubt, all these works evidence a 'public turn' Harvey first took around twenty years ago.[10] Several books have been translated into other languages. Since *The New Imperialism*, he's only published two substantial 'scholarly' works. They are *Paris, Capital of Modernity*, an extended presentation of his earlier research into the remaking of France's largest city (Harvey, 2003b), and *Cosmopolitanism and the Geographies of Freedom* – a meaty exploration of freedom in the context of both neoliberalism and a diverse post-socialist Left in a multi-cultural world (Harvey, 2009a).[11]

The other clear evidence of Harvey's public turn is his now substantial website (https://davidharvey.org). The site was launched in 2007–2008 courtesy of a (then) graduate student called Chris Caruso. Initially, it was intended to make Harvey's annual seminar about Marx's *Capital*, volume one, available to people beyond CUNY. But it's evolved to become much, much more than this. The site has three principal components. There are video courses given by Harvey that lead viewers through virtually all of Marx's late works. Then there's a large and growing set of podcasts and videos by Harvey about various key events and issues of our time (edited transcripts were published in *The Anti-Capitalist Chronicles* in 2020). Finally, there's a full listing of all his books.[12] Harvey is also a regular user of Twitter (with over 150,000 followers). It's worth noting too that, until the COVID-19 virus restricted physical movement, Harvey had for many years engaged in face-to-face discussions with political activists and other Leftists beyond academia. One especially interesting aspect of his recent career was him accepting an invitation from the government of Ecuador to co-direct the National Strategy Center for the Right to the Territory (CENEDET, 2013–2017).[13]

Making sense of David Harvey's Marxism

In retrospect, we can see that that Harvey's career has had three stages, two of which were resolutely academic. He's been very effective throughout. There was a pre-Marxist stage (ending around 1970), then a stage focussed on understanding and adding to Marx's theory of capital accumulation (1970–2000), and a recent phase of putting the theory to work to understand current world affairs (and doing so as much outside academia as within it, see Figure 2.6). Today, Harvey is one of the world's chief advocates for (classical) Marxism. His energy is undiminished well into his eighties. Though in some senses they are a thing of the past, Harvey can legitimately claim to be a public intellectual – at least among Left-leaning sections of the public in the United States and beyond. His stature now transcends academic Geography and academic Marxism. This said, the institutional foundation for all his work has been academic tenure: continuing professorial positions, with the accompanying right of intellectual freedom, have been hugely enabling. As Harvey noted in interview over thirty years ago, 'I'm a privileged academic, writing in privileged circumstances. I have the possibility to take-on very long term projects if I so wish in ways that probably other people couldn't' (in Peake and Jackson, 1988: 14). In this, he's hardly alone: other influential Marxists have likewise used this privilege to great analytical advantage (for instance, Hans-Georg Backhaus, John Bellamy Foster, Nancy Fraser, Werner Bonefeld, Robert Brenner, Michael Burawoy, Terry Eagleton, the late Stuart Hall, Michael Lebowitz, Fredric Jameson, Richard Wolff, the late Ellen Meiksens Wood and Göran Therborn).

Looking back on his long career, it's possible to identify some signal characteristics of Harvey, his writing and his many spoken presentations (over and above his obvious capacity for hard work). One is his intellectual consistency. Where many notable thinkers change course over time, Harvey has been unwavering since his first embrace of classical Marxism in the 1970s. While he's evolved his historical-geographical materialism in some respects (to be explored later in this book), fundamentally it remains unchanged since *The Limits*. Harvey returns again and again to Marx's original works and has paid little attention even to significant new Marxist works appearing since *Social Justice* (such as Moishe Postone's *Time, Labor and Social Domination* [1993] or several key works by Bob Jessop). It's an open question as to whether this is admirable or reflective of an insufficiently open mind (on which see Gregory, 2006, among others). Second, Harvey is clearly possessed of great tenacity. He's kept the flame of Marxist thought alive through many difficult years, including the present ones when opposition to the capitalist order is manifesting in distinctly

Figure 2.6 David Harvey in 2011.

morbid ways (e.g. as right-wing populism in the United States, Hungary, Brazil and elsewhere).

In the third place, Harvey is completely committed to theory – not for theory's sake, but as a 'cognitive map' that can illuminate the key processes driving the dizzying changes we have seen in the nineteenth, twentieth and twenty-first centuries. Theory is what gives all of Harvey's work a panoramic quality, both analytically and empirically (see Chapter 3). Indeed, after Marx, he has talked of its 'luminous summit'. If this makes his theory 'totalising' then, as Harvey would have it, this merely reflects the promiscuous and colonising behaviour of capitalism rather than over-reach on his part. Fourth, Harvey has always insisted that geography matters. The relative location and connectivity between and material character of phenomena on the Earth's surface are very important for Harvey, but in more than the banal sense that everything must exist or occur somewhere. Instead, his work as a Marxist shows us how geography is both effect and cause in the grand story of capitalism. It is, that's to say, *constitutive* not epiphenomenal. This deep interest in 'social process and spatial form' carries over from his 1960s conversion to spatial science.

Fifth, since *The Condition* Harvey has paid more attention to how capitalism intersects with the many non- or proto-capitalist elements of contemporary life. This has enriched his Marxism, without diluting its analytical coherence. In the 1990s and early 2000s, in particular, he sought ways to build bridges between the cognitive and normative agenda of Marxism and the agendas of the many anti-capitalist movements for whom Marx is not a reference point. We might then say that his early interest in capitalism per se gave way to a concerted interest in capitalism within a 'more-than-capitalist world'.

Sixth, Harvey's work is animated by a critical sensibility, as one would expect from a card-carrying Marxist. In *Social Justice and the City*, he wrote the following lines, which stirred a generation of geographers and urban analysts: 'There is an ecological problem, an urban problem, an international trade problem, and yet we seem incapable of saying anything of depth or profundity about any of them' (1973: 129). Since then, Harvey has sought to make plain the destructiveness, injustice and waste caused by the capitalist pursuit of growth. It's not that he claims everything about capitalism is bad (hardly possible since Harvey himself has benefitted considerably from living in a capitalist world). It's more that he deems the price of capitalist 'progress' too high to bear for many people and for the planet.

This said, and in the seventh place, it's nonetheless true that Harvey's work has leaned more towards explanation and diagnosis than towards political analysis and prognosis. As we will discover in the next chapter, his critical theory of capitalism is adept at finding fault. But Harvey has devoted less attention to questions of political goals, political strategy or political programmes – this despite the many interesting and important things he has said about justice, rights and other key normative ideas (see Chapter 8). Finally, it's obvious that Harvey believes in the motivational power of systematic thinking and evidence-based analysis. As Derek Gregory long ago noted, 'Harvey may not be an activist, but he is keenly aware of the active power of ideas to shape the world in which we live and die' (2006: 24). In an era of misinformation, misrepresentation and multiple framings of reality, Harvey has been very determined to get the Marxist take on things noticed far and wide. This is especially evident since around 2007 when his website was launched. The communist dictator Josef Stalin is reputed to have once said, 'Ideas are far more dangerous than guns. We don't allow our enemies to have guns, so why should we allow them to have ideas?'. While no enemy of free thinking, Harvey recognises that ideas can be extremely potent in the hands of both the powerful and those who oppose them (see Chapter 3).

These various characteristics of Harvey's life and work will, we hope, shine through in the rest of this book. As noted, he's now in his twilight years, but still going strong. He's received virtually every academic accolade a social scientist can receive (except a Nobel Prize for Economics, for obvious reasons).[14] He has a global readership and profile, supported by his website, translations of his recent books and his deliberate move to 'pitch' to general audiences since around 2007. He also, we hope, has many more years ahead of him.

Conclusion

Having surveyed David Harvey's life and major works in this chapter, it's readily apparent why we've written this book. His *oeuvre* is now so large that only a few people could willingly commit the time and energy to understanding it. This said, Harvey's intellectual consistency does mean that reading one of his books or major essays offers certain insights into almost all of the others. Even so, no part of Harvey's huge body of work can fully illuminate the whole. In the chapters to follow, we do not exhaustively delve into all of Harvey's major writings (there are far too many). But, based on a close acquaintance with fifty-plus years of his writing, we're able to highlight the principal themes, innovations over time and reactions to his brand of geographic Marxism. Throughout, we seek to 'read him on his own terms' as Harvey himself has sought to read Marx (2010b: 7). Our hope is that we're as sure a guide to Harvey's work as Harvey is to Marx's. His writing is hardly the last word on capitalism, past and present. But it does offer important tools to understand it critically in an age when the underbelly of capitalist 'progress' is so very clearly malignant.

Further reading

Barnes, T. (2006). Between deduction and dialectics: David Harvey on knowledge. In N. Castree & D. Gregory (Eds.), *David Harvey: A Critical Reader* (pp. 26–46). Blackwell.

Barnes, T. & Sheppard, E. (2019). Baltimore as truth spot: David Harvey, Johns Hopkins, and urban activism. In T. Barnes & E. Sheppard (Eds.), *Spatial Histories of Radical Geography: North America and Beyond* (pp. 183–209). Blackwell.

Harvey, D. (2000a). Reinventing geography. *New Left Review*, 4, 75–97.

Harvey, D. (2002a). Memories and desires. In P. Gould & F. Pitts (Eds.), *Geographical Voices: Fourteen Autobiographical Records* (pp. 149–188). Syracuse University Press.

Harvey, D. (2021a). Reflections on an academic life. *Human Geography*. OnlineFirst. https://doi.org/10.1177/19427786211046291

Toscano, A. (2007). Reflections: David Harvey interviewed by Alberto Toscano. *Development and Change*, 38(6), 1127–1135.

Williams, L. J. (2007). The geography of accumulation: an interview with David Harvey. *Minnesota Review*, 69, 115–138. https://doi.org/10.1215/00265667-2007-69-115

Notes

1. Notably, an interview with the editors of *New Left Review* (Harvey, 2000a), along with two autobiographical pieces (Harvey, 2002a, 2022a).
2. George Orwell famously and vividly captured the depredations of the era in the first half of his 1937 book *The Road to Wigan Pier*, which focussed on the life conditions of the northern English working class. In the United States, where Harvey would later relocate to, the iconic literary record of the Great Depression was John Steinbeck's Pulitzer Prize winning novel *The Grapes of Wrath* (1939).
3. With Chatterjee, Harvey also examined the local government enforcement of building codes in Baltimore, showing how they inadvertently made things worse for inner-city renters (see Harvey et al., 1972).
4. Only in the early 2000s was *The Limits* accorded wider recognition as what Bob Jessop (2004: 480) called 'a classic post-disciplinary text with a message that goes well beyond geography'.
5. It's worth noting that in his time in Baltimore Harvey developed a real affection for that troubled city, involving himself in various local political initiatives since his arrival there in 1969. For instance, he was a founding member of Research Associates in Baltimore in 1982 (https://rafbaltimore.org/about/), which set up the Progressive Action Center by converting the Enoch Pratt Library in

Waverly into a Left library and political action space staging public events and educational activities. The building was sold in 2014 and Harvey resigned from the executive board at that time.

6. Two outstanding analyses of the period are Andrew Gamble's *The Free Economy and the Strong State* (1988) and Robert Pollin's *Contours of Descent* (2005).
7. Harvey's Marxist critique had been foreshadowed by a long essay written by literary critic Fredric Jameson in *New Left Review* (1984). Jameson went on to publish his own book, *Postmodernism, or the Cultural Logic of Late Capitalism* (1992), although this lacked the political-economic heft of *The Condition*.
8. A decade later, Harvey wrote an introduction to a reissue of the *Manifesto* (Harvey, 2008a).
9. This book was informed by the 2004 Hettner Lecturers that Harvey was invited to deliver at the University of Heidelberg in Germany. The written versions of the lectures appeared with a more general essay about 'space' in the short book *Spaces of Neoliberalization* (2005b). Published by Franz Steiner Verlag, it was reissued in 2006 by Verso under the title *Spaces of Global Capitalism*.
10. In a small way, this turn was presaged during his time at Oxford University. A few years after his return to the UK, he was invited to make three programmes for BBC Radio 4 about modern cities. The details are BBC News and Current Affairs (Radio Four): 'City Lights/City Shadows', three radio broadcasts, 10th October, 17th October and 24th October 1993, produced by Sallie Davies, scripted and narrated by David Harvey.
11. There's also a somewhat hard to get short book about the rise of China and its epic investments in infrastructure since around 2000, titled *Abstract from the Concrete* (Harvey, 2016a), which contains an interview with Harvey.
12. Since the website went live in June 2008, it has received more than four and a half million page views according to Google Analytics. The website's geographical reach extends to over 120 countries. Since the materials on the website are published under a creative commons license, the content can be and is widely replicated on many other sites.
13. The Center was part of El Instituto de Altos Estudios Nacionales (IEAN) in Quito, Ecuador. It was conceived as an action research and training centre for civil servants and activists. Harvey was very involved in its establishment and expansion in the 2013–2015 period, making extended annual visits there. The Center was disbanded in 2017.
14. Aside from the earlier mentioned Anders Retzius Medal, Harvey has received the Patron's Medal of the Royal Geographical Society and the Vautrin Lud International Prize in Geography (France). He was also made a fellow of the British Academy in 1998 and was elected to the American Academy of Arts and Sciences in 2007. In 2018 he received the Leverhulme Gold Medal of the British Academy for creative contributions to the social sciences. Harvey has also had several visiting positions, for example he was a Miliband Visiting Fellow at the London School of Economics, 1998–2002. In addition, he's received several honorary doctorates.

3 Between philosophy and political practice

The power of critical theory

The abstract and the concrete; A basic theory of capitalist accumulation (that's rather less 'basic' than it initially seems); The battle of theory; The detour of philosophy; Down to earth: theorising the local, comprehending geographical variety; In what sense a critical *theorist?; Conclusion*

As noted in Chapter 2, Harvey concluded his pre-Marxist book *Explanation in Geography* with the injunction to his geography colleagues: 'By our theories you shall know us' (Harvey, 1969a: 486). He's taken this to heart in a profound way ever since. Virtually all his written works since *Social Justice and the City* are overtly theoretical, and even his close empirical studies of nineteenth-century Paris are directly animated by theory. In one sense, this may seem odd. After all, one meaning of the word 'theory' is unverified speculation, as in 'my theory is that there are aliens from outer space disguised as humans among us'. But Harvey's career is anything but an extended exercise in cerebral guesswork. For him, theory comprises a set of concepts able to describe, explain and criticise the key processes and relationships that structure our world.[1]

As a Marxist, Harvey's central focus has been the structuring power of the capitalist mode of production. For him, theory is an essential tool of both analysis and evaluation. Without theory we risk being confused or deceived about the realities of a fast-changing, often befuddling world. But Harvey is well aware that theory is only valid when properly anchored in the empirical realm, lest it shade into detached theoreticism. As he noted forty years ago, 'theory that cannot shed light on history or political practice is surely redundant', even if it cannot

DOI: 10.4324/9780429028120-3

ultimately 'procure [us] a full understanding of singular events' (1982a: 451, 450). Given its centrality to his life's work as a Marxist, we devote this chapter to examining the nature and purposes of theory as Harvey understands it. As we'll see, theory has analytical and critical aspects, or cognitive and normative purposes.

The abstract and the concrete

If theory is an effort to identify the 'signals in the noise', then what can we say about the reality that we (and Harvey) must reckon with each and every day? It is true, if banal, to observe that the world is a complicated place. Things are only ever 'simple' if one intentionally ignores a chain of causes and a cascade of events that led to any one particular object (e.g. a plastic bottle of Evian spring water) or situation (e.g. the massive 2020 explosion in the Port of Beirut due to improperly stored ammonium nitrate) being the way it is (or was). It's also true, if banal, to say that people perceive the world from different angles of vision, which can alter over time as their life circumstances change. Our sense of who we are (aka 'identity'), and our understanding of the world near and far, are shaped by many things. For instance, the life of Jeff Bezos (founder of online retailer Amazon) has been manifestly different to that of a Uyghur blacksmith living in rural northwest China or a Hindu teenage girl raised in predominantly black Soweto, South Africa. Even the wealthiest people are to a large degree place-bound – they live and work in one or other locality for extended periods of time. These places inevitably leave their mark. This said, in our internet age, most people's understanding of self and world is increasingly shaped by things, people, information and ideas hailing from afar, as much as it is by what's close to hand (e.g. parents, the local landscape or schoolmates). There are always exceptions, of course (especially in countries with government-controlled news and social media). But in a world of nearly nine billion human beings, affordable telecommunications and transportation have created a real sense of a global village for many.

To add to the complexity, and the wide range of experienced realities, there are two other things to consider. One is that most people rarely have the time, energy or (in many cases) the desire to better understand the world they inhabit. Only a relative minority of people study things like economics, politics or sociology to degree level. Even then, there are competing perspectives in the academic world about the 'right' way to comprehend phenomena such as Brexit or the inability of national governments to slow the rate of global warming. It's tempting to throw one's hands in the air, declare that 'it's all just too confusing' and leave it at that.

Another thing to consider is this: without the assistance of 'experts' to help them make sense of the world, the everyday realities of life do not allow people to see the key forces that drive continuity and change over time. In other words, our mundane experiences – such as buying petrol for a car, working as a dental assistant, volunteering in a housing shelter or paying our mortgage – do not, in themselves, offer us much insight into a larger and wider set of connections we know they're somehow a part of. Only disciplined inquiry can make these connections plain. As we saw in Chapter 1, Harvey is among those to devote years of their lives to such disciplined study so that others can understand what lies behind and beyond their everyday experiences. Inevitably, a certain responsibility comes with this. To claim to understand the grand forces of history and geography demands a commitment to rigour, honesty and open-mindedness in the face of new evidence (or criticism from detractors). Accordingly, good theory should reflect this commitment.

In sum, we might say that, for Harvey, theory promises to (i) replace a complexity we don't properly understand with one that we do, (ii) reveal processes and relationships that aren't normally perceivable in people's everyday lives and (iii) show how these processes and relationships connect, and create commonalities among, places as different as Beijing, Bombay, Brisbane, Bogota and Boston (see Figure 3.1). On more than one occasion, Harvey has used a cartographic metaphor to depict theory as a 'cognitive map' (e.g. 1989b: 2) that allows us to look down from on high. The map does not seek to depict everything but, rather, the main topographic features, their relative position (where they exist) and the lines of connection between them. Theory, then, is selective like any map. It uses concepts to cut into the connective tissue of reality to reveal the metaphorical bones, organs and arteries. In *The Grundrisse*, his posthumously published notebooks from the 1850s (published in English in 1973 by Pelican Books), Marx famously wrote that 'The concrete is concrete because it's the concentration of many determinations, hence [the] unity of the diverse' (p. 101). But we cannot, like laboratory scientists, conduct experiments to identify the nature and relative importance of these determinations. Like Marx, Harvey disaggregates the concrete *conceptually* to represent in thought the key determinations characteristic of a capitalist society. To phrase this differently, Harvey utilises the 'power of abstraction'.

You're a terrorist? Thank God. I understood Meg to say you were a theorist.

Figure 3.1. Armchair theory, harmful theory? Some regard 'theory' as hopelessly abstract or else a form of attempted brainwashing (as in recent criticisms of 'woke' critical race theory). But Harvey sees theorising as a positive human capacity.

Source: Cartoon by Anthony Haden-Guest (2004). Redrawn by Felicity Brasset.

A basic theory of capitalist accumulation (that's rather less 'basic' than it initially seems)

'To abstract' is to remove from, separate or disentangle. It involves illuminating specific processes, relationships or phenomena whose nature may otherwise be difficult to understand. But the word 'abstract' also means non-specific or general. In Harvey's case, much of his theorising in the first sense of the term is especially abstract in the second sense of the term. That is, his cognitive map is based on a remote view of the world, one more akin to orbiting the planet than flying in a helicopter or even a passenger jet. While we often regard remoteness in negative terms, in Harvey's case the intention of abstract theory is not to distance us from the world but, rather, to improve our understanding of its everyday aspects. As we will see later in the book, this is not at all paradoxical.

Starting in the 1970s, and following Marx's *Capital*, Harvey has theorised capitalism as a mode of production with the following fundamental qualities (regardless of time or place):

$$M{-}C <^{LP}_{MP} \ldots P \ldots C{-}M + \Delta M$$

Money (M) is used to purchase two kinds of commodities, namely workers (who sell their labour power [LP] for a certain period of time each day, week, month and year) and means of production (MP: buildings, technologies and direct material inputs to production). Commodities are things that can be sold and bought in return for money. The commodities of LP and MP are combined in a production process (P) wherein new goods and services are created (C′). These are then sold to various consumers, the aim being to supplement the original money advanced (M) with an increment (profit: Δ). As Harvey noted in *The Limits*: 'The capitalist form of circulation rests upon an *inequality* because capitalists possess more money … at the end of the process than they did at the beginning' (1982a: 21).[2] This cycle of accumulation begins again once those who own firms, and employ workers, deploy money earned (or else money received from bank loans, shareholders, asset sales etc.) in a new round of commodity production. Harvey calls this the 'primary circuit of capital' (or capital for short). Capital is about *metamorphosis* between money and commodity forms.

This conceptual depiction of capitalism may seem almost laughably simplistic when one considers the realities of actually existing capitalism (with its hedge funds, central banks, government bonds, private equity firms, stock markets, patent laws, millions of self-employed workers and numerous trading agreements). However, it cuts through all the empirical detail in a way that's both useful and more sophisticated than it appears to be. As Harvey asserted in *The Urbanization of Capital* (1985a), where he considered pre-capitalist cities, this depiction of the DNA of capitalism helpfully communicates its differences from other modes of production, past and present. For one thing, it shows that the central social relationship is based on a general institutionalisation of *private property*: a class of people own the means of production, while another class are 'free' to sell their labour power in order to live. Production is organised according to wage labour and employment contracts, implying both a class distinction and a class relation.

Second, it shows that capitalism is *expansive*: its guiding (and we might say very odd) logic is 'accumulation for accumulation's sake'. Producers are not aiming for a steady state; instead, they seek to enlarge their coffers. This is the GOD imperative (Grow or Die!) for individual capitalists and the system as a whole. Third, since there are many capitalists in the world, the circuit of capital diagram above shows that *inter-firm competition* is a key mechanism for the production of goods and services in capitalism. Fourth, in turn, this drives constant *innovation* in both production processes and product offerings, as firms seek to cut costs and enlarge their market share. For Marx and Harvey, the pressure to grow, compete and innovate gives capitalism a 'law like' character so far as producers and workers are concerned. The pressure confronts those who make commodities as an external force which is neither created, nor regulated, by any one actor in the drama of capital accumulation. Scottish philosopher and economist Adam Smith famously called it the 'hidden hand' of the market. For Marx, and Harvey, it's at least as much an 'iron fist'.

Fifth, theorising capitalism as, at base, a process of expansion predicated on employing workers to make goods and deliver services shows it to be *contradictory*. For instance, in aggregate it's obvious that workers are both a cost of production for employers but also a mass of consumers whose shopping with the wages they earn is necessary to help to keep capitalism afloat by ensuring that demand matches expanding commodity supply. Finally, the circuit diagram above shows us that, in capitalism, economic wealth takes several forms rather than one principal one (such as gold metal). For instance, means of production can be assets for commercial property owners if they rent office space to, say, a financial services company. Meanwhile, a billionaire like Virgin Group founder Richard Branson sees his company bank balance grow year on year but may also own shares in other firms which may yield a higher return than putting money into a savings account. In short, wealth in a capitalist society is variable and fluid because the accepted practice of exchanging all manner of things for money renders otherwise different phenomena (paintings, precious metals, houses etc.) *commensurable*. So long as a thing has a potential market (i.e. can be sold), it has a chance of being a specific material embodiment of wealth that's convertible to other forms. So long as capital circulates, that is, there's a chance that very many things will increase in their monetary value.

We now begin to see that Marx and Harvey's 'primary circuit of capital', for all its apparent conceptual simplicity, is in fact rather complicated. It represents a specific political economy: that is, a particular way in which wealth is defined, created and distributed in an economy organised according to historically created, and culturally and legally instituted, relationships between groups understood as 'producers', 'employees' and 'consumers'. In reality these groups are highly differentiated, of course, and operate in tandem with landlords, money lenders, unemployed workers and other social groups. Following Marx, Harvey deploys a set of concepts to help us understand the complications. Chapter 1 of *The Limits* is one of several places where he adumbrated these concepts, distilling the early chapters of volume one of *Capital*.

Some of these concepts we have already mentioned, such as mode of production and labour power. Others are familiar to people with a basic acquaintance with Marx's work, though those new to Marxism may find these venerable concepts variously strange or intriguing. The concepts include use value, exchange value, value, abstract labour, concrete labour, material wealth, social wealth, socially necessary labour time, commodity fetishism, alienation, class relations, class struggle, class-in-itself, class-for-itself, the formal and real subsumption of labour, organic composition of capital, surplus value (relative and absolute), relative surplus population and crises of accumulation. We will explore several of these in the next chapter, where we examine Harvey's understanding of capitalism's 'irrational' tendency to undermine the accumulation process.

For now, though, we focus on just five concepts to help further explain the nature and utility of theory as Harvey understands it. They are the concepts of use value, exchange value, value, surplus value and fetishism. Commodities are qualitatively different and have specific uses – for instance, an electric washing machine is nothing like a tennis ball or a leather handbag. But they are exchangeable at certain prices for a commodity whose special role is to enable commensuration among these various use values. This commodity – money – allows commodities to have an exchange value (i.e. to be worth a particular amount of dollars, Euros etc.). But, following Marx, Harvey reasons that price must represent something that commodities have in common, despite their qualitative differences. After Marx, he calls this something 'value'. Marx described it as real but immaterial (or invisible), rather like gravity. Far from being cryptic, Marx was referring to the fact that a capitalist economy requires a general 'substance' to permit daily determination of the relative worth of multifarious commodities. Mainstream economists have, in the past, called this metaphorical substance 'utility' as determined by contingent relations between buyers and sellers. Marx and Harvey demur and maintain that value is the abstract social form assumed by all manner of concrete labour practices when the commodities they produce are brought to market. Put differently, value is emergent from the unity of commodity production and sale (exchange) in the context of class relations (where most people sell their capacity to work in order to live). It is thoroughly social and, so Marx and Harvey argue, made possible by the common metric of twenty-four-hour clock time, whose universalisation since the seventeenth century has allowed the commensuration of disparate and far-flung acts of concrete labour (with workers paid for a certain number of hours each day and week).

While this is not the place to defend Marx's question-begging 'labour theory of value',[3] our brief discussion of use value, exchange value and value serves to illustrate some important additional elements of Harvey's approach to theory more widely. One is *conceptual systematicity*. Like the late Marx, Harvey insists that concepts must have a *necessary* relationship to each other and thus be 'organically related'. In the early parts of *Capital* volume 1, and *The Limits*, neither Marx nor Harvey could fully 'prove' the existence of value. But the simple decomposition of all commodities into two forms of value led them logically to the conclusion that, for routine exchange to occur, there *must* be a qualitative, universal something that allows material differences to be expressed as monetary quantities. The something cannot be the material form of money (since money is a variable token: coins, notes, precious metals, beads, shells etc. can serve as money) but, rather, something that particular forms of money make flesh.

Likewise by way of systemic reasoning, Marx and Harvey derived the insight that capitalists collectively appropriate wealth from workers. In general, things are exchanged for 'what they are worth' given prevailing demand and supply conditions. Thus, the profit that motivates capitalists cannot be acquired by being seen to 'rip off' workers (though there are, undoubtedly, very many instances of underpaid employees in the world). To achieve social stability, labour market exchange (i.e. wages paid for the purchase of an individual person's working time) must be perceived to be broadly fair. Where, then, does profit come from? How is it, that what comes *out* of the capital circulation process is more than went *in* at the start? For Marx, and Harvey, the answer is that 'surplus value' *must* be created by workers. For if capitalists really did pay workers the wage (price) that's equal to the value they create in production then, *ipso facto*, production would be egalitarian and capitalists would simply be giving back to workers exactly what they put in. There would be no profit.

Yet we know that capitalists routinely capture surplus value, and we know that to make profits they must sell goods and services to living people. It follows that, for Marx and Harvey, there's one logical conclusion: labour power (work performed in return for a wage) must be capable of creating more value than the value represented in workers' combined salaries. Surplus value is generated across the economy as a whole, though it's perfectly possible for individual firms to be loss-making and for there to be extremely well-paid workers in particular industries. Final commodity sales (acts of exchange) thereby each day *realise* surplus value, whereas only collective labour power *creates* it in the productive sphere.[4]

As this discussion indicates, Marxist theory presents to the reader a logical unfolding of an argument that, by the end, reconstructs in thought a complex reality that does not present itself to us in this logical, systematic way. Note the implication for how to interpret Marxian concepts. Each concept is *not* self-sufficient. This is why Italian economist Vilfredo Pareto (1848–1923) once memorably described Marx's concepts as akin to bats: for in them one can see both birds and mice. The concepts thus cannot be viewed as metaphorical bricks cemented together in rows to make a theoretical house. Instead, each concept only makes sense *relationally*, in the context of all the other concepts to be presented in a particular book, chapter or article written by Harvey. This means that a *linear presentation* of theory must be counteracted by a *non-linear reading* of the theory: Harvey wants us to appreciate the conceptual whole, the *compages*, not merely the parts. This places certain demands on his readers because a book like *The Limits* 'begin[s] with what in effect is a conclusion' (1982a: 1; see Castree, 1996). In volume one of *Capital*, Marx expressed the difficulty of reading his book as 'climbing up a steep summit'. As geographer George Henderson has noted, the ascent is arduous because the Marx-Harvey mode of 'theorizing has a sort of levelling effect. Every twist, turn, and stopping point matters equally, because these are *all* co-constitutive' (2004: 445, emphasis added).[5]

This mention of the relational nature of Marxian concepts brings us to a final important element of Harvey's approach to theory. Here a fifth signifier – commodity fetishism – is helpfully illustrative. While use value and exchange value are concepts describing *visible* aspects of our capitalist reality, the value concept describes something that's real but *hidden* (or virtual). The notion of fetishism is the point of connection. To fetishise something is to attribute to it qualities or powers that, in fact, exceed the thing in question and arise from its relationships. For Marx, in capitalist societies consumers tend to regard commodities as simply things-in-themselves (e.g. a Hyundai motorcar or an Apple iPhone). This is because they are presented to us as such (e.g. through TV advertising), as objects or services to be purchased and used. We also use them as discrete goods or services that we consider to be ours. But the fully developed concept of value (achieved at the end of *Capital*, volume 1, and *The Limits*) challenges fetishism and 'thingification'. The concept invites us to see commodities as *material expressions of social relationships between workers and employers realised through 'blind' market exchange of diverse goods and services*. In a capitalist world we wrongly, but understandably, fetishise commodities, misrecognising that their qualities partly reflect (or 'contain') a vast economic process without which they would be otherwise or simply nothing at all. This misrecognition is systemic and insidious: people are 'trapped' in a world of commodity appearances.

The battle of theory

So much for the nature and aims of theory in Harvey's writing. Clearly, his goal is to reveal some key truths about the world. Indeed, for several years (in the 1980s), he often referred to classical Marxism as a 'science', echoing Marx (who was a huge admirer of evolutionary biologist Charles Darwin, whose fundamental discoveries challenged theological explanations of how humans came to be a 'higher species'). 'Truth', however, is a highly contested thing: are there absolute truths, partial truths, perspectival truths and therefore plural truths? Sensibly, Harvey has never waded too far into these deep philosophical waters. But he's long been sensitive to the actual or potential *consequentiality* of theories that lay claim to be truthful, accurate or otherwise realistic. Given that there are many such theories across the disciplines and professions, this points towards a possible clash of theories. Whose theories are people to believe? Author of the magisterial *General Theory of Employment, Interest and Money* (1936), John Maynard Keynes – commenting on his own discipline and its wider influence – once said that 'practical men who believe themselves quite exempt from any intellectual influence are usually the slaves of some defunct economist' (2013: 383). Like Keynes, Harvey understands that the presence or absence of certain theories can make a big difference to how people think and act.

This was already the case fifty years ago. In justifying his initial turn to Marxism, Harvey offered some interesting insights into what we might call 'the battle of theory'. Two (now classic) essays remain of particular interest. One was published in the Leftist academic journal *Antipode* (Harvey, 1972b) and then reprinted in *Social Justice* where it was titled 'Revolutionary and counter-revolutionary theory in Geography and the problem of ghetto formation' (Harvey, 1973: Chapter 4). The other essay was published in the journal *Economic Geography* and entitled 'Population, resources and the ideology of science' (1974a). Both repay reading even after half a century. Both speak to Harvey's enduring belief that theory matters in society, not only in the world of academia or think tanks.

The first essay asked how we should explain the existence of run-down inner-city neighbourhoods like those Harvey encountered in Baltimore from 1969 onwards.[6] Needless to say, accurate explanations can inform appropriate solutions to a society-wide problem. Before he answered the question, Harvey offered some general insights about knowledge. One insight was that some forms of knowledge inevitably serve to sustain the existing social order. Mainstream social science, he said, 'formulates concepts, categories, relationships and methods which are … the product of the very phenomena they are designed to describe' (1973: 125). At first glance, this statement sounds utterly vacuous: after all, isn't the point of good social science precisely to 'correspond' with social reality? But Harvey was alerting readers to the biases built-in to knowledge, *especially* when it claimed be objective. For instance, he noted that in the late nineteenth century efforts were made to replace the study of political economy (Marx's concern) with the supposedly scientific study of 'economics' (1973: 127). Economics narrowed the field of analytical and political vision to questions of supply and demand, interest rates, wage levels, inflation etc. and their relationships. As such, it made it less possible to discuss questions of how social relationships, power and uneven wealth distribution are integral to the functioning of a capitalist economy.

In light of this insistence that 'expert' social science is not uninfluenced by the world it claims to study dispassionately, what did Harvey have to say about the 'ghetto' (i.e. run-down inner-city areas)? Harvey recounted how leading analysts of modern Western cities in the 1960s explained common spatial patterns shared between places as diverse as Chicago and Sydney. For instance, in *Location and Land Use* (1964), William Alonso had focussed on the locational decision-making of diverse actors endowed with varying amounts of monetary resources. He envisaged urban land use as governed by patterns of 'bidding' whereby actors compete to buy or rent parcels of land (or buildings) according to their interests and goals. For instance, retailers will want to locate in the central business district (CBD) in order to have access to large numbers of consumers; meanwhile, professionals may want large houses and a leafy residential environment and can afford to commute to work in the CBD, thus gravitating to the suburbs. In between, inner-city 'donut' areas existed because poorer urban residents need access to jobs concentrated in (or near) the CBD and cannot readily afford the transport costs of commuting from the suburbs to work. Overall, in Alonso's view, a 'rational geography' ensues that can be explained with reference to resource-constrained decisions made by actors with diverse 'preferences' for land use. In the detail, this rational geography would vary somewhat from city to city, so Alonso thought. In each case, information about locational decision-making would be gathered in which variables like price, time availability, ease of access and so on would be measured. The theory of urban land use could thereby be tested.

Harvey took issue with this way of studying the internal geography of cities, inspired by Marx's critique of the capitalist mode of production. As intimated earlier in this chapter, this critique situates urban actors in sets of social relations, norms and regulations that confront them as 'structures' that, though far from natural, are difficult to alter. One is the norm of private property, enforced through all manner of regulations upheld by the law and police. In this light, common and problematic features of Western cities – inner-city poverty, high unemployment, crime and related maladies – are not the unfortunate result of 'constrained preferences' among the poor. Instead, they are geographical expressions of the systemic inequality integral to the functioning of capitalist societies. For instance, landlords able to afford inner-city housing legally enjoy the power to charge people relatively high rents (per unit area), leading to high population densities, or lower rents for poorly maintained properties. Either way, inner-city residents born into such conditions find it hard to escape them without serious intervention by governments in the name of social justice.

Harvey's point about theory and theory testing, then, was both simple and powerful. He argued that the 'realities' one is seeking to shed light on are not simply 'out there' awaiting discovery through unbiased use of suitable techniques, like social surveys, informed by a sound theory. Instead, as his critique of Alonso showed, methods and data are the servant of the way one 'carves up' the world theoretically prior to any empirical research. As noted earlier, abstraction (and *how* we abstract) matters. For instance, instead of focussing on supposedly sovereign urban actors with their bundles of resources, preferences and locational options, as a Marxist Harvey urged analysts to focus on relations of power and inequality between employers, rentiers, workers and government. Methodologically, such a focus might, for example, yield ethnographic research into landlord–tenant interactions or interviews with local government officials about the politics behind public housing provision over time (e.g. the lobbying of mayors by certain construction companies). Or the focus might be on how the decisions of powerful urban actors (e.g. mortgage lenders or government regulatory officials) impinge on the locational circumstance of the poor (see Harvey and Chatterjee, 1974, on Baltimore).

On the basis of this argument, Harvey distinguished between *revolutionary*, *status quo* and *counter-revolutionary theory*. All are anchored in reality (they are not mere 'wishful thinking'). The second offers insights that serve to perpetuate current reality; the first challenges that status quo by identifying the causes of problems and openings for meaningful solutions; meanwhile, the third actively resists the first, offering concepts and arguments that may serve the interests of elites in society at the expense of those who are harmed by the status quo. Nailing his post-positivist colours to the Marxist mast, Harvey declared that 'The intellectual task is to identify real choices as they are immanent in an existing situation and to devise ways of validating ... these choices through action' (1973: 149).

Harvey's paper 'Population, resources and the ideology of science' covered much the same ground, only with the neo-Malthusian theory of 'over-population' as its target. This theory, in various ways, informed a lot of discourse about the need to control birth rates in the 1970s. But there were two changes of emphasis in Harvey's article that are worth highlighting relative to the piece on urban theory. The first was his use of the term *ideology* to characterise neo-Malthusianism. This is a key idea in post-classical Marxism, and one Marx and Engels used on many occasions (see Eagleton, 1991). Though Harvey didn't unpack the idea in his article, it's another, quite pointed way of designating status quo and counter-revolutionary thinking. Any social order can only reproduce itself if that order is rationalised and legitimated by those who benefit the most from it. This is the function of ideology (or what Antonio Gramsci, writing in the 1930s, helpfully termed 'hegemony' to describe the socially negotiated 'common sense' of any period and place). In lay terms, Harvey's critique of ideology took the form of posing the rhetorical question about capitalist elites: 'well they *would* say that, wouldn't they?'.

Second, Harvey strongly emphasised the fact that all theories secrete certain *philosophical* beliefs about the basic nature of reality. Consumers of theory are implicitly invited to take these beliefs for granted. The beliefs are, if you like, the hidden dimension to ideology, whereas theories and supporting evidence (as with neo-Malthusianism) are the visible aspect of ideology. Harvey took aim at what he called the neo-Aristotelean thinking taken-for-granted in Western societies.[7] Such thinking, which is still very much with us today, sees reality atomistically. That is, it presumes the world is chock-full of objects (or sets thereof) that can be abstracted from their relations to other objects. In the case of neo-Malthusian thinking, this took the form of positing 'natural resources' (a set of biophysically given entities of a renewable or non-renewable kind) and the number of people utilising them ('population'). If resources are fixed in quantity and quality then, for neo-Malthusians, it followed that there are definite *limits* to population growth. The two variables or 'factors' collide. However, reasonable though this simple claim may seem, Harvey cautioned against its hidden philosophy. He urged an appreciation of the interrelatedness of supposedly discrete chunks of reality wherein some become *intrinsic* to each other in key respects.

For instance, he argued that 'resources can be defined only with respect to a particular technical, cultural, and historical stage of development, and that they are, in effect, technical and cultural *appraisals* of nature' (Harvey, 1974a: 272, emphasis added). Likewise, he argued that scarcity is not simply absolute and determined by nature (as with a lack of water in a desert). Instead, it's 'inextricably social and cultural in origin. Scarcity presupposes certain social ends, and it is these that define scarcity just as much as the lack of natural means to accomplish these ends' (1974a: 272). Having challenged the philosophical taken-for-granted animating neo-Malthusian theory, Harvey then invited his readers to criticise the theory on an alternative philosophical basis:

> Let us consider a simple [neo-Malthusian] sentence: 'Overpopulation arises because of the scarcity of resources available for meeting the subsistence needs of the mass of the population'. If we substitute our definitions into this sentence we get:
>
> > 'There are too many people in the world because the particular ends we have in view (together with the form of social organisation we have) and the materials available in nature, that we have the will and the way to use, are not sufficient to provide us with those things to which we are accustomed'.
>
> (1974a: 272)

In short, Harvey urged his readers to see that the 'battle of theory' was also a battle of philosophical worldviews – albeit a somewhat subterranean one.

The detour of philosophy

Since the early 1970s, Harvey has done battle with a widespread 'billiard ball' view of the world that abstracts things from their constitutive relationships, positing those relationships as somehow external and contingent. Because his non-atomistic philosophy undergirds his work as a theorist, it's worth briefly exploring its core elements. In a small number of writings, he's made these elements explicit, so we draw upon these writings here.

Philosophy is often defined as the pursuit of timeless, highly abstract truths about (i) the nature of reality (ontology) and the way (ii) people can develop trustworthy means of making sense of that reality (epistemology). But Marx criticised the 'idle speculation' of much European philosophy in his own day and argued for a materialist worldview mindful of both the biological *and* social aspects of humanity's existential condition. Accordingly, Harvey already acknowledged in *Social Justice* that 'there are no [purely] philosophical answers to philosophical questions ... [because] the answers lie in human practice' (1973: 13). In the conclusion to that book, he was clear that 'Marx appealed to history as proof and affirmation of his ontology' (1973: 296). Harvey also, as we've seen, rejected epistemologies that presumed cool detachment from the world: 'It is irrelevant to ask whether concepts, categories and relationships are "true" or "false". We have to ask, rather, what it is that produces them and what is it that they serve to produce?' (1973: 298). Broadly, then, Harvey has long been 'post-foundationalist' in his philosophical beliefs – he eschews the idea that anybody can specify once-and-for-all dimensions of human existence (except, perhaps, at a level of abstraction that borders on being meaningless). He is also, clearly, secular (i.e. he doesn't believe that deities exist with the power to shape reality).

But this broad post-foundational commitment aside, what else is there to say about Harvey's philosophical worldview? Though he wrote precious little about it in the years after *Social Justice* was published, in the mid-1990s he did, at last, venture some formal statements (e.g. Harvey, 1993a, 1995a). The most complete of these statements was presented in his most abstract book *Justice, Nature and the Geography of Difference* (1996a: Chapters 2–5, hereafter *JNGD*).[8] The timing was no accident: at that point in his career, Harvey was being criticised in some quarters for being too fixated on capitalism, as if little else in the world really mattered. In this context, his attempt at philosophical self-explanation was a form of self-defence, taking the form of both standing his ground while also conceding some ground to his constructive critics.

As he explained in *JNGD* (especially in Chapters 2 and 3), Harvey adheres to a philosophy of internal relations when it comes to understanding capitalism. This involves both a *dialectical ontology* and a *reflexive, open-ended dialectical epistemology*, with both expressed via Marxist theorising (as per previous sections of this chapter). Glossing, the ontological claims are as follows: processes, flows and relationships are as important as objects, entities and things; processes are, as capitalism demonstrates, often structured into totalities, systems or wholes; these totalities can be contradictory in their operation, creating forces of stability and change; specific parts or 'moments' within a system offer insights about the whole because they, in effect, internalise all other parts or moments; relatedly, parts and moments of a bigger system can be both causes and effects interchangeably; and processes do not simply have a history and a geography but can *constitute* their own spatio-temporality. Epistemologically – and again we are glossing here – Harvey made a set of corresponding claims, as follows: the process of analysis must represent a dynamic, unified yet contradictory capitalist reality by identifying key processes and relationships; such analysis can reasonably focus on any part of the wider capitalist system because the key processes and relationships are 'contained' in that part;[9] dialectical logic, mirroring a dialectical reality, allows the analyst to track where and how 'moving contradictions' manifest in a system that's growth-orientated and looking to 'entrain' presently non-capitalist phenomena; and this dialectical tracking forces the analyst to extend and modify their understanding of a capitalist-infused world, so analytical closure is only ever temporary.[10] In all this, Harvey's philosophical outlook has been deeply informed by the work of American Marxist Bertell Ollman, among others. Harvey calls his view a 'strong' version of relational dialectics (1996a: 57) (see Table 3.1).

Younger readers will no doubt find the term 'dialectics' to be terribly arcane (which it is!). Some older readers will be aware of its venerable roots in the writings of the ancient Greeks and, much later, those of German philosopher Georg W. F. Hegel (among others). Is Harvey arguing that our present-day reality is *predominantly* dialectical, that is an open system driven to change its forms of appearance due to opposing forces within it? Yes, he certainly has argued this (rightly or wrongly) for many years. But this is not the same as proposing that capitalism squeezes other things out *altogether* or else wholly *reduces* those things to its own peculiar logic. We live in an 'over-determined' world, one where a dynamic confluence of different social relationships, forms of power, institutional rationalities, biophysical conditions and ethno-cultural values govern our daily lives. To suppose otherwise would be to inflate the power of capitalism unduly, as argued in J-K Gibson Graham's (1996) classic work *The End of Capitalism (As We Knew It)*.

The philosophy of 'critical realism', first developed by the British scholar Roy Bhaskar (1944–2014) in the 1970s, in effect formalised this over-determinist view for social and natural scientists. In the world of academic Marxism, Americans Stephen Resnick and Richard Wolff have done a great deal to make Marxist dialectics consistent with an over-determinist ontology (for instance, see their now classic book *Knowledge and Class*, 1987).

Table 3.1: Dialectical thought in David Harvey's work

Ontological dialectics	**Epistemological dialectics**
Internal relations and wholes exist and matter	Rational abstractions necessary to dissect complex realities and avoid chaotic conceptions
Contradiction seen as a motor of change	Linear representations of synchronic realities need to be treated with caution
Process and material form are co-constitutive	Systematic tracking of real contradictions allows a reconstruction in thought of unfolding realities

Some doubt whether Harvey's philosophy (and theoretical practice) can, in fact, serve to understand the articulations between capitalism, patriarchy, racism, religion and other things (see, for instance, geographer Cindi Katz's very sympathetic critique from 2006). But what we can say is that Harvey's is not a 'philosophy of everything', meaning that – for him – there's definitely more to life than the dialectics of capitalism. He would thus surely endorse Terry Eagleton's amusing observation that 'Marxism is not some Philosophy of Life or Secret of the Universe, which feels duty-bound to pronounce on everything from how to break your way into a boiled egg to the quickest means to delouse cocker spaniels' (2003: 33). We live in a pluriverse, albeit one where capitalism seeks to profit by incorporating into its ambit all manner of things that are not reducible to it.

Down to earth: theorising the local, comprehending geographical variety

We've seen that Harvey's approach is to abstract from 'on high' in order to reveal encompassing, contradictory processes. We've seen too that he predicates his theoretical work on a philosophy of internal, dialectical relations. To repeat: Harvey's theoretical and philosophical propositions are designed to shed light on real-world complexities and potentialities. His central interest is in the *concrete* (or empirical) as 'the concentration of many determinations', and as a constantly changing 'unity of the diverse'. 'The concrete', of course, is the totality of everything at all temporal and geographical scales. It encompasses what's empirically visible and also what's real but not readily perceivable day to day. Strictly, it's impossible to fully understand (there's simply too much going on to account for). To make the analysis of the concrete more tractable, social analysts have for decades homed-in on the *local* scale of things. Harvey's in-depth studies of nineteenth-century Paris (and to a lesser extent Baltimore and Oxford) place him among these analysts. And yet he's expressed strong reservations about certain ways of studying the local. It's instructive to consider the nature and point of these reservations. They shed light on Harvey's understanding of the theory-empirical relationship in a world of multiple, overlapping, and interconnected towns, cities, rural areas and regions.

A key reference point is Harvey's mid-1980s essay 'Three myths in search of a reality in urban studies' (1987a), which inspired a lively debate in the journal *Society and Space*. Having just returned to the United Kingdom, Harvey's focus was a shift in urban and regional studies among a cadre of erstwhile Left-leaning British social scientists (including human geographers).

These researchers were trying to understand why, how and with what effects the British economy was being restructured (a process which accelerated after around 1973 as the Fordist-Keynesian regime of accumulation unravelled). Two notable instances of this were Marxist geographer Doreen Massey's influential book *Spatial Divisions of Labour* (1984) and a large, multi-locality, multi-project team programme of research funded by the Economic and Social Research Council (ESRC). The programme was called CURS (the Changing Urban and Regional System of the United Kingdom – see Cooke, 1986). Independently of each other, Massey and the many CURS researchers grappled with the spatially uneven patterns of economic crisis, decline and renewal. Yet Harvey saw two commonalities in this work that he found troublesome.

One was the relegation of the claims made by Marxist theory to the 'general context' for understanding local-scale developments (as opposed to the theory being used to directly explain some of those developments). The other was a fixation on local-scale events and trends in all their seeming particularity and complexity (e.g. in the coalfields of Nottinghamshire versus the service town of Cheltenham versus the former docklands of east London). As Harvey expressed it, 'There's nothing ... to guard against the collapse of scientific understandings into a mass of contingencies exhibiting relations and processes special to each unique event' (1987a: 373). His former doctoral student Neil Smith (1987a) echoed Harvey's concern that same year. In an article in the journal *Antipode*, Smith – commenting on the CURS localities programme – opined that

> It is what we make of the empirical data that counts, and this implies that the shared theoretical perspective must be an ever-active ingredient; theory cannot function simply as a backdrop to an unfolding empirical play but must be a co-star on the front of the stage. If the comparability of the results between the different localities is not stressed, the danger is that the CURS project will do little more than repeat the empiricist locality studies of an earlier generation [of geographers] which deliberately examined individual places for their own sake, and did not attempt to draw out theoretical or historical conclusions.
>
> (1987a: 62)

There's no need here to determine whether Harvey and Smith's concerns about the research of Massey and others were entirely justified (see Massey, 1991, for a partial rebuttal).[11] It's the concerns themselves that matter. Harvey and Smith were cautioning against (i) an analytical fixation on the local scale, (ii) a local-scale theory-light process of fact collecting and

(iii) a failure to conduct relational, cross-case inquiry that tracks common processes, relations, pressures and contradictions among otherwise different localities. Research that ignores these three cautions can lead to theoretical and empirical parochialism, effectively denying the globality of capitalism and the political implications of that. That was the worry expressed by Harvey and Smith. As geographer Alan Cochrane put it at the time: 'If each place [studied] is [empirically] unique, then each conceptualisation seeking to explain industrial location ends up having to be unique, too' (1987: 357).

In the years since this late-1980s 'localities debate' (as it became known), Harvey has been consistent in his critique of analytical (and political) localism. It came through in his analysis of the campaign to save jobs in Cowley, near Oxford (Harvey and Swyngedouw, 1993); in his critique of the post-modern celebration of 'difference' (e.g. Harvey, 1989a); and in any number of his 'global' analyses since *The New Imperialism* was published two decades ago. Note, then, two things. First, 'the concrete' for Harvey is not synonymous with the local (or micro) scale. It's there to be analysed at *all* spatio-temporal scales, from the world to the individual human body. Second, while he's understandably emphasised capitalist processes that cross-cut multiple scales, theorising is not, in fact, synonymous with 'general' or global analysis. As Kevin Cox and Andrew Mair (1989) wisely observed, as part of the localities debate, it's necessary to theorise key mechanisms, institutions and relations that are partly or wholly local in their mode of operation. This isn't something Harvey has made sufficient mention of. Theorising is *not* selective in scalar terms (e.g. one can theorise in very abstract terms about place-specific phenomena). Good theory should thus be able to conceptually present a mesh of global, national *and* local-scale phenomena via a set of relational and 'rational' abstractions (see Table 3.2).

Table 3.2: Theory, empirical research and spatial scale. It's often mistakenly thought that abstract theory focusses on the global scale and that empirical research is local or regional in scale. Harvey's view is that capitalism's multi-scalar nature requires matching *all* levels of theoretical and empirical analysis

Abstract theory	Local-scale phenomena	Regional-scale phenomena	National-scale phenomena	Global-scale phenomena
Meso-level and concrete theory	Local-scale phenomena	Regional-scale phenomena	National-scale phenomena	Global-scale phenomena
Theoretically informed empirical research	Local-scale phenomena	Regional-scale phenomena	National-scale phenomena	Global-scale phenomena

In what sense a *critical* theorist?

We've almost completed our exposition of the nature and aims of theory in Harvey's Marxism. But there's one final, important element that we need to explore. Clearly, Marxists seek to understand the world, but they also wish to change it. They're not interested in knowledge for knowledge's sake. As books like *Social Justice* and *The Limits to Capital* signal in their titles, Harvey wants to move beyond 'the rule of capital'. How realistic this aspiration is will be considered later in this book (see Chapters 8 and especially 9). Here we simply focus on what makes Harvey's classical Marxist theory 'critical'. To use his language from fifty years ago, in what ways is the theory 'revolutionary', that is – as he expressed it in *The Limits* – about 'the unity of rigorous science and politics' (1982a: 37)? Somewhat strangely for a political radical, Harvey has never been too forensic in his discussion of the evaluative dimensions of theory. In this he mirrors Marx, whose comments about socialism and communism were fairly episodic, brief and usually non-specific.[12] Accordingly, we venture an interpretation of our own based on long acquaintance with Marx and Harvey's writings.

To criticise is to find fault, while also implying – or else stating explicitly – a preferred state of affairs that could or should eventuate. In Harvey's case, his critique is of certain non-Marxist theories (as we have seen above) and the changing realities of a resolutely capitalist world. At the level of theory, this critique is necessarily abstract, unless or until the theory is used to assess potentialities for political change in concrete situations at various spatio-temporal scales. It seems to us that Harvey's abstract critique of capitalism is necessarily an *immanent* one. That is to say, his theoretical writings (and theory-informed analyses of nineteenth-century Paris and the present epoch) show that capitalism is, in effect, *self-critical* when seen through Marxian lenses. Harvey's criticism is not 'external' to its object nor glibly utopian (e.g. 'wouldn't it be nice if people shared their wealth more equitably'). This has two aspects.

First, like Marx, Harvey shows that central concepts of capitalist society, such as 'equality' and 'freedom', are more limited in their practical meaning than they appear to be. For instance, commodity exchanges are supposed to be fair and voluntary transactions between owners (e.g. of money or cars) wherein the 'right' price is paid for something in light of prevailing demand and supply conditions. As we've seen above, Marx's analysis of the primary circuit of capital shows that, in fact, workers as a whole produce more value than they receive back in their collective wages. Because Harvey replicated that analysis in *The Limits* and elsewhere, it can be said that his critique is categorial: that is, it uses logical reasoning to show how hollow many common-place concepts employed to justify capitalism actually are. The concepts capture only a part of capitalist reality, not nearly enough of it: the formal equality that exists between the buyer and seller of labour-power in the labour market, for example, also explains but obfuscates the substantive exploitation of the working class in the labour process.

Second, like Marx, Harvey's theory pushes beyond a conceptual critique to highlight the 'irrationality' of, and harm caused by, capitalism in practice. For instance, the revelation that capitalism is contradictory as part of its normal functioning indicates that it constantly fails millions of people (including capitalists, and not only workers). Economic crises are the most acute instances of this, be they regionally specific or more global in nature (see Chapter 4). Inter-capitalist competition in the context of the growth imperative and the employment of wage workers (who are both a cost of production but also consumers of commodities) leads to periodic mismatches. Surplus material wealth (stockpiles of rice, clothes and laptops, for instance), or surplus monetary wealth (accumulated in bank accounts and on investors' balance sheets), can find no immediate market or use, despite the existence of surplus labour-power (e.g. in the form of high unemployment). Need and plenty thus sit side by side. As theory predicts and history shows, spectacularly in the 1930s Great Depression and more recently the global financial crisis of 2007–2009, capitalism is a disequilibrium economy. It *necessarily* – rather than incidentally – creates poverty and homelessness, disinvestment in specific places, and so on, as much as it enhances many people's lives through skilled occupations, well-paid jobs and remarkable commodities available for purchase (like smart phones and VR gaming headsets). The 'madness of economic reason' (Harvey, 2017a) arises from apologists' attempts to deny and justify the massive harm caused by punctuated, geographically uneven, endless economic growth.

In this twofold light, then, Harvey's critique of capitalism is immanent because he shows that

> if it is essential to a normative standard [like liberty] that attempts to realise it in practice backfire, that is plausibly a problem with the standard itself. And since the standards in question partly constitute the practices and institutions they govern, to revise such a standard is *ipso facto* to revise the structure of the practice or institution itself.
>
> (Diehl, 2022: 679)

But does such immanent critique vouchsafe a better future?

Critics of Marxism, going back many decades, have attributed to it a determinist view of history in which the working class will unite and act as 'the grave diggers of capitalism'. There's little evidence this was ever Marx's position, and it certainly isn't Harvey's (see Chapters 7 and 8). At the level of theory, Harvey's critique only identifies the *potential* for political revolution seeded by the creative destruction that's endemic to capitalist accumulation. It does not predict that workers become an insurgent 'class *for* itself' rather than a 'class *in* itself'. This distinction refers to the 'objective' and 'subjective' elements of class, the former being necessary but insufficient to engender class-based political action among working people. Whether revolutions eventuate, or else reformist projects designed to soften the hard edges of capitalism, are questions for empirical research rather than for theory as such. This much has been obvious since late 2007, when the world's financial system went into meltdown. The ensuing crisis, in which millions of people lost their jobs, lost their homes and saw their governments print money willy-nilly (while taking on huge debts in most cases), has not precipitated revolutions in countries like the United States of America, where the crisis originated. As such, it was a not an epochal 'moment of truth'. This highlights the need for an analysis of 'social formation' (evidentially) not merely the mode of production (conceptually).[13]

In short, a *concrete critique* is necessarily an empirical critique, albeit one that should be informed by sophisticated theory. Such critique can identify all sorts of reasons why capitalism is producing misery and discontent, without presuming any progressive political outcomes will emerge. Many of Harvey's 'public' books published since *The New Imperialism* (2003a) are critiques in this sense, albeit less microscopic than his study of Paris in the years 1850–1870 (Harvey, 1985a). Does this mean that all is broadly well with Harvey's underlying theoretical critique of capitalism? Not exactly. As we intimated in our above comments about over-determination and levels of abstraction, even at the level of theory it's important to identify how capitalism articulates with other major components of contemporary life (such as gender relations, or ethno-racial prejudice against minority groups).

Harvey acknowledged this in *JNGD*. There, he engaged with the writings of socialist-feminist political theorist Iris Marion Young (1949–2006), among others. In her influential book *Justice and the Politics of Difference* (1990), Young had distinguished what she called the 'five faces of oppression' and argued that late-twentieth-century Left politics had to reckon with their complex interaction. Harvey concurred, and accordingly his subsequent work has made frequent mention of a broad 'anti-capitalist' politics as opposed to a more narrow sounding 'class politics' (see Chapter 7 of this book). Even so, the fact remains that Harvey hasn't engaged in systematic conceptual thinking about a 'more than capitalist critique' to match the rigour of a capital-centric work like *The Limits*. This is rather odd because 'race' was so integral to the inequalities he railed against in his first Marxist book, *Social Justice and the City*. In this, he compares unfavourably to a figure like Nancy Fraser, another American socialist-feminist philosopher. In *Justice Interruptus* (1997) and elsewhere, Fraser has brilliantly analysed the intersections between various axes of social power, different forms of social identification, different modalities of justice, and different sorts of social relations, structures and processes.[14] She gives them equal conceptual weight so as to clarify the normative stakes in ensuring that a complex Left politics comes to fruition in practice. A careful theoretical analysis of these intersections remains vital in order to properly grasp both empirical events and political possibilities (see Chapter 8).

Conclusion

'Representations and ideas', writes Italian social scientist Federico Brandmayr, 'are not merely an epiphenomenon but play an active role in shaping social reality' (2021: 1). Clearly, David Harvey shares this view. As we've seen, he places special emphasis on theory as a vehicle for consciously shaping social reality. For him, rigorous theory – connected to evidence – is necessary but always insufficient. Of course, there are no guarantees that any theory will be broadly influential, including his own. For decades, the kind of research Harvey conducted was known only among a relatively small number of academics in Geography and Urban Studies. This was consistent with a broader trend in which Anglo-European Marxist thinking became concentrated in universities after 1945. Contrast this with Marx's later years, and the decades after: Marxist ideas changed the world for the best part of a century by being embedded in mass political movements (though, sadly, in ways that warped the key cognitive and normative insights of Marx, Engels and the best Marxist analysts of the early twentieth century). As capitalism has changed its spots over the decades, so too has the critique of capitalism had to evolve to keep up. Harvey's 'public turn' – the focus of Chapter 9 – is his attempt to make Marxist theory count for more beyond the academy at a dangerous moment in the dysfunctional life of the capitalist system.

As Harvey is all too aware, those dedicated to preserving capitalism have done a rather good job of it in recent decades. Sometimes, they've referred publicly to theory in their explanatory rhetoric – an example being American Republican politicians referring to the Laffer curve theory in the 1990s to justify tax cuts.[15] Other times, they've benefitted from the undoubted complexity of national and world affairs: citizens are easily misled by sound bites and slogans that offer reassuring (but erroneous) renderings of reality. Mostly, though, capitalist elites have altered the basic terms of public discourse – for instance, in most countries the term 'socialism' is now perceived to be quaint or else a dangerous throw-back to a much less liberal era. Relatedly, many critics maintain that the discourse successfully 'interpellates' people so that they come to *identify* personally with capitalism in its current neoliberal phase. Meanwhile, the intellectual and political Left has had to adapt to all this, in the process becoming a largely ineffective opposition as capitalism both multiplies and divides those negatively affected by it. This raises important empirical questions about how capitalism has been able to weather very serious crises during the five decades that Harvey has been writing and lecturing about it.[16] But to approach the answers (see Chapters 7 and 8), we first need to understand why and how crises manifest as a structural necessity. It's to this topic, which is central to Harvey's work, that we now turn.

Further reading

Benhabib, S. (1984). The Marxian method of critique. *Praxis International*, 3, 284–298.

Castree, N. (2006). The detour of critical theory. In N. Castree & D. Gregory (Eds.), *David Harvey: A Critical Reader* (pp. 247–269). Blackwell.

Harvey, D. (1973). Revolutionary and counter-revolutionary theory in Geography and the problem of ghetto formation. In *Social Justice and the City* (pp. 120–152). Johns Hopkins University Press.

Harvey, D. (1989b). Introduction. In *The Urban Experience* (pp. 1–16). Blackwell.

Harvey, D. (1996a). Dialectics. In *Justice, Nature and the Geography of Difference* (pp. 46–68). Blackwell.

Riva, T. R. (2021). Value. In B. Skeggs, *et al.* (Eds.), *The Sage Handbook of Marxism*, volume 1 (pp. 85–101). Sage.

Notes

1. Four years before Harvey published his most theoretical work – *The Limits to Capital* – the distinguished British Marxist historian E. P. Thompson had published *The Poverty of Theory* (1978). It was a critique of *theoreticism*, not theory as such; and the sort of theory Harvey advanced was more in keeping with the empirically testable kind that Thompson approved of – not the more abstract kind proposed by French duo Louis Althusser and Étienne Balibar, the focus of Thompson's ire.

2. He was, of course, referring to capitalists in aggregate (at any one time many who own companies and employ workers might well be *losing* money, though rarely would most of them be).
3. Even more than 150 years since *Capital* volume one was published, there are highly technical debates about key elements of Marx's political economy – a recent example is the exchange between American Marxist Fred Mosely (2021) and Sraffan political economist Robin Hahnel (2021). Harvey, following Diane Elson (1979), prefers to talk about the 'value theory of labour' rather than the opposite (see Harvey, 1982a: 35–38). That is, he believes Marx's aim was not to show that *only* workers create *all* forms of economic value but that, in capitalist societies, economic value is an alienated form of wealth whose origins lay in the utilisation of paid labour. Harvey acknowledges that there are many forms of value in all societies, and that wealth also assumes many material and symbolic forms. F. Harry Pitts' (2020) book *Value* offers an explanation and defence of Marx's value theory relative to other notions of value proffered by economists and fellow travellers. The US geographer George Henderson (2013) has published a brilliant analysis of the manifold forms and effects of 'value' in Marx's work.
4. The two best places in Harvey to read about 'the labour theory of value' are Chapter 1 of *The Limits to Capital* (Harvey, 1982a) and the appendix to *Marx, Capitalism and the Madness of Economic Reason* (Harvey, 2017a). The implication that it is a *separate* theory within Harvey's wider theory is not true – it's a set of conceptual propositions that lie at the heart of Harvey's wider theoretical anatomisation of capitalism. As intimated in the previous note, value theory in Marx and Harvey is not a trans-historical statement that *all* workers create 'value', nor that *only* workers create value (since value comes in various forms). Nor is it a theory of commodity prices, since prices are tethered to capitalist value but not determined by it in the detail. Harvey tackles the price-value relation lucidly in the *Madness of Economic Reason* book.
5. For instance, when reading *Capital* it is vital to know that in volume one Marx presumes and brackets all sorts of things that are only dealt with in volumes two and three. Where volume two deals with value *realisation* and volume three with value *distribution*, volume one deals with value *production*, yet the insights of each volume affect the others. So only by readers modifying their understanding as they proceed can they make adequate sense of Marx.
6. It can usefully be read alongside Chapter 5 of *Social Justice*, called 'Use value, exchange value and the theory of urban land use'.
7. He has sometimes referred to this worldview as Cartesian after the famous French philosopher René Descartes (1596–1650).
8. Since then, he's largely resisted making formal statements of philosophical belief, although philosophical propositions do pepper several books including and since *Spaces of Hope* (2000a) and *Cosmopolitanism and the Geographies of Freedom* (2009a).

9. To prove the point, he went on to publish a journal article that showed how a single working-class person's body can reasonably be seen as the site of an 'accumulation strategy' within modern capitalism (Harvey, 1998b).
10. For example, *The Limits to Capital* uses dialectical logic to tackle topics that Marx barely got to grips with, which Harvey described as 'filling empty boxes' in Marx's conceptual matrix (e.g. pertaining to fixed capital).
11. A very fruitful debate about theory, geographical variation, scale, the empirical and the global unfolded in the pages of *Antipode* between 1987 and 1990. It was a response to the Harvey-Smith critique.
12. In his lifetime Marx was a critic of 'utopian socialists' (especially in France) and felt that it was pointless to try to predict the post-capitalist future without detailed understanding of capitalism's real historical geographies.
13. In our view, Harvey's 'critique-as-crisis-theory' has two elements. One is a focus on class struggle and the possibility of a social revolution being a means for billions of working-class people to 'reappropriate' the wealth they collectively create and collectively 'alienate' (allowing the capitalist class to profit from it). The other element is a focus on the systemic domination of most people on the planet by the 'blind' forces of capital accumulation. During moments of crises, these forces have devastating consequences for hundreds of millions of people, wage workers and non-wage workers alike. The first critique operates in the name of workers as a constituency; the second critique operates in the name of a highly differentiated humanity, along with the non-human world (which has been massively damaged by capitalism over the centuries). In both cases, truly moving beyond the rule of capital would involve a change to people's self-conceptions, as much as to the material arrangements within various post-capitalist modes of production.
14. In her latest book *Cannibal Capitalism* (2022), Fraser integrates an anti-capitalist politics with a politics of 'nature', social reproduction and identity in a magisterial normative-political synthesis.
15. American economist Arthur Laffer (born 1940) theorised that, up to a point, cutting taxes would, in fact, increase overall tax revenues for governments. While this proposition is hardly new in economics, Laffer's several roles in Republican governments since the early 1970s allowed him to shape both public policy and political rhetoric about taxes and government spending. This was a period when American public debt ballooned, and a number of people criticised 'big government'. Laffer's advocacy for a lightly regulated capitalism can be found in Laffer, Moore and Tanous (2008). A rather disastrous enactment of Laffer's ideas occurred in the state of Kansas between 2012 and 2017, under the auspices of then Governor Samuel Brownback. The American economist Paul Krugman has been an outspoken critic of these ideas and policies in the public domain, though to little effect it seems.
16. Many analysts have sought to answer these questions, such as Colin Crouch (2011) in the United Kingdom and Wendy Brown (2019) in the United States of America.

Contradiction, perpetual change and crisis

The DNA of capitalism

4

Capitalism in periodic crisis: the theory; Falling profits: the first layer; Over-accumulation: the second layer; Finance to the rescue?; Time, history and capitalism; Conclusion

In a recent *New Left Review* article, Harvey (2020b: 115) likens the circulation of capital to the Earth's water cycle. It's a felicitous analogy. Just as water assumes different forms – liquid, gas and ice – so too does capital (e.g. money, infrastructure and commodities for sale). Just as the availability of water varies temporally and spatially – a flood here, a glacier there – so too are the pathways that capital takes uneven in length, width and direction. The most significant interruptions to the stable circulation of capital are crises. Here, significant numbers of working people, a great many capitalists and many local or national governments find themselves badly affected by disruptions in the circuit of accumulation. Jobs are suddenly lost, houses are repossessed, money is in short supply, debts go unpaid and so on. As Slavoj Žižek once expressed it (2002: 554–555), 'a crisis occurs when reality catches up with the illusory, self-generating mirage of money begetting more money'. Crises are structural in their causes and impacts (they largely elude the control of various actors) and also inter-subjective (many people experience them as shared moments of serious stress and loss). That is to say (in the language of sociologists), capitalist crises involve 'system disintegration' and coincident 'social disintegration' at the level of peoples' everyday lives. At this level, to use another analogy, people are made to feel like tiny cogs in a vast, erratic machine that most of them barely understand and certainly don't feel they can influence. Crises put them under considerable strain.

DOI: 10.4324/9780429028120-4

In this chapter, having touched upon it towards the end of the last, we adumbrate Harvey's theory of systemic crisis. We draw primarily on four of his books: namely, *The Limits to Capital* (1982a), *A Brief History of Neoliberalism* (2005a), *The Enigma of Capital and the Crises of Capitalism* (2010a) and *Seventeen Contradictions and the End of Capitalism* (2014a). We explain how Harvey, true to Marx, shows crises to be *endemic and necessary features of the process of capital accumulation*. They are, quite simply, unavoidable. This puts the emergence and eventual management of crises at the heart of Harvey's historical-geographical materialism. It leads us to consider how the 'primary circuit of capital' (aka 'production') connects to other spheres of economic activity, especially finance. It allows us to see that inherent contradictions and attempts at their resolution spur capitalism on historically: its evolution is punctuated by rounds of growth, stability, breakdown, restructuring and renewed expansion. While crisis and contradiction are fundamental to how Harvey integrates geography into classical Marxism, in this chapter we largely bracket the geography. Our focus is mainly on how capitalism not only unfolds through time but *uses* time strategically. We thus emphasise Harvey's *historical* materialism here more than his historical-*geographical* materialism. We also bracket important questions of how various people and institutions (e.g. national governments) seek to legitimise capitalism as an economic system during periods of crisis. Their various legitimation techniques are crucial to minimising revolt against the system, and radical reform agendas too. These techniques involve judgements about whether and how to label a particular episode a 'crisis' at all (on which see Janet Roitman's excellent book *Anti-Crisis*, 2013).

Capitalism in periodic crisis: the theory

Crisis and crises: definitional, conceptual and empirical issues

A crisis is a low frequency, high magnitude event: it represents a radical and painful departure from 'normal' times. To be sure, even in such 'normal' times, there are always certain individuals, institutions and even whole regions suffering difficulties of various sorts. But in such times, capitalism *as a system of circulation and accumulation* is not in significant difficulty. It is functioning relatively smoothly. During periods of structural crisis, by contrast, the circulation of capital is thrown into disarray in one or more countries. This can manifest in all sorts of ways, impairing capital in all its different forms. Manufactured commodities prove unsellable and their price plummets, sending their producers into bankruptcy. Banks relying on those producers to repay loans advanced to buy machinery that now lies idle are no longer able to issue new loans or to redeem customer deposits. Nor do they receive mortgage payments from home-owning workers whose jobs at the aforementioned manufacturing companies have been jettisoned. In short, through a cascade of causes and consequences, the whole system (or major parts of it) experiences shock and instability. The larger the system happens to be at any one moment in time, the greater the potential for more people and places to be impacted by it.

There will always be debate over what does and doesn't constitute a crisis for capitalism, but two criteria are essential. A systemic crisis is no momentary blip in time. (The UK Treasury defines a recession – one common word for an economic crisis, the other, more serious, being 'depression' – as two or more consecutive calendar quarters of contraction in economic output). And it is non-local and pan-economy: it's not isolated either geographically (to a particular place or handful of localities) or sectorally (to one or a small subset of industries).

Perhaps the most famous crisis in the history of capitalism was the Great Depression of the 1930s. Although it began, as crises typically do, in one place – the United States – it ultimately enveloped all of the capitalist world. Between 1929 and 1932, global economic output fell by approximately 15 per cent – a reduction that was unprecedented, and to which the world has never again come close, even with COVID-19, which by comparison saw just a 3 per cent fall in global output (from 2019 to 2020). All manner of additional metrics can be rolled out to evidence the sheer magnitude of the meltdown and its human impact. Rates of unemployment rose to far above 20 per cent in dozens of countries. The volume of international trade more than halved, as governments responded to the pressures on domestic industry with protectionist economic policies that restricted imports from overseas. And it took a full twenty-five years for the main US stock market index, the Dow Jones Industrial Average, to regain its previous peak of September 1929.

Harvey's crisis theory is an outworking of Marx's ideas from a century earlier. Though we refer to it here as a 'theory of crisis', that's actually something of a misnomer. Conceptually, it's not a 'theory within a theory' – which would suggest separability from Harvey's wider analytical framework. Rather, it's simply part-and-parcel of Harvey's holistic account of capitalism; we might say that his theory of capitalism *is* a crisis theory (though much else besides). In any event, much like Marx (who was witness to early capitalist crises in Europe in the 1840s and 1850s), Harvey has himself lived through multiple crises of capitalism. While he's certainly interested in the specific details of different crises, his intellectual interest is wider and more ambitious: it is in explaining the root causes of *all* capitalist crises. What is it about capitalism that makes it prone to crisis formation? Harvey elaborated a multi-layered answer in *The Limits to Capital* (1982a), and has held fast to that answer ever since, drawing on it in subsequent books to show how it helps us understand the various crises that have since occurred. He does not suggest that the theory can predict the timing of crises, nor that it can explain their exact empirical form – all crises are 'conjunctural' and empirically specific, even if varieties of the same 'species'. But his theory *can* help anticipate crises and account for their actual emergence.

The theory is rooted in Harvey's depiction of capital's primary circuit (see Chapter 3). The M → C ... P ... C′ → MΔ circulatory process *looks* straightforward on paper, but it rarely is in reality. To produce commodities, the question is: can the capitalist find the right raw materials, instruments of production and labour power and at the right price? Can she control the production process itself in such a way that surplus value can be captured? And are there sufficient consumers with sufficient financial wherewithal and the right demand profile to enable the capitalist to sell her product and earn a profit? Encountered at sufficient scale by enough capitalists, all of these challenges harbour crisis tendencies. Examining capital this way, Harvey powerfully depicts capitalist crisis tendencies in terms of capital's (in)ability to navigate a series of niggardly bottlenecks or chokepoints. Those crucial links in the chain – where M becomes C becomes M – are, if you like, capital's weak points or Achilles heels, where its flow is liable to being disrupted.

At the heart of Harvey's theory is the claim that crises are a necessary and endemic component of capitalism, an integral feature of this mode of socio-economic organisation. We may not be able to determine when, where and exactly why the next crisis will come along, but we can be sure that it *will* come. We will get to the question of why shortly. But it's worth highlighting that this understanding of capitalism is far removed from mainstream economic views. That the economy tends towards conditions of 'equilibrium' in which relevant economic forces are in balance is a mainstay of economic orthodoxy. Moreover, it's also believed that economists understand the economy sufficiently well to be able to help maintain such equilibrium. Most famously, in 2003 (just four years before the global financial crisis), the Nobel prize-winner Robert Lucas announced in his presidential address to the American Economic Association that economics' 'central problem of depression prevention has been solved, for all practical purposes' (Lucas, 2003: 1). Such hubris is anathema to a Marxist like Harvey. Crises can't be prevented, because they are inevitable.[1]

Why do crises inevitably occur?

The reason that capitalism is crisis-ridden is its inherent contradictions. Harvey, after Marx, identifies all manner of antinomies within capitalism. A very important one, and thus a good example to illustrate with, is the contradiction between exchange and use value. In *Seventeen Contradictions* (2014a), Harvey argued that this was one – but only one – of the roots of the 2007–2009 financial crisis, which began in the overheated US housing market when property prices tumbled (by around 20 per cent nationwide and more than 40 per cent in cities such as Phoenix and Las Vegas) and large numbers of homeowners were unable to pay their mortgages. Over 'the last 30 years or so', Harvey (2014a: 20) explained, 'housing has become an object of speculation' for households and investors alike. In other words, its exchange value had come to be treated as more important than its use value (the provision of shelter). Culminating in the bursting of the speculative bubble, the reckless pursuit of housing's exchange value ultimately 'destroyed … access to housing use values' for the approximately 10 million US individuals whose homes were repossessed by their mortgage lenders (2014a: 22). Housing is 'a perfect example', for Harvey, of how the simple difference between exchange and use value 'can evolve into an opposition and an antagonism before becoming so heightened into an absolute contradiction as to produce a crisis not only in housing but throughout the whole financial and economic system' (2014a: 23). Too many people invested in housing as a means to make money, only to be caught out when a number of homeowners could no longer afford to pay their mortgages because of insufficient wages, job losses and higher interest rates.

Meanwhile, if the reason that capitalism is crisis-ridden is that it's contradictory, the reason it is contradictory largely has to do with class. Its classed basis *renders* capitalism contradictory. The basic logic, laid out most extensively and systematically in *The Limits* – Harvey's crisis book *par excellence* – runs something like this. Capitalism's class character seeds essential tensions that impose important limits to capital circulation and accumulation: limits to how much profit it can generate, how much of that profit can be successfully reinvested and so on. In turn, crises represent the most acute manifestations precisely of those limits. That class is integral to all of this is something that Harvey repeatedly reminds his readers. 'The class analysis of *Capital*', Harvey insisted in *The Limits* (1982a: 33), 'is designed to reveal the structure of [the contradictions that] prevail at the heart of the capitalist mode of production'.

The paramount class-based contradiction is of course that between the owners of the means of production and the workers they employ.

Capitalists seek to capture surplus value that *originates* with workers by way of commodity sales which, in the end, are *realised* in large part by those self-same workers. But Harvey maintains that to understand capitalism and its crisis tendencies, there are other class-related contradictions to bear in mind too. Consider his early-1970s work with Lata Chatterjee on the Baltimore housing market, referenced in the previous chapter. Poor tenants suffered negative outcomes because they lacked power vis-à-vis landlords who were relatively wealthy. This also was a class relationship. Housing rent was in practice nothing like the 'clean', individualised market exchange envisioned by mainstream economics. It was instead thoroughly social, being the payment 'which accrues to the monopoly power of landlords *as a class* vis-à-vis the collective power and condition of the tenantry. It is set, in short, by a "class" conflict within a restricted geographical area' (Harvey and Chatterjee, 1974: 33, emphasis added).

What's more, the class contradictions of capitalism are 'horizontal' as well as 'vertical'. Specifically, there's a contradictory relation between individual capitalists and capitalists as a class. In other words, what's in the interest of a particular firm is not always in the interest of firms collectively. Harvey has given many examples. One, following Marx himself, concerns historic struggles over the length of the working day. Individual capitalists, 'each of them acting in his or her own self-interest and locked in competitive struggle with each other' (Harvey, 1982a: 34), are incentivised to push workers to their physical and mental limits to maximise the production of surplus value. But taken to its exploitative extremes, this process endangers the very physical (human) basis for capital accumulation and thus for the successful reproduction of the capitalist class itself. So capitalists must come together as a class, 'usually through the agency of the state', to temper competitive struggle and prevent the excessive exploitation of workers (1982a: 34). And that's what they have historically done. An early example was the English Factory Acts of the 1800s, which restricted the length of the working day. The 1833 act, for instance, stipulated that children of 9–13 years should work no more than nine hours a day, and children of 13–18 no more than twelve hours.

Once in train, crises are rarely simply left to work themselves out. Interestingly, some economists believe that this is what should be allowed to happen. During the global financial crisis that began in 2007, for example, some, so-called libertarian economists, argued that besieged banks – the immediate capitalist casualties of the turmoil in housing and mortgage markets – should have been allowed to go bankrupt. The libertarian logic, essentially, is that failure is an important part of capitalism, and that a Darwinian 'purge' of inefficient organisations renders capitalism more efficient and robust in the long term. But this hands-off approach is seldom if ever taken, and it wasn't in 2007–2009: only one financial institution of any real note, Lehman Brothers, was allowed to fail; others were bailed-out in one way or another by various governments. The bailouts in the United States alone cost an estimated $500 billion (Lucas, 2003). In times of capitalist crisis, the powers-that-be intervene to try to shore-up markets and institutions and prevent a crisis from becoming a catastrophe.

Harvey argues that this is inevitable: it is what a *capitalist* state will always do in crisis circumstances – that is, step in to try to stabilise accumulation and secure the reproduction of the status quo. This state-interventionist role is a crucial element of Harvey's theory of crisis. But it's important to note something of an inconsistency here. For while the state is at the heart of his crisis theory, Harvey has never articulated a convincing 'state theory' per se – a theory of the role of the national and local state in capitalism. He did write one very short paper on the topic in the 1970s (Harvey, 1976), in which he conceptualised the state not as 'some mystical autonomous entity' but as a system of interacting institutions (after the British Marxist Ralph Miliband), as a set of social relations (after Bertell Ollman) and, in particular, as a process of 'exercising power' – via a range of institutional arrangements and through diverse (e.g. administrative, judicial) channels. He embellished these remarks somewhat in *The Limits*, highlighting the state's interest (and not only in times of crisis) in 'the regulation and control of capital, albeit in the interests of the capitalist class as a whole' (1982a: 322). But as a 'theory', it's decidedly thin. The lack of a meaningful theory of the state is one of the most obvious lacunae in his work, certainly when considered alongside contemporary Marxist political economists (such as Bob Jessop) who have devoted significant attention to the topic.

The one element of the state's role vis-à-vis crisis management that Harvey *has* theorised at some length concerns its interactions with what he calls 'finance capital', by which he means the finance sector. As we shall see later in the chapter, finance, and the credit system in particular, play a decisive role in Harvey's crisis theory. Finance is both a product of capital's attempts to deal with its internal contradictions *and*, ironically, a mechanism for exacerbating those very contradictions. Alongside his theorisation of capitalism's geographies, Harvey's work on finance and crisis represents arguably his most important and original contribution to understanding the contradictory dynamics of capital accumulation.

And here's the thing: the state is integrally bound-up in the mechanisms of finance, *especially* in times of crisis and crisis management. It can make emergency loans. It can enact credit constraints or rationing. Above all else, there are the crucial 'quasi-state' financial institutions that are central banks.

Charged with managing currencies, overseeing private banking sectors and (increasingly) with ensuring financial stability, central banks such as the US Federal Reserve and the European Central Bank are 'independent' of the state in theory but only modestly so in practice – they derive their authority from governments and are directly accountable to them. As Harvey observed in *The Limits*, central banks actually represent the direct integration of finance capital with the state apparatus and are arguably the one state form that is not 'even *relatively* autonomous of capital' (1982a: 322). If Marx's famous description of the state as 'the executive committee of the bourgeoisie' can be applied meaningfully to any arm of the state, then the central bank, Harvey maintains, is it.

In *The Limits*, Harvey put central banks front-and-centre in crisis management. Real-world events surely inspired him in this: the Federal Reserve played a key role in dealing with the US recession of 1980–1982, the period during which Harvey was completing the manuscript. But not even Harvey himself could have imagined how right his claims about central banking and crisis management would turn out to be. Central banks have indisputably been *the* pivotal actors internationally in the state response to both the 2007–2009 financial crisis and the 2020–2021 COVID-19-inspired economic crisis. *Monetary policy* – the central banks' remit, and focussed on managing the supply and cost of money, the latter registered in interest rates – has been significantly more important than *fiscal policy* – the catch-all term for government spending and taxation. Indeed, already by 2013, scholars observing events were being moved to write about 'central bank-led capitalism' (Bowman et al., 2013).

Whatever role the state and other actors adopt in crisis management, however, the results are always imperfect. Contradictions and crisis tendencies, in Harvey's theory, are never really 'solved'. They cannot be. Whether actively managed 'well' or badly or not at all, crises do not eradicate underlying contradictions, so much as tend to dampen some – thus potentially stabilising capital accumulation for a period of time – but thereby inflame others. Returning to Harvey's hydrological analogy, crisis management is akin to the apocryphal Dutch boy sticking his finger in the leaking dyke: sealing off one leak merely increases pressure elsewhere in the system, eventually leading to another leak springing at another weak point. 'Contradictions', as Harvey likes to say, 'have the nasty habit of not being resolved but merely moved around' (2014a: 4).

And so Harvey's theory of crisis is at once a theory of history – and, as we will see in the next chapter, of geography. In highly simplified and stylised form, it runs broadly as follows. Periods of relatively smooth capital accumulation always come to an end because capital confronts material contradictions internal to it. A crisis occurs, during which capital – abetted by the state – attempts either to temporally defer (this chapter) and/or spatially displace (Chapter 5) those contradictions. Relief is found, in the shape of a new regime of relatively stable accumulation, but only ever temporarily. For the contradictions have only been 'moved around', and often also magnified in the process: one crisis thus irrevocably sets the stage for the next. In sum, Harvey's theory of history (and geography) is a theory of capitalism lurching from one crisis to the next, groping forward in time (and expansively in space) in search of what is always an elusive solution to what *cannot* ultimately be fixed. In the rest of this chapter, we'll explore and flesh out the theory in more detail, exposing it in 'layers', bracketing for now the crucial geographical aspects, while for illustrative purposes connecting the theory to real-world crisis events of the past century.[2]

Falling profits: the first layer

The first layer of Harvey's crisis theory is focussed strictly on the dynamics of the production process. Marx called this – the P at the centre of the primary circuit of capital – capitalism's 'hidden abode'. What he meant by that was that most economists in the early and mid-nineteenth century did not pay much attention to it. Instead, they were preoccupied with understanding other spheres of economic activity, in particular exchange (the buying and selling of commodities in markets) and distribution (how industrial companies, landlords and financiers divided-up profits). By contrast, Marx argued that production was at the heart of things. Venturing into this hidden abode, he uncovered the secrets of the creation of value and surplus value (see section two of Chapter 3).

But Marx also uncovered something else: contradictions and crisis tendencies. The most important alleged such tendency was for a progressive fall in the rate of profit among capitalist producers. In the *Grundrisse*, Marx went so far as to call this 'the most important law of modern political economy' (1973: 748). This 'law' says that there is an ineluctable tendency within capitalism for the rate of production of surplus value (and thus profit) to decline. Note that Marx's 'profit rate' is a relative concept. It indexes not the quantum of profit per se – say, an absolute amount of dollars – but the amount of profit *relative* to the amount of capital invested in production. 'Return on capital employed' is the equivalent measure in today's business world. Given that capitalism is a system oriented in the first and last instance towards profit creation, an inherent propensity for profit rates to fall is nothing if not a crisis tendency.

Marx's proposition is, as Harvey admitted, 'both brilliant and simple' (1982a: 177). The rate of profit on production, Marx says, is decided by two factors. One is the rate of exploitation – in other words, how successfully workers are being exploited, measured as the amount of surplus value extracted from a given amount of labour power. The other factor is what Marx termed the 'organic composition of capital', which represents the ratio between the value of the 'constant capital' (machinery, raw materials, etc.) and 'variable capital' (labour power) involved in production. An increase in the rate of exploitation lifts the rate of profit. But an increase in the organic composition of capital depresses it. This stands to reason: if workers are the source of surplus value, replacing workers with technology will eventually squeeze profitability. In sum, the relative movement of the two factors over time determines the movement of the profit rate.

So, how do the two factors move? On the one hand, Marx claimed, the organic composition rises without restraint, and it does so because it is always in firms' individual interest to innovate technologically to remain competitive, thus displacing workers (see Chapter 3 on competition as a 'coercive' force).[3] In Harvey's technical phrasing, 'the capacity to produce surplus value relative to the total value circulating as capital is diminished over time by the very technological revolutions that individual capitalists institute in their pursuit of surplus value' (1982a: 180). On the other hand, the rate of exploitation can only increase at a decreasing rate. Again, here's Harvey: 'The increasing difficulty in squeezing higher rates of exploitation out of an already severely pauperised work force, the state of class struggle and the need to maintain a modicum of working-class consumption exercise a restraining influence' (1982a: 177).

The cumulative upshot is obvious: if, as Marx insists, the rate of exploitation increases more slowly than the organic composition, profit rates must fall. And it's equally obvious that this is fundamentally about contradiction and class. It's about the abovementioned contradiction between *individual* capitalists and capitalist *class* interests, insofar as the former are impelled 'to generate a technological mix that threatens further accumulation' (1982a: 188). And it's about the related contradiction – Marx called it an 'incompatibility' – between the 'forces of production' (the technological imperative to *displace* workers) and the 'relations of production' (the social imperative to *exploit* workers). Thus, Marx noted:

> The growing incompatibility between the productive development of society and its hitherto existing relations of production expresses itself in bitter contradictions, crises, spasms. The violent destruction of capital, not by relations external to it, but rather as a condition of its

> self-preservation, is the most striking form in which advice is given it to be gone and to give room to a higher state of social production.
>
> (Quoted in Harvey, 1982a: 179)

In *A Brief History of Neoliberalism* (2005a) and *Seventeen Contradictions and the End of Capitalism* (2014a), Harvey has argued that it's largely in these terms that we can understand the crisis tendencies that engulfed North Atlantic capitalism in the 1970s. To appreciate his argument, we firstly need some basic familiarity with the 'surface' forms that the 1970s crisis took.

In 1971, rapidly rising inflation saw the US government impose a series of emergency measures, among them import surcharges and domestic controls on wages and commodity prices. That the economy was very much in crisis was underscored by President Richard Nixon's momentous decision the same year to suspend the convertibility of the dollar into gold. The reason this was so important was that it effectively sounded the death knell for the Bretton Woods system – the framework of rules and institutions within which commercial and monetary relations among Western nations had operated (with relative stability) since the end of the Second World War. Hard on the heels of this came the 1973 oil shock: an export embargo imposed by the Organisation of the Petroleum Exporting Countries (OPEC), whose member nations were concentrated in the Middle East and North Africa, caused massive increases in energy prices in capitalism's heartlands. Western governments introduced measures that seem barely believable today – restrictions on how much gasoline motorists could buy, bans on non-essential driving and the like. The mid-1970s were scarred by stock-market collapses and economic recession across much of the West. Continuing high inflation combined with rising unemployment to give rise to the crisis phenomenon for which the 1970s are perhaps best known – 'stagflation'. The United Kingdom (where one of the present authors lives) was as hard hit as any country, its government suffering the ignominy of having to rely on the IMF for a bailout in 1976, and subsequently imposing wage controls that culminated in widespread strike action by public-sector trade unions in 1978–1979's 'Winter of Discontent' (refer back to Figure 2.3).

To understand all this with Harvey, recall, first of all, one of the essential premises of his crisis theory: namely, that crises elicit responses from capital and the state that often deal successfully with immediate tensions, but which nonetheless aggravate other contradictions and hence store-up trouble for the future. To grasp what happened in the 1970s, then, it's necessary according to Harvey to go *back* to the crisis that preceded it and consider the actions that were taken to address it.

With global war (1939–1945) following the Great Depression, the fifteen-year period beginning in 1930 was effectively one long crisis for much of the capitalist world economy. When the West emerged battered and bruised from the Second World War, its leading national governments took unprecedented steps to try to secure peace not just militarily but economically. The economic policies they pursued were predominantly 'Keynesian', named after the English economist John Maynard Keynes (1883–1946). Keynes argued that the main reason the Depression had been so deep and long-lasting was a lack of aggregate demand in the market. Governments could ensure such demand in future both through their own spending and by boosting working-class consumer power. Keynesian policy thus aimed to achieve full employment (or something close to it) and to ensure that workers were sufficiently well paid. As the French political economist Thomas Piketty (2014) has famously shown, the late nineteenth and early twentieth centuries had been characterised by very high levels of income and wealth inequality. Keynes recognised that such sharp inequalities were a threat to social and economic stability and needed to be dampened. He was, to be clear, no Marxist – he believed in liberal capitalism. But he also believed that capitalists couldn't be left to their own devices, and that excessive income and wealth differentials benefitted no-one in the long run, least of all capitalists themselves. Restraints needed to be placed on markets and corporations in order to ensure worker welfare and to limit poverty, allowing for more stable accumulation. In short, capitalism needed to be 'embedded' in a system of strong government and a form of class compromise.

Between 1945 and the mid-1970s, Harvey (2014a: 81) has observed, the advanced capitalist countries therefore 'tended towards a demand-management stance' of the type advocated by Keynes, designed to bolster demand including by supporting working-class wage claims. This stance represented a relatively cohesive example of what the French regulation theorists Robert Boyer and Alain Lipietz – whose language Harvey occasionally employs – have termed a 'mode of regulation': an historically and geographically specific set of policies and norms designed to stabilise patterns of capital accumulation. But as Marx could have told governments (and Keynes), what was good for workers would not ultimately be good for corporate profits. As Harvey further explained, the Keynesian mode of regulation, insofar as it tolerated and even encouraged 'a well-organised and politically powerful working-class movement' (2014a: 81), increasingly seeded problems in the production of surplus value.

This was quintessentially a story of the falling rate of profit. As demonstrated by Michael Webber and David Rigby (fellow geographers, on whose exhaustive analysis of the period Harvey has frequently drawn), the

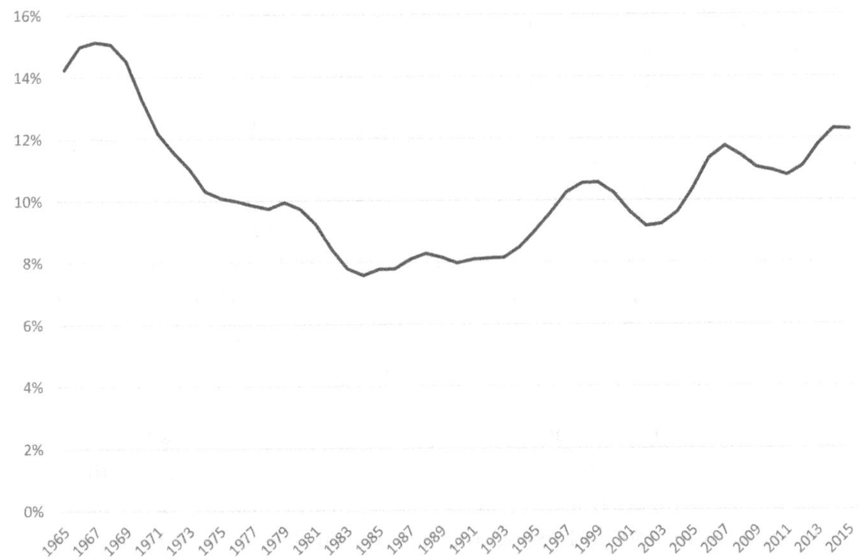

Figure 4.1. The rate of profit in the US corporate sector, 1965–2015.[4]

Source: Bureau of Economic Analysis.

organic composition of capital was increasing strongly during these post-war decades, putting pressure on profit rates (Webber and Rigby, 1996). But not only, meanwhile, was Marx's 'rate of exploitation' of workers not increasing fast enough to counteract this effect. It was *decreasing*, as a result of the relative empowerment of workers affected by Keynesian approaches: declining proportions of the value created by workers were captured by their employers. Thus, eventually and inevitably, profit rates fell. In the United States, the fall was underway already by the mid- to late 1960s (Webber and Rigby, 1996: 499) (see Figure 4.1). And in the 1970s, things finally came to a head. Both higher unemployment and higher inflation – the 'twin evils' of the decade – stemmed from this crisis in corporate profitability, in the former case due to a resulting decline in business investment and in the latter case because firms reacted to diminishing profits by raising prices at a growing pace.

Over-accumulation: the second layer

If the response to the Great Depression and World War II was Keynesianism, the response to the economic crises of the 1970s was something altogether different. Across the Western world, right-of-centre political parties took power from the Left and implemented policies that represented wholesale rejections of Keynesian orthodoxy. Margaret Thatcher, who became the UK prime minister in 1979, and Ronald Reagan, who became the US president two years later, were in the vanguard. Where Keynesianism represented a 'demand-side' approach, Thatcher and Reagan pursued a 'supply-side' program geared to maximising economic growth by way of tax cuts and reduced regulation of business activity. Though similar approaches were introduced earlier in certain other countries, notably under the dictator Augusto Pinochet in Chile from 1975, Thatcher and Reagan are today widely regarded as the original poster children for this distinctive political-economic program that emerged phoenix-like from the ashes of the crisis-ridden 1970s.

This program is now usually labelled 'neoliberalism'. Taking different forms in different countries and mutating over time, neoliberalism is a slippery beast and in the voluminous scholarly literature dedicated to it, it has been identified and explicated in any number of different ways. For many observers, the key to neoliberalism is its emphasis on markets as purportedly superior mechanisms of resource allocation: the kernel of neoliberal policy, according to this understanding, is the replacement of the state by the market in the management of economic affairs, backed by laws to reduce government 'interference' and other 'distortions'.

Though he's acknowledged the ascendancy of markets, however, Harvey's own primary analytical emphasis is elsewhere in *A Brief History of Neoliberalism* (2005a), his book on the phenomenon. We will have more to say about Harvey's analysis of neoliberalism in Chapter 6. For now, we limit ourselves to the bearing of that analysis specifically on Harvey's crisis theory. As Harvey saw it, the crux of neoliberalism was – and indeed, still is – its reversal of Keynesianism specifically in the realm of class relations. If Keynesian policies affected a class compromise of a sort, neoliberalism has categorically obliterated it and restored the untrammelled power of the capitalist class. One outcome, today, is the large number of billionaires, like Jeff Bezos. This restoration of capitalist class power has been cloaked in the neoliberal language of 'freedom' for all people (in the economic, civic and political spheres). And it has inevitably had profound implications for the dynamics of capital circulation and accumulation. It's seeded a new set of crisis tendencies, turning on a different set of contradictions. It is these crisis tendencies and contradictions that Harvey has put at the heart of Western capitalism's periodic downturns since the 1970s, including the great crisis of 2007–2009.

Especially in the United Kingdom and the United States but also to varying degrees elsewhere in the West, neoliberalism has represented from the very start a sustained, decades-long assault on organised labour (for Thatcher, breaking the back of the trade unions was nothing less than a personal mission), resulting in a progressive squeeze in real wages. In the United States, for example, the share of total national income accounted for by workers' wages fell from 70 per cent in 1979 to 60 per cent in 2007. The corollary of this decline was a sustained recovery in the share of income accruing to capitalists, driven overwhelmingly by a rise in the rate of profit (Bivens et al., 2014) (see Figure 4.1). The resulting increase in income and wealth inequality in North America and Europe, in particular, is well evidenced in Piketty's (2014) *Capital in the Twenty-First Century*.

With profits booming, on the face of things there was nothing now for capitalists to be worried about. But there was nonetheless a creeping problem. The workers who create products and services and value for capitalists are ultimately the same people to whom firms must sell those products and services in order to keep capital successfully circulating and accumulating. Thus, if wages are forced downwards in order to augment profits, the ability of workers to fulfil their mutual role as consumers is inevitably compromised. It's another core contradiction: between the imperatives of value *creation* (in production) and *realisation* (through sale on the market). Marx himself put it best, in *Capital*, saying that the sale of commodities and thus the realisation of value 'is restricted not by the consumer needs of society in general, but by the consumer needs of a society in which the great majority are always poor and must always remain poor' (cited in Harvey, 2014a: 81). If, due to the squeeze on wages, aggregate effective demand dries up, capitalism eventually will face a crisis of 'over-accumulation' – not a *dearth* of surplus value creation but an *excess*, relative that is to opportunities to profitably reinvest that surplus in markets with positive demand profiles.

In Harvey's view, this was the predicament that capital in the core capitalist countries increasingly faced in the 1990s and 2000s: that is, 'a chronic and enduring problem of over-accumulation' (Harvey, 2004a: 64). Courtesy of the neoliberal response to the economic malaise of the 1970s, capitalism had simply staggered from one type of crisis condition to another. By 'reducing real wages, crushing working-class organisation and generally disempowering workers', neoliberalism successfully 'resolved the pre-eminent problems of surplus value production' – but 'it did so at the expense of creating problems of realisation in the marketplace' (Harvey, 2014a: 81–82).

What we can see, then, is that Harvey has a wide-ranging crisis theory, one that allows for multiple proximate crisis causes and manifestations. He's not of the view that every crisis that capitalism experiences occurs for the same reason. Rather, 'crises come in many shapes and forms' (Harvey, 2018b). This stance has seen Harvey subject to criticism from other Marxists. Alex Callinicos, Andrew Kliman, Paul Mattick, Michael Roberts and others are all especially critical of Harvey's insistence that the sphere of exchange – wherein firms sell commodities on the market, thus *realising* the value and surplus value created by workers in the production process – plays a material role in crisis formation. Mattick (2008), for example, has disparaged Harvey's analysis of insufficient consumer demand and the corresponding problem of over-accumulation as a brand of 'left Keynesianism' – inasmuch as Keynes, as we've seen, also regarded shortfalls in demand as integral to capitalism's crisis tendencies. For Mattick and other classical Marxists, 'correct' Marxist crisis theory is that which explains crisis formation strictly with reference to the sphere of production, and specifically the 'law' of the falling rate of profit.

The hostility is somewhat explicable. Marx can certainly be read in different ways. Furthermore, theory is political (as we saw in Chapter 3). If – as per Mattick and others – capitalism's repeated descent into crisis is fundamentally about contradictions in the relations between capital and labour in production, then the only solution is to reform those relations, which basically means overthrowing capitalism. Keynes's gambit had been to suggest otherwise: post-war Keynesian economic policy 'sought to overcome the crisis-tendencies of accumulation by intervention at the level of distribution and exchange, *while leaving the social relations of capitalist production intact*' (Clarke, 1990: 443, emphasis added). Little wonder that some Marxists are extremely wary of any crisis theory that smacks of Keynesianism.

Harvey has defended himself robustly against such criticisms (e.g. Harvey, 2018b). To our minds, two points about the critique seem worth making here. The first is that, contra Mattick et al., Harvey's theory of crisis does not, in fact, posit crisis tendencies as residing in production (falling profits) *or* realisation (over-accumulation). Instead, the tendency towards crisis ultimately resides in what Harvey calls the 'contradictory unity' between the two. The production and realisation of value constitute a 'unity' insofar as neither is possible without the other: value cannot be realised unless it has been produced; and the value created in production is only *potential* value until it is realised. And this unity is contradictory because what's good for the production of value (worker exploitation) is not good for its realisation – and vice versa. Second and relatedly, Harvey clearly is not a Keynesian! He definitely does not think the social relations of capitalism should be left intact.[5] And he has shown emphatically, as we saw above, that the demand-focussed Keynesian approach to crisis management does not (and cannot) work – it produced the crisis of the 1970s. Capitalism, in short, is for Harvey perpetually caught in a catch-22:

> It can either maximise the conditions for the production of surplus value, and so threaten the capacity to realise surplus value in the market, or keep effective demand strong in the market by empowering workers and threaten the ability to create surplus value in production.
>
> (Harvey, 2014a: 81)

With Western capitalism suffering from conditions of chronic over-accumulation since the 1980s, the capital-state nexus has, says Harvey, responded with multiple forms of crisis firefighting – all (necessarily) imperfect. Insofar as the 'problem' of over-accumulation is the existence of surpluses of capital that cannot be profitably reinvested in the primary circuit of commodity production, attempts to address over-accumulation have commonly entailed doing something *else* with that capital to avoid its immediate devaluation. The language Harvey uses here is very vivid and, as is often the case, is hydrologically inflected. Warding off crises of over-accumulation is about 'absorbing' or 'mopping up' capital surpluses.

In Harvey's theory, this can occur in one of two ways. The first is *spatial*: surpluses can be absorbed through *the production of new spatial configurations of capital circulation and accumulation*, for instance by 'opening up new markets, new production capacities and new resource, social and labour possibilities elsewhere' (Harvey, 2004a: 64). These new spatial configurations are part of the focus of Chapter 5. The second way in which over-accumulated capital can be absorbed is *temporal*. Essentially, what Harvey means here is that instead of money being thrown into commodity production in the here-and-now in anticipation of an immediate return, it is invested instead in such a way as to support future commodity production. One example given by Harvey is long-term capital projects, such as a power plant or a factory. Another is social expenditures such as education or research. The point is that in both cases, surpluses are absorbed in the present but are not required to yield a return – via indirect increases in corporate profitability – until *later*. Such investments overcome crisis tendencies through temporal deferral. In a very real sense, they *buy time* for capital. 'By stretching out the tendency to over-accumulate far into the future', Harvey (1985c: 140) has asserted, 'crises can perhaps be staved-off for many years'. He's called such deferral a 'temporal fix' for capitalism.

Ultimately long-term investments merely postpone rather than eliminate crisis tendencies, however. Take the example of 'fixed capital', those instruments of production – such as the aforementioned power plant or factory – that support production over an extended time period. Sometimes, the capital 'stored' in these infrastructures is devalued due to premature obsolescence. After all, capitalism is always advancing technologically. Invest money in fixed capital, and you run the risk of that infrastructure being superseded by technological change; hence Marx's description of fixed capital as 'value imprisoned within a specific use value' (cited in Harvey, 1982a: 237), one associated with commodity production under historically specific technological conditions. Oil rigs and the rest of the vast legacy infrastructure of fossil-fuel extraction represent a striking contemporary example of this imprisonment. But even if the 'stored' capital *is* eventually realised through future commodity production, unless the original underlying problem of over-accumulation has been resolved, that stored capital simply 'flows back from storage to combine with excess capital in current production to create ever-greater pools of surplus capital' (Harvey, 1985c: 139).

Finance to the rescue?

Money and finance are pivotal to Harvey's theory of capitalist crisis. To say this is to say much more than that crises are largely *experienced* 'financially' – in the form of reduced monetary incomes, inability to pay debts and so on. Rather, it's to say that money and finance are integral both to the ways that crises form and the ways they are managed. Each of the 'layers' of Harvey's crisis theory elaborated earlier in this chapter is suffused with monetary and financial dynamics: finance mediates profit rates and over-accumulation tendencies. Harvey's basic proposition vis-à-vis finance and crisis is that finance is at once the solution *and* the problem. Capitalist finance 'is a product of capital's own endeavours to deal with the internal contradictions of capitalism [... and yet] ends up heightening rather than diminishing the contradictions' (1982a: 239). Let's see how.

Harvey understands finance – which he terms 'finance capital' – in two connected ways. The first is as an *institutionalised power bloc*. If industrial capitalists (the producers of commodities) represent one 'fraction' of the capitalist class, and 'merchant capitalists' (firms like retailers or wholesalers specialising in buying and selling commodities rather than making them) are another, 'finance capitalists' are a third. They run the institutions that manage and control the financial system, ranging from simple high-street banks (focussed on taking deposits and making loans to households and companies), through investment banks (which help companies with matters such as issuing the shares that are traded on global stock markets), all the way to 'asset managers' such as private-equity and hedge funds (which invest money on behalf of capital-rich institutions like pension schemes and insurance companies).

The second way in which Harvey understands finance capital is as *a process of circulation*. At the heart of this is the credit system – society's vast array of interlocking relationships of credit and debt, whereby economic actors lend money to one another at interest. Harvey has argued that most credit represents what he terms, after Marx, 'fictitious capital'. This is money advanced by one party to another without anything being provided in the other direction other than legal title to a future income stream of some sort. In the case of debt, that future income comprises interest plus – at the end of the loan term – capital repayment. Where the capital is company shares ('equities'), the future income is a portion of profits, paid out as dividends. Other types of fictitious capital examined by Marx and Harvey include government debt, which represents a claim on the government's ability to tax private income. In all cases, fictitious capital is created in anticipation of *future* value creation; it is precisely in the sense that the value has not yet been produced that the value of the legal title is 'fictitious'. Fictitious capital, and the circulation thereof in an array of different financial markets, plays an important role in Harvey's crisis theory.

The first thing that Harvey has asserted about the credit system and fictitious capital more generally is that it's nothing less than essential to capitalism. Imagine, he says, trying to go into business *without* access to credit. To purchase machinery, raw materials and so on – let alone to make investments in factories – one would need instead to hoard money. But hoarding withdraws money from circulation, which if it occurs on a large scale is highly disruptive to capital accumulation. Harvey has thus cited Marx on fictitious capital's utter necessity to capitalism as we know it: it permits 'an enormous expansion of the scale of production' and 'accelerates the material development of the productive forces' (quoted in Harvey, 1982a: 288). 'Without credit', in Harvey's own words, 'the whole accumulation process would stagnate and founder' (1982a: 264).

More generally, fictitious capital helps coordinate capitalism's moving parts in such a way as to smooth the contradictions between them. It is, in fact, the preeminent 'co-ordinating force in capitalist society', its 'central nervous system' (1982a: 278, 284). For one thing, it provides a means to manage the contradictory relation between individual capitalists and capitalists as a class: if the former act in such a way as to threaten the overarching interest of the latter in balanced accumulation, the financial system can effectively discipline such errant behaviour – interest rates can be raised, share prices marked down. By way of further example, consider also the crucial contradiction between production and realisation discussed in the previous section. If pressure on wages leads to a shortfall in effective demand and thus capitalist difficulty in realising value in the market, the provision of consumer credit can help bridge the gap. In sum, Harvey concludes that the credit system contains the potential to straddle capitalism's thorniest antagonisms (1982a: 285–286). *But it is only potential.* After all, crises still occur. Why? Harvey's answer, again following Marx but also substantially embellishing his insights, is that fictitious capital is Janus-faced. It has a 'double-edged role', wherein its circulation is simultaneously 'the saviour of accumulation' *and* (in Marx's words) 'the fountainhead of all manner of insane forms' (1982a: 270). There are numerous reasons for this, of which three are paramount.

First, control of the credit system gives financiers enormous power, and there is absolutely no guarantee that they will use that power in the aforementioned positive coordinating fashion. As 'representatives' of the capitalist class more widely, finance capitalists such as bankers 'should, presumably, allocate money capital to facilitate accumulation in general', yet, 'as individuals, they are bound by competition to act in their own immediate self- or factional interest' (1982a: 286). Thus, they often do things explicitly to the detriment of smooth accumulation: as Marx said, they 'despoil industrial capitalists' or 'interfere in actual production in a most dangerous manner' (quoted in Harvey, 1982a: 287). Marx wrote those words a century before the advent in the 1970s and 1980s of so-called asset stripping by private-equity firms and the like, whereby such investors acquire firms and auction-off their assets in a bid to pay-off debts and increase their own financial worth. But Marx's words apply to such practices of despoliation and interference with uncanny precision.

Second, fictitious capital, by its very nature, encourages speculation. Its creation *assumes* that sufficient value will ultimately be created out of which the income promised by a legal title such as a share certificate can be paid, but it doesn't *guarantee* it, and as such it's 'ever a risky business' (1982a: 266). In such a situation, it's all too easy for the accumulation of these claims on future commodity and value production to run far ahead of what actual production can or does deliver. As Harvey has said, such claims can indeed readily circulate 'even though they may have no basis in actual production' (1982a: 287). As long as there is a willing buyer of the title, the merry-go-round of financial speculation can happily proceed – until such a time as it is brought to a shuddering halt by the collective realisation that the claim is worthless. A famous example was the 1990s Bre-X scandal, when the eponymous Canadian company announced to the world that it had discovered 57 million ounces of gold reserves on the island of

Borneo. Speculation in its shares sent its market value soaring to more than $4 billion, only for independent analysis to find that there was in fact no gold. The value of Bre-X and its shares was quite *literally* fictitious.

Third, finance can never actually resolve the immiseration of large numbers of workers and the negative implications of this immiseration for effective demand. When workers take-on growing volumes of debt in order to be able to consume capital's products and services, the contradiction between production and realisation encouraging such increased debt assumption is not banished but instead 'is internalised within the credit system' (Harvey, 2014a: 83). Unless the debt is actively relieved, it has to be paid-off eventually. The use of debt to 'resolve' the contradiction delays the moment of reckoning while also making that reckoning more violent by augmenting the ability of capitalists to produce commodities without due heed to market demand.

For Harvey, all of these key mechanisms by which finance capital foments crisis tendencies came together in remarkable fashion in 2007–2009. For three decades, the financial sector, especially in the United States, had been exploiting its enormous power not principally to coordinate capital accumulation more broadly so much as to concentrate the accumulation of wealth in its own hands, in a process widely referred to as 'financialisation'. Financialisation involves an increase in profit-making via financial products and mechanisms relative to the so-called real economy of, say, food, clothes and furniture manufacture. As Harvey said, this wave of financialisation was 'spectacular for its predatory style', and in the United States, it saw the financial sector's share of total corporate profits rise from around 15 per cent in 1970 to approximately 40 per cent by 2005 (2010a: 245, 51). Balanced economy-wide accumulation this most certainly was not.

Simultaneously, those three decades saw an explosion in consumer debt as credit restrictions were roundly swept away by financial liberalisation and deregulation, enabling workers subject to the neoliberal squeeze on real wages to turn to their credit cards to make do. In the United States, for example, total consumer debt (excluding mortgages) climbed from only around $300 billion at the end of the 1970s to over $2.5 *trillion* by 2007 (Figure 4.2). Mounting problems of insufficient underlying effective demand had not gone away, of course – they were merely 'papered over by a credit-fuelled consumerism of excess' (Harvey, 2010a: 118). Meanwhile, Harvey adds that such consumerist excess in places like the United States and Europe encouraged a too-rapid, unsustainable expansion of commodity production in Asia in general and China in particular.

And to top it all, there was massive speculation in housing by both developers and households, in countries ranging from the United States

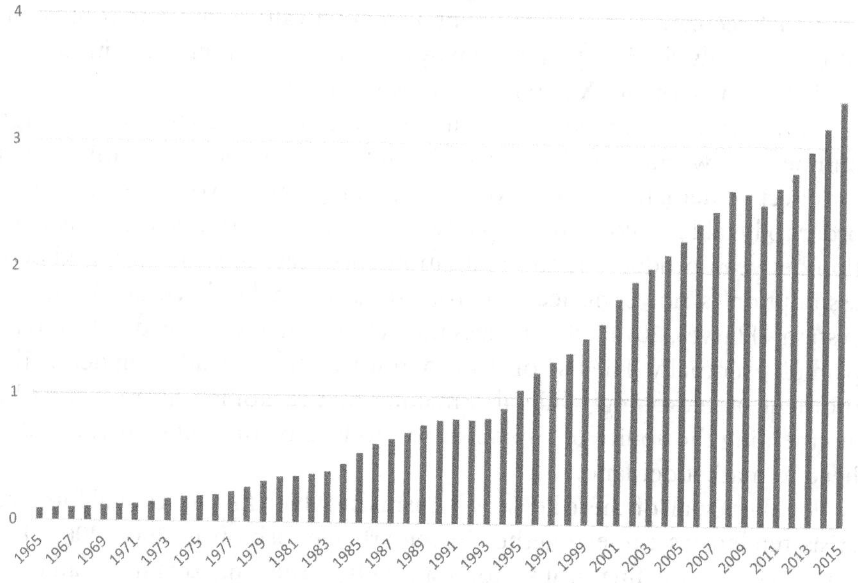

Figure 4.2. US consumer credit, households and non-profit organisations, 1965–2015 ($tn).

Source: Board of Governors of the US Federal Reserve System.

to Spain and Ireland. Crucially, the finance sector fuelled both sides of the bargain, 'lend[ing] to developers to build speculative tract housing while lending mortgage finance to consumers to purchase that housing'. The problem, needless to say, is that such practices 'can all too easily produce speculative bubbles' (Harvey, 2014a: 82), and that's what happened in the run-up to the financial crisis. In 2007, the bubble finally burst. Housing-market speculation was, if you like, the straw that broke the proverbial camel's back (with catastrophic results, see Figure 4.3). The broader, deeper issue, Harvey's theory submits, was finance capital's multifaceted role in heightening the very contradictions within capitalism to which it represents a nominal solution.

What's important to recognise is just how emphatically this distinguishes Harvey's account of crisis in general, and the financial crisis of 2007–2009 in particular, from the accounts offered by more mainstream commentators and which have garnered considerably wider attention. We'll focus our brief comments here on *Crashed* (2018) by the Columbia University historian Adam Tooze, a book widely regarded as the authoritative account of 2007–2009 (and indeed the years that followed). But one could just as easily make much the same comparison with say *Fool's Gold* (2009) by the

Figure 4.3. Foreclosed housing. In September 2010, at the peak of the crisis in the United States of America, 12,000 homes were repossessed in just one month.

Financial Times journalist Gillian Tett, which was arguably the most influential account of the crisis until Tooze's book appeared.

For Tooze (and Tett), the crisis was essentially a failure of risk management. Banks such as Bank of America, Bear Stearns, Citigroup and Lehman Brothers invested billions of dollars in complex financial products that essentially comprised bundles of homeowner mortgages. This would all have been well and good, Tooze (2018: 59–61) intimates, if those banks had shared the risk of such investment with others and had financed the investment through judicious means. But they did neither. To fund investment in mortgages that by their nature would generate returns only over a very long period – most US home loans are for thirty-year terms – the banks borrowed money that typically had to be paid back just ninety days later. When the market realised that lots of the mortgages would probably never be honoured (they were 'subprime'), the banks' ability to continue to borrow and thus to satisfy existing repayment obligations suddenly dried up.

Tooze's is certainly a compelling narrative of what happened. And it's likely Harvey would deny none of it – indeed, the details of ruinous speculation enumerated by Tooze fit relatively seamlessly into Harvey's theoretical architecture. But that's the point: when one considers the two accounts side by side, Harvey's looks very much like a wood and Tooze's more like some of the trees within it. As the leading Marxist Perry Anderson (2019) has observed, Tooze – and we would add, Tett – is fantastic on *how* finance brought the world to its knees but has less to say about *why* the world had arrived at the situation in which it was in a position to do so. Rather, *Crashed* 'takes the hypertrophy of finance … as a situational given, without structural explanation' (Anderson, 2019: 71). For Tooze, finance's failures are themselves the story. For Harvey, they are not. The crux of his story is instead why capitalism under neoliberalism – a capitalism of resurgent class division and chronic over-accumulation – generated in the first place a maladaptive financial system that only ever *appeared* to be able to resolve its contradictions.

Time, history and capitalism

Following Marx, we can now see how and why Harvey is an 'historical materialist'. The capitalist mode of production – a very particular way of defining, creating and distributing wealth – does not simply 'have a history'. Instead, it restlessly *makes* history by locking hundreds of millions of people into activities that change the world. This unsettled history, as we've seen in this chapter, is necessarily non-linear. It proceeds through phases of economic growth and relative stability for many parts of the globe, followed by shorter crisis periods that are materially destructive and experientially distressing for a great many people. Politically, the phases involve a different balance of class forces, with no guarantees that the mass of wage workers across the world will have their interests well served. What unifies these phases is *ceaseless change*, its pace varying over time. As Marx and Engels famously said in *The Communist Manifesto*, 'all that is solid melts into air' in a capitalist world. Inter-capitalist competition and profit-seeking lead capitalism to devalue stasis, tradition and efforts to conserve both present and past arrangements. Specifically, Harvey – like Marx – has shown that a structural compulsion to realise value in an unknown (or very uncertain) future drives ever-changing activity in the present. Finance capital is at the heart of this future-facing drama in which, one might say, time is a strategic 'resource' or pressure valve (used consciously to defer crises for several years).

If this was all that Harvey had to say about time and history, it would certainly be enough to command one's attention. But there is, in fact, much more than this going on in his many writings since the 1970s. We end this chapter by briefly recounting Harvey's other important insights into time and history in a world dominated by the capitalist mode of production.

These insights are somewhat complex but can be gleaned by reading across multiple publications since *The Limits to Capital* was published forty-plus years ago. They're not only interesting in their own right but are also essential if we're to properly understand how and why geography matters for Harvey (the subject, in different ways, of Chapters 5–8 of this book).

First, Harvey is insistent that time is not – contra Isaac Newton – merely a universal and objectively given phenomenon that escapes all social influence. Instead, for him time is socially constructed when it comes to understanding human activity and experience. This comes through loud and clear in *The Condition of Postmodernity*. 'The objectivity of time', he there wrote, 'is given in each case by the material practices of social reproduction, and to the degree that these vary geographically and historically, so we find that social time [... is] differentially constructed' (1989a: 204). It was also a major theme in *Justice, Nature and the Geography of Difference* (1996a: Chapters 9 and 10). There Harvey observed that 'social constructions of time operate with the full force of objective facts to which all individuals and institutions necessarily respond. To say that something is socially constructed is not to say it is personally subjective' (1996a: 211–212). So, Harvey's view is that different societies or communities 'construct' time in different ways and institute those constructs via a set of techniques, norms, rituals and other practices. Times are plural, and any singular time could only entrain all people worldwide through acts of force or persuasion. There's ample anthropological evidence of this, and Harvey has referenced it at some length. For example, in the two above-mentioned books he dwells on Pierre Bourdieu's (1977) monograph about the North African Kabyle people, and on Nancy Munn's (1986) study of an isolated island community near Papau New Guinea. These rich inquiries show that different societies fashion time in ways that can border on the incommensurable.

This, though, does not address the meaning of the 'time' being constructed. What *counts* as time, and so too its 'content', presumably differs according to the definitions and practices that take hold in different societies at different moments in history, making a generic definition of time virtually impossible. While this is indeed Harvey's view, one can nonetheless identify two ways in which he's specified the importance of socially constituted time as an 'objective fact' in different social formations. One way is time as *measure*: societies partition and space the flow of time in different ways. For instance, from the seventeenth century onwards, Europeans (and now pretty much everybody) divided time according to seconds, minutes, hours, days, weeks and months. Ever more precise clocks were manufactured to tell the time so that its passage could be quantified precisely. This time was 'empty' and constructed as 'external' to any particular events that it served to pinpoint chronologically. Harvey has cited Tamara Hareven's (1982) book *Family Time and Industrial Time* several times over the years to make this point about time as measure.

The other way time matters, according to Harvey, is closely linked to this: temporal measures are used to coordinate and structure human activities in different places.[6] This is time as a *regulatory or disciplinary force*. For example, as Britain underwent its passage from a rural-agricultural to an urban-industrial society two centuries ago, people were subject to a new kind of working day. As English historian E. P. Thompson showed in his famous essay 'Time, work-discipline and industrial capitalism' (1967), the early capitalists used clock time to schedule the length and intensity of paid employment in the new factories and mines. Citing Thompson in several of his books, Harvey has noted that workers progressively fought against the worst aspects of this – for instance, six or seven-day working weeks marked by long hours, few breaks and low hourly pay. The nature, duration and pace of work for a certain amount of money became a key consideration for workers in the early decades of capitalism.

These two general points about time, illustrated with reference to capitalism's reliance on twenty-four-hour clock measurement, bring us to one of Marx's most important arguments about the specificity of time within this mode of production. It's a point that has been absolutely central to Harvey's own work since *Social Justice and the City*. This is the claim that time functions as a *real (or concrete) abstraction*, as elaborated in Chapter 1 of *The Limits to Capital* (1982a), in Chapter 1 of *Consciousness and the Urban Experience* (1985b) and in many other places since. What does the claim entail? As noted above, capitalists have long relied on clock time to measure, coordinate and structure various concrete acts of making, moving, concentrating, selling, recycling and disposing of commodities. In the two senses just discussed, clock time might be regarded as a sort of *tool* or *device* that allows capitalists, workers and others to agree what do to do when and how quickly or slowly to do it. In this sense, time is overt and people are conscious of it. For instance, from the perspective of capitalists, 'time is money'. They will strive to make and sell more in less time, perhaps by using smart twenty-four-hour machines to replace workers who become fatigued and need to sleep. But the notion of time as a real abstraction within capitalism goes much further than this instrumental use of time.

In Chapter 3, we showed that for Harvey and Marx money is the phenomenal form of the invisible but real thing called 'value', which in turn is the dynamic totality of acts of concrete labour as unified through processes of market exchange. Exchange realises value, whereas the combined efforts of geographically dispersed wage workers create value. But not all capitalists are able to make a profit through their ensemble of products, working practices, marketing decisions and so on. This begs the question: how can the endeavours of these capitalists and their workers be compared in practice? Who's the most creative, competitive and entrepreneurial? Economists point to supply and demand: consumers will decide on the relative worth of various commodities depending on the quality and volume of commodities coming to market. On this basis, some firms will prosper, others will not. Prices (or exchange values) then become the commensurating mechanism that all market players respond to. For Harvey and Marx, though, this puts the cart before the proverbial horse. Prices are not mere epiphenomena of shifting consumer evaluations of the worth of commodities. Instead, prices complete a process of commensuration among diverse and competing commodity producers that has *already* begun, and which is ceaseless. It is *time*, not market-determined prices, that enables this commensuration to occur. And this involves more than time as a common measure or reference point, as with our global system of time zones.

To make this sound less cryptic, Marx famously formulated the notion of 'socially necessary labour time' in his later works. This notion references a qualitative and quantitative reality enabled (but not *caused*) by the use of clock time in the capitalist mode of production. In essence, competing capitalists strive to beat the 'average' time taken (at an average wage cost) to produce commodities in particular economic sectors. In *The Limits* and elsewhere, Harvey has made the point that commodities take time to get to market, not only to produce, and so talks about the 'socially necessary turnover time' of capital. This is the total time commodities take to complete a 'circuit'. But the essential point is the same as Marx's. For competing capitalists to beat out their rivals, there needs to be a real and ongoing – rather than nominal or ephemeral – basis for comparing their diverse endeavours. That basis, for Marx and Harvey, is the 'moving average' of total labour time involved in making, transporting and selling commodities so as to realise the value committed to bringing those commodities to market. The average moves because capitalists vie to beat it and thereby serve to reduce it in aggregate. This labour time is socially constituted, qualitatively particular (because based on clock time) and, in theory, measurable quantitatively (should anyone bother to do the mathematics across the economy as a whole).

In this light, we see that for Harvey *capitalist time* operates in no less than three registers. It's an 'empty' and quantitatively precise measure (clock time) that's now globally hegemonic; it's a measure used practically to coordinate and structure billions of concrete acts within firms and society at large; and it's an abstract, invisible but very real force that acts upon capitalists, workers and others as a 'guiding hand' to determine who makes a profit, where and for how long. This layered conception of capitalist time has been explicated quite brilliantly by the late American Marxist Moishe Postone (1942–2018) in his remarkable book *Time, Labor and Social Domination* (1993). While Harvey has not explicitly discussed Postone's *magnum opus*, his scattered discussions of time seem to us to amount to something similar to what Postone sees in Marx's later works.

However, where Postone focusses squarely on capitalism in abstraction from its 'more than capitalist' integument, Harvey has long been alive to how other sorts of time (and many other things) are configured in relation to capitalist temporality. During, before and after capitalist crises, these different registers of time matter, to varying degrees, to different people as part of their individual and collective existence. They may be inspired by religion, morality or cultural traditions and may be speculative and imaginative in the ways they structure, and lend significance to, past, present and future. In *The Condition* and *JGND* in particular, Harvey pointed to the importance of these other temporalities in a world suffused with capitalist time. He noted their political, moral and affective dimensions for people who may, or may not, take issue with the chronic instability engendered by capitalism.

To conclude, we said earlier that capitalism makes history rather than simply having a history. What we've seen in this section is that, for Harvey, capitalist history – the particular sequence of events occurring since its European inception in the eighteenth century – has been shaped deeply by the specific way that time is defined, and made to matter, within this mode of production. Socially constituted and materially effective, capitalist time is a force to be reckoned with, not merely a framework for recording the unfolding of events across the decades. For those possessed of a lot of money, they can buy time to escape the daily routines that billions of others are locked into. Indeed, they can substantially affect the routines of others, as the investment decisions by today's plutocrats in the United States of America, China, Russia, India and elsewhere reveal so well. Other registers of time are forced to accommodate themselves to capitalist time or, for those able to escape the system, to serve as refuges from its rigours.

Conclusion

As this chapter has explained, Harvey – after Marx – is a crisis theorist. He's shown how and why capitalism's evolution is necessarily punctuated. Capitalism is compelled to grow and to change, with periodic crises being the 'irrational rationalisers' of a dynamic system. Crises involve: commodity use values being un-utilised, under-utilised or even destroyed; exchange values being significantly depreciated; and, ultimately, the shrinkage of value within the system as a whole. The human costs can be enormous for workers: jobs are lost, homes are repossessed by mortgage lenders, personal savings diminish, credit card bills go unpaid and anxiety soars. Meanwhile, many capitalists suffer too as firms go bankrupt, share prices plummet and so on. Governments and financiers are obliged to step in to find ways to manage the impacts of crises and set capital accumulation back on a growth path. Yet some capitalists prosper at the expense of others during crisis episodes (Figure 4.4), which in turn can fuel the already-burning fires of dissent in the wider society. As we've seen, capitalism's bumpy evolution does not simply unfold through time. Instead, time is defined, measured, organised and responded to in very specific ways that mark out this mode of production. Capitalism not only throws itself forward into an uncertain future; its temporal frame seeks to dislodge other registers of temporality in any society insofar as they might impede capital accumulation. For instance, the 'temporal fix' discussed by Harvey is not simply about

Figure 4.4. Hard times. Critics, like Harvey, pointed to how some capitalists prospered from a global financial crisis they played a huge role in causing. Meanwhile, ordinary people faced real hardship.

Source: Cartoon courtesy of Max Gustafson.

deferral into an 'empty future' but, instead, an attempt to *colonise* future economic action by hitching it to interest rates and specified return times on investment.

Of course, it would contravene Harvey's relational philosophy and theory if issues of time and history were somehow separated from issues of space and geography. It's to these latter issues that we now turn. To revisit the hydrological analogy used to introduce this chapter, in the next chapter we want to explore where H_2O moves to and how it assumes different 'fixed' forms like ice and ocean water as it circulates far and wide, dissolving and evaporating over time before condensing once again.

Further reading

Harvey, D. (1982a). Money, credit and finance. In *The Limits to Capital* (pp. 239–282). Blackwell.

Harvey, D. (2005a). Freedom's just another word ... In *A Brief History of Neoliberalism* (pp. 5–38). Oxford University Press.

Harvey, D. (2014a). Prologue: the crisis of capitalism this time around; Introduction: on contradiction. In *Seventeen Contradictions and the End of Capitalism* (pp. ix–xiv & 1–11). Profile Books.

Postone. M. (1978). Necessity, labor, and time: a reinterpretation of the Marxian critique of Capitalism. *Social Research*, 4(4), 739–788.

Notes

1. It's worth noting here that while Harvey, like Marx, rejects the idea that all the interacting and competing influences and forces in the economy can ever be in balance – a theoretical condition known as 'general equilibrium' – he, again like Marx, sometimes assumes specific equilibrium outcomes among particular sets of forces or influences in order to conduct his thought experiments. This is all part of his complex dialectical mode of theorising: one set of conditions is held steady while another set is interrogated, only for the former assumption subsequently to be relaxed and itself explicitly and critically examined.
2. Of course, there are other triggers for crises of various kinds than events internal to capitalism. Examples of 'external' triggers include volcanic eruptions, wildfires, tsunamis, floods, landslides and earthquakes. The crises that result can be hugely profitable for some capitalists – dubbed 'disaster capitalists' by critics – by clearing a path for new lending and new investment. The COVID-19 pandemic of 2020–2022 (a crisis which seriously affected global capitalism, as well as driving large pharmaceutical firms to create vaccines very quickly) arguably belongs in this 'external' category, although many observers, Harvey

included, maintain that the pandemic is in fact 'internal' to capitalism in the sense of resulting from capital's encroachment on and disruption of natural ecosystems and habitats: 'I would conclude that COVID-19 is Nature's revenge for forty years of Nature's gross and abusive mistreatment at the hands of a violent and unregulated neoliberal extractivism' (Harvey, 2020a: 183–184). The same debate – internal or external to capitalism, or perhaps occupying a blurry boundary region? – applies to phenomena such as wars, which of course can be equally disruptive of 'normal' economic processes, fomenting economic crises on regional, national or international scales.

3. There is an implicit assumption here that technical change undertaken in the service of cost reduction always means substituting variable with constant capital. It turns out that this is one of many assumptions on which Marx's 'law' of the falling rate of profit actually relies. In view of the evident debatability of several such assumptions, Harvey has never given the 'law' his full endorsement. He thinks of it much more as a *tendency*, albeit one that applies only under certain historical and geographical conditions. As such, and as we will shortly see, for Harvey the falling rate of profit can only be *part of* a wider crisis theory, not the totality thereof.
4. This is shown as a five-year moving average to smooth the trend (i.e. the figure shown for 1965 is the average profit rate for 1961–1965) and is calculated as corporate profits with inventory valuation and capital consumption adjustments divided by the net stock of corporate fixed assets.
5. Equally, however, Harvey – unlike many other Marxists – does not believe that an abrupt, revolutionary overthrow of capitalism would be beneficial (still less likely). The reason, he says, is that such large proportions of the world population are today dependent on the ongoing circulation of capital that, were it to suddenly break down, so also would social reproduction as we know it. People would starve on a massive scale. In other words, any transition away from capitalism would have to be gradual and orderly in order to not be enormously destructive. All this means that although Harvey does not support the maintenance of capitalism in the long term, he concedes its necessity – albeit provisionally and conditionally – in the short term (see Harvey, 2020a: 11–13).
6. Excellent studies on the globalisation and institution of twenty-four hour clock time are provided by Dohrn-van Rossum (1996), Maier (1987) and Ogle (2015).

5 The restless and uneven geographies of capitalism

Core propositions; Between fixity and motion; The spatial fix; Inter-place competition; Rent and the market for land; Putting geography into Marxism (and Marxism into geography); Conclusion

David Harvey is a Marxist, but he's also a geographer. Neither of the labels is more important than the other when it comes to understanding his work. Not all of his writing is explicitly 'spatial' by any means. But much of it is. More significantly, any engagement with Harvey's work that does not foreground his geographical analysis misses an essential component of his understanding of capitalism. For this, there's a simple reason: according to Harvey himself, if you don't understand capitalism's geographies, you don't understand capitalism itself. Its geographical dynamics are as integral and constitutive as its social and temporal dynamics. They help to make capitalism what it is, in all its contradictory and combustible reality. If one were pressed to say what Harvey's most original and important scholarly contribution has been, it would be difficult to look beyond his incorporation of geographical dynamics into the Marxist understanding of capitalism. This, we are sure, will be his most lasting legacy: long after he has passed, people will be learning from and citing his studies of the geographies of capital accumulation and class struggle. In this chapter, we aim to introduce you to these studies.

This chapter is not, however, an examination of Harvey's thinking about 'space' or 'geography' in its totality. Following the French Marxist Henri Lefebvre, Harvey has distinguished three dimensions of 'space': *material space*, which comprises the physical fabric of the world we inhabit and experience, such as roads, housing developments, industrial parks, airports,

DOI: 10.4324/9780429028120-5

electricity grids, public squares, shopping malls and so on; *representations of space* – formal depictions of space in 'words, graphs, maps, diagrams, pictures, etc.'; and *spaces of representation*, namely 'the lived space of sensations, the imagination, emotions and meanings' experienced by people day in, day out (Harvey, 2006a: 279). Harvey is interested in all three and in how they interrelate but in practice has largely focussed on the first dimension. In the present chapter, we follow his lead (though we don't deal with all aspects of material space here either). Drawing on and extending Marx, Harvey challenges and upends the conventional idea that geography is merely the variegated arrangement of phenomena at local or regional scales: instead, it is a vast, complicated and ceaselessly changing material landscape that's produced by capital, the state and others, and which in turn shapes those actors. We begin the chapter with the basic propositions that animate Harvey's theorisation.

A quick and important note on terminology. In Harvey's writings it's not always clear to unwary readers which of the three definitions of 'space' above applies, or at what geographical scale. Sometimes space refers to the global scale (as opposed to the local); other times it refers to the built environment; still other times it refers to all the 'objective' and perceived aspects of the myriad constructed environments that capitalism creates and, over time, devalues and destroys. In this chapter, we use 'space' and 'geography' interchangeably to refer to the created material geographies of capitalism, for which Harvey now and then also uses the term 'landscape'.

Core propositions

First, Harvey has long maintained that the material spaces that matter to capitalism are multifaceted. His project is, as he wrote in a seminal 1980s essay on 'The geopolitics of capitalism', to theorise the 'historical geography of capitalism' (Harvey, 1985c: 144), by which he means its conjoined spatial and temporal dynamics. This necessitates considering the 'stuff' of geography from a bewildering array of perspectives. It means the market for land. It means transportation and communication networks during and after their construction. It means the geographical mobility of the different forms in which 'capital' materialises in practice: money, labour power, machines and commodities. It means the specificity of particular places with their concentration and juxtaposition of certain people, organisations and so on. It means the connections *between* places, not to mention the differences between them. It means buildings of all kinds. No wonder, then, that when Harvey pondered the theoretical task he had thereby set himself, he quivered. 'Bravely said, but hard to do', was how he put it in the aforementioned essay (1985c: 144). To capture this vast diversity of geographies, Harvey has often invoked the umbrella concept of 'spatial configurations' (although he also often simply uses the term 'space', as noted above, which is confusing when he counterposes it to 'place'). *Spatial configurations* is a helpful concept: that capitalism has a distinctive (though complex) set of spatial forms, alongside and connected to its characteristic social configurations (not least, the relation between classes), is indeed one of Harvey's main claims.

Second, Harvey has started from the premise that classical Marxism's preoccupation with temporal relations and dynamics has come at the expense of an understanding of geographical dynamics. It's this lacuna he's sought to rectify. But it's important to be clear about what exactly Harvey means by this. He does not mean that Marx dismissed geography out-of-hand and was ignorant of its importance. No: Marx 'frequently admits of the significance of space and place in his writings' (1985c: 142). Marx discussed, among other things, the opposition between town and country, the regional differentiation of labour markets, the concentration of factory-based production in urban centres and, last but not least, the importance within capitalism of reducing spatial barriers through developments in communication and transportation technologies – a tendency that Marx referred to as the 'annihilation of space by time' and Harvey (1989a) has in turn described as 'time-space compression' (see Chapter 6). But crucially, Marx's comments on geography were *ad hoc* rather than systematic: 'none of this', Harvey (1985c: 143) observed, 'is really integrated into theoretical formulations that are powerful with respect to time but weak with respect to space'. Effecting precisely such systematic theoretical integration hence has been Harvey's major objective.

Third, Harvey maintains that the geographical landscape that capitalism creates is much like the social and economic landscape that it creates – specifically, it's a locus of contradiction and tension rather than an expression of harmonious equilibrium, as tends to be the case in mainstream economics (Harvey, 1975a). 'I am primarily concerned', Harvey wrote in *Consciousness and the Urban Experience*, 'with how capitalism creates a physical landscape of roads, houses, factories, schools, shops, and so forth in its own image and what the contradictions are that arise out of such processes of producing space' (1985b: xvii). Capitalism, like anything, cannot exist on the head of a pin as a somehow ageographical process unfolding through time.

Fourth, however, this is by no means the end of the matter. Yes, capitalism creates spatial configurations in its own image. But to leave it at that would be to suggest that 'geography' is somehow passive in the capitalist drama of accumulation and class struggle. And that is the very opposite of what Harvey argues. Spatial configurations are much, much more than 'a mere reflection of the processes of accumulation and class reproduction', Harvey insisted in *The Limits to Capital* (1982a: 374). They are not the mute container or receptacle of historical socioeconomic dynamics; they *shape* those dynamics as much as they *express* them. Thus, Harvey theorised the production of spatial configurations as 'an "active moment" within the overall temporal dynamic of accumulation and social reproduction' (1982a: 374).

Of course, Harvey is not alone in this. Other well-known geographers made comparable claims about the role of space in social and economic life around the same time. The American geographer Edward Soja, for example, published an influential article claiming that social and spatial processes and forms exist in a reciprocal relationship with one another, comprising what he termed a 'socio-spatial dialectic' (Soja, 1980). And British geographer Doreen Massey's 1980s work was similarly rooted in the insistence that geographical 'facts' – 'distance, betweenness, unevenness, nucleation, co-presence, time-space distanciation, settings, mobility and differential mobility' – not only 'affect how specified social relations work; they may even be necessary for their existence or prevent their operation' (Massey, 1991: 272). But *how* Harvey theorised all this has been different and distinctive. As we'll see, contradictions play a pivotal role, just as they did in our previous chapter. In short, for Harvey, capitalism by its nature produces spatial configurations that themselves harbour disharmonious tendencies, the (imperfect) resolution of which is affected by the production of *different* and, over time, *malleable* spatial configurations. The space economy is restless, conflictual and forever being reconstituted anew. It is, Harvey averred, 'beset by counter-posed and contradictory tendencies' that compel capital constantly 'to produce new forms of geographical differentiation' (Harvey, 1982a: 416–417).

This, and more, will become clearer as we proceed. Equipped with these four basic propositions, we can now explore in detail Harvey's wide-ranging theorisation of capitalism's material geographies, especially as they enable and impede the circulation and accumulation of capital.

Between fixity and motion

'From the standpoint of the circulation of capital', Harvey (1985c: 145) argued, 'space appears in the first instance as a mere inconvenience, a barrier to be overcome'. This, if you like, is Harvey's starting point, ground-zero in his theory of the historical geography of capitalism. The reason has to do with time as much as with space. As we have seen (Chapters 3 and 4), the production of value and surplus value occurs through a process of circulation whereby money is advanced and is transformed through the production process into a greater sum of money. This takes time, and the time it takes for money to return to the capitalist in its expanded form – for M to become MΔ, which Marx termed the 'turnover time of capital' – is a loss for capital, mainly because, as Marx put it, 'time passes by unseized' (cited in Harvey, 1982a: 86). Capitalists thus strive to reduce the turnover time to as close as possible to (again, in Marx's words) 'the speed of thought'. The quicker your money returns to you with a profit, the quicker it can be put to work to exploit further profitable investment opportunities. Any impediment to the reduction of turnover time is thus a problem to be surmounted.

And space itself is one such crucial impediment. After all, accumulation is always distributed across and between places that in some cases can be relatively close to one another but in others far apart. As such, spatial integration – the linking of commodity production and exchange taking place in different locations – is a fundamental dimension of capitalism and is achieved through the *physical* circulation of capital in all its different physical incarnations. *The quicker capital can circulate geographically, the quicker it can circulate economically.* This is the basis for Marx's famous, above-cited observation that it's in capital's interest to annihilate space with time. Improved communication and transportation technologies do not shrink the actual geographical distance between places, but they do shrink the distance as registered and experienced in the time taken to traverse it; and that, to capital, is what matters.

How spatially mobile *is* capital? Following Marx, Harvey suggested that in each of the states it assumes, capital has 'a special and uniquely defined capacity for geographical movement', and that these respective mobilities 'interact in the context of accumulation and so build, fragment and carve out [distinctive overall] spatial configurations' (1982a: 405, 416). Physical commodities are the simplest to deal with: their mobility depends on transportation systems, as modified by the attributes of the commodity in question. (A cup and an aeroplane are not equally mobile.) Capital-as-money moves with varying levels of ease. Money-as-credit is vastly more mobile than physical cash, for example; its mobility is limited only by telecommunications capabilities and any barriers posed by convertibility between national currencies. And what of human labour power? Here, Harvey was writing about capital's contradictory priorities decades before critics of neoliberalism would make the same essential points. On the one hand, capital does indeed encourage workers' geographical mobility, albeit always in the service ultimately of its own freedoms: the free movement of labour helps capitalists avoid labour shortages insofar as people can go where jobs are, and an influx of migrant labour into particular sectors or local labour markets can serve to intensify competition between workers and reduce labour costs. On the other hand, capitalists tied to particular places aren't keen on labour mobility if it means potentially losing workers to better employment opportunities elsewhere: hence the frequent adoption of strategies 'to bind preferred workers to particular firms and locations' (1982a: 382).

That just leaves to be considered capital in the productive state: that is, when raw materials and workers and so forth have been assembled and commodity production takes place. Production, too, is characterised by incentives to be as mobile as possible – to seek out lower production costs in new locations, for example. Indeed, this has been one of the most notable trends in the global economy since the 1970s. Companies headquartered in Western Europe and North America have in recent decades widely 'offshored' large parts of their productive operations to locations in the Global South offering lower land, labour, and regulatory costs. The likes of Apple, for example, actually do very little in their home markets – principally strategy, design and marketing. Component parts for Apple's products are manufactured all over the world, while almost all its phones, laptops and tablets have been assembled in China.

But production is not always mobile. One of the main reasons for this is the reliance on what Harvey, after Marx, calls 'fixed capital'. By this, he means instruments of production employed over an extended period of time, such as factories or the machinery they contain (see also Chapter 4). Some such capital is very difficult and expensive to move around; and some can't be moved around at all. If a producer relocates and leaves behind fixed capital that's not yet at the end of its useful life, and for which a buyer cannot be found, that capital is devalued. Thus, industries employing relatively large amounts of fixed capital – think steel production or car manufacturing – find it particularly difficult to relocate. Their fixed, immobile capital restrains them. One implication is that the more such industries can off-load responsibility for constructing, maintaining and owning the relevant buildings and machinery to third parties (principally the state), the more mobile and nimble they are.

And as Harvey has said, it is in fact not just capital-in-production that depends upon such immobile physical infrastructures. 'Each form of the geographical mobility of capital', he wrote (Harvey, 1985c: 148), 'requires fixed and secure spatial infrastructures if it is to function effectively'. The mobility of employable workers depends on workers' health and education, and hence on houses, hospitals and schools. Money can only move from New York to Hong Kong in the twinkling of an eye if the necessary, secure telecommunications infrastructures exist in both places to enable the transaction. And the capacity to move commodities similarly depends upon the existence of a fixed, efficient and stable transportation system facilitating not just mobility *per se* but also safe warehousing.

From all this Harvey draws three important conclusions. The first and most immediate is that there's an obvious paradox. For capital to be in a position to transcend spatial barriers and thus achieve the desired spatial integration, it has to produce *immobile* spatial configurations of various kinds. Or, in Harvey's pithy formulation: 'The ability to overcome space is predicated on the production of space' (1985c: 149). Of course, it's not physically possible for the *same* elements of capital to be both spatially fixed and spatially mobile. Rather, what happens in practice is that there are trade-offs: 'A portion of the total capital and labour power has to be immobilised in space, frozen in place, in order to facilitate greater liberty of movement for the remainder' (1985c: 149). The jet-setting of, say, the banker is indirectly *predicated upon* the immobility of the airport facilities he uses and of the people who service those facilities. Nevertheless, viewed in the round, what we see is 'a tension within the geography of accumulation between fixity and motion, between the rising power to overcome space and the immobile spatial structures required for such a purpose' (1985c: 150).

The second conclusion is that this inherent tension between fixity and motion manifests as chronic instability in the medium-to-long term. How could it be otherwise? The social and physical landscape that suits capitalism's needs at a particular point in time is already passé months or years later as the quest to tear down spatial barriers proceeds apace. The stimulus to produce a certain material configuration of accumulation at one historical and geographical conjuncture is necessarily matched by a stimulus 'to undermine, disrupt and even destroy that landscape at a later point in time' (1985c: 150). Harvey thus envisions capitalist development constantly negotiating a 'knife-edge' between alternately preserving and destroying the values of capital commitments sunk in the physical landscape – between forces of geographical inertia and progression. One only need think of places such as the US Midwest, Germany's Ruhr valley and England's northeast, whose vast infrastructures of industrial production were pivotal to capital accumulation in the 1960s and 1970s only to be rendered essentially redundant from the 1980s onwards, to grasp the knife-edge to which Harvey alludes. No wonder Harvey has invoked the Austrian economist Joseph Schumpeter's vivid concept of 'creative destruction' to capture this process of restless formation and re-formation of geographical landscapes. For in annihilating space by time, capitalism dissolves 'the created spaces of capitalism, the spaces of its own social reproduction' (1989b: 192).

Third and lastly, there is a violence and destructiveness to this process that is inevitably social as much as spatial. It is not just physical landscapes that get devalued – so too do the businesses and lives rooted in those landscapes. The perpetual reshaping of the geographical landscape of capitalism is, Harvey (1989b: 192–193) has said, 'a process of violence and pain', provoking 'many an anguished cry' from various quarters of society. Harvey has appealed to classical historical literature to give voice to the anguished – to writers like Charles Baudelaire, Henry James and Émile Zola, among others. But one could just as easily cite cries from contemporary popular culture, from the British film *The Full Monty* (1997) – featuring Sheffield's declining steel mills and desperate former steelworkers – to another heart-wrenching 'social realist' movie, *I, Daniel Blake* (2016).

The spatial fix

The relationship in Harvey's work between contradictions and crisis tendencies on the one hand, and the production of new spatial configurations on the other, is multi-layered and rather complicated. At the risk of oversimplifying, we can say that the production of new spaces – whether it's a new factory complex, a new export market or a new transportation network – exists, for Harvey, in two different relations to contradiction and crisis. Either it *seeds* contradiction, and hence crisis tendencies. Or it is a *response* to such tendencies. In examining his ideas about fixity and motion, we've been focussing on the former sort: the production of fixed infrastructures against the backdrop of a general drive to overcome spatial barriers creates a chronic contradiction between the respective imperatives to preserve and destroy the value of those infrastructures. Now, however, we turn to new spatial configurations of the latter sort – those representing responses to contradictions and crisis tendencies. Harvey's arguments in this regard have generated one of his most famous concepts – the so-called spatial fix.

Outward geographical expansion as a spatial fix

Ironically, given the name and its etymological proximity to 'fixity', the spatial fix as Harvey first theorised it is not about immobility, but rather its obverse – mobility, or more specifically, geographical *expansion*. To understand what Harvey originally meant by the spatial fix – he first wrote about it in a paper published back in 1981 (Harvey, 1981a) – we need to recall an idea we discussed in the previous chapter: that of 'over-accumulation'. Let's assume, Harvey said, that there's an emerging crisis in the form of an excess of capital relative to opportunities to employ that capital profitably. In such a situation, devaluation looms – through inflation in the case of money, growing stockpiles and falling prices in the case of commodities, or simple idleness in the case of productive capacity.

But geography, Harvey argued, provides a potential way out. The looming crisis can be averted through geographical extension into other territories. Harvey theorised three such possibilities, but without suggesting this was an exhaustive list. First, money that's surplus at 'home' can be lent abroad as a means of payment to buy-up surplus commodities produced domestically. Arguably, this is what all the money that China has been lending to the United States and its consumers in recent times represents, at least in part. Second, surpluses of money can be lent abroad to create fresh productive powers there – new factories and machinery and so forth. This, certainly, is what happened throughout the British Empire in the nineteenth and early twentieth centuries, not least in the still young USA, and it's what happened when the United States itself began lending to the southeast Asian 'tiger' economies (Singapore, Hong Kong, South Korea and Taiwan) from the 1960s. And third, domestic capital can access overseas-based reserves of labour and put them to work either there or (via immigration) domestically – the latter having occurred in much of the Global North in the post-war era. In any event, whatever the exact mechanism, Harvey (2001a: 24) reckoned that capitalism has an 'insatiable drive to resolve its inner crisis tendencies by geographical expansion'. Globalisation since around the mid-1980s, for Harvey, represents in considerable part the manifestation of that drive.

The first thing to say about Harvey's spatial fix idea is that it was in some respects an unfortunate choice of term. It could be – and sometimes has been – taken to imply that through such geographical expansion, capitalism *did* successfully 'fix' its inherent crisis tendencies. It resolved them. But a proper reading of Harvey's 1981 text shows that this was never his meaning. Whichever mechanism of expansion was employed, Harvey demonstrated that the underlying contradictions eventually resurfaced, such that any crisis relief was only short-lived. As he put it twenty years later, the ultimate effect of the spatial fix is simply 'to project and replicate the contradictions of capital onto an ever-broadening geographical terrain' (2001a: 27). There *is no resolution* in the long run. The 'fix', he suggested in the same essay, is akin to that sought by an addict, in the sense that 'the resolution is temporary rather than permanent, since the craving soon returns' (2001a: 24). A 'spatial bandaid' would perhaps have been a better term.

A second point to note is that the concept of the spatial fix arguably falls prey to one of the main criticisms of Harvey's work more generally –

that it's overly 'structuralist', even functionalist (e.g. Duncan and Ley, 1982). What this means is that individual institutions, let alone individual people, have little obvious active or volitional role to play in the capitalist drama as Harvey depicts it, being reduced to the functional status of mere 'carriers' of an overarching structural logic that's irresistible. The spatial fix occurs *because capital deems that it must, that it's needed.* Critics also here suggest that Harvey's logic is back-to-front. Instead of empirically identifying a problem (over-accumulation) and tracing the actual response to it (geographical expansion), he can be read as observing a phenomenon (geographical expansion) and deducing that it must be a result of a condition of over-accumulation – without ever, in fact, showing that there *is* over-accumulation in the first place.

Third, if we combine the 'spatial fix' with capitalism's above-mentioned oscillation between fixity and motion, we can see already that Harvey is building towards an overall theorisation of capitalism's geography that posits it as not only restless but deeply uneven. The map of the economic landscape will combine local pockets of fixed investment with multiple vectors of expansionism; some places will be invested in heavily, others not so much, and others still will be invested in but then later left behind. In short, capitalism develops unevenly geographically as well as socially. Interestingly, Harvey has written about uneven geographical development under capitalism multiple times, but without ever quite furnishing an overt explanation of such uneven development *per se*.[1] Such a theory was provided instead by one of Harvey's most influential graduate students, the late Neil Smith, in an eponymous book (Smith, 1984).

'Internal' geographical reconfiguration as a spatial fix

In the years since he first introduced the term, Harvey has broadened the meaning of the 'spatial fix' quite substantially. So too have others who borrow the concept (e.g. Herod, 1997; Wyly, Atia and Hammel, 2004). As such, what originally had quite a specific connotation – geographical *expansion* into new territorial production sites and consumer markets – has come to encompass a much wider range of phenomena, embracing all manner of new spatial-economic configurations. In particular, Harvey has argued that in response to conditions of over-accumulation, expansion is not capital's only possible 'spatial' response. It can also 'internally' reconfigure the geographies of the territories it already dominates.

We have already touched on part of this. As we saw in Chapter 4, Harvey has argued that one way in which capital surpluses are 'mopped up' is through long-term investments in the fixed capital of machinery, factories and the like – a 'temporal fix' in the sense that crisis tendencies are thereby deferred. Harvey has then extended this preliminary argument in two crucial ways. First, he's said that to absorb surpluses in this manner, capital not only can invest in buildings used for commodity production, it can also erect buildings used for social reproduction, not least housing. Second, he's argued that because in doing so capital reconfigures the geographical foundations of the economy and society, this is a spatial fix as much as it is a temporal one.

More exactly, it is a predominantly *urban* spatial fix, since the built environment whose construction facilitates surplus capital absorption is largely, and increasingly, city based. Harvey has used the term 'capital switching' to refer to this process whereby excess money capital that cannot be profitably reinvested in commodity production is diverted instead into city (re)building. He's argued that this was what happened in response to over-accumulation in, for example, the United States in the 1950s and 1960s, during which decades a whole new suburban landscape was created in concrete (Walker, 1981).

When Harvey has written about the 'urbanisation of capital', therefore, as he did for instance in the eponymous 1985 book (Harvey, 1985a), he is not just saying that, over time, processes of capital circulation and accumulation have more and more occurred in cities. Capital increasingly circulates *through* cities, too: that is, through the very physical fabric that constitutes them. Capital, then, is also urbanised in the more fundamental sense that the buildings that make up cities (and the parcels of land on which those buildings sit) become commodities like any other, their production, distribution and exchange being organised essentially according to the same logic as other commodities – the logic of value production and expansion.

So significant a dynamic is this for Harvey that, drawing heavily on the insights of Henri Lefebvre, he's used another important concept to denote it – the so-called secondary circuit of capital. If the primary capital circuit is the one we have already examined, in Chapters 3 and 4, whereby the route from M to MΔ is through simple commodity production, the secondary circuit sees capital absorbed into the physical infrastructures of factories, housing, schools and roads. There is likewise a Harvey term for the *social* infrastructures of capital accumulation, such as health and education, which he similarly regards as a convenient sink for surplus capital: the 'tertiary' circuit (see Figure 5.1).

Once again, Harvey's theorisation of city-building-as-surplus-capital-absorption has been regarded by some as altogether too mechanical and functionalist: the idea that the making of the built environment reflects the

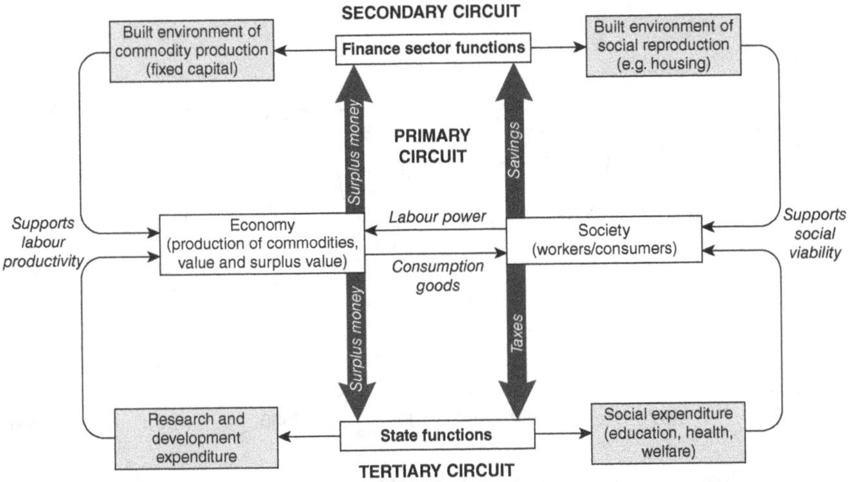

Figure 5.1. The primary, secondary and tertiary circuits of capital accumulation.

Source: Reproduced in modified form from Harvey (1985a: 9).

deep-seated 'requirements' of an arguably phantasmic over-accumulated capital does not sit easy with those who prefer more tangible explanations, rooted for instance in the strategic decision-making of the property development industry. To be fair to Harvey, though, he never did suggest that *all* city-building is a function of capital-switching. Sometimes a wave of new construction occurs simply because new office space or factory space or housing is actually needed in a particular place. This for example was clearly the case, Harvey has said, in the formative era of industrial capitalism in nineteenth-century Europe. Early industrial cities such as Manchester in England developed as they did because they aggregated in one location the key components necessary for large-scale machine-based commodity production: producing agglomerations of factories and housing (in Harvey's secondary circuit) *enabled* the mass production of textiles (in the primary circuit), furnishing dense concentrations of wage labourers. Similarly, Paris was rebuilt between 1850 and 1870 specifically in order to replace a legacy built environment 'that bound it so tightly to an ancient past' with one that would be more 'compatible with the increasingly sophisticated and efficient capitalist organisation of production emerging in the new manufacturing towns not only in Britain – France's main commercial rival – but also in Belgium, Germany, Austria, and even in certain other regions of France' (Harvey, 1985b: 67, 65).

But in the 'post-industrial' cities of today's West, the primary and secondary circuits interact very differently. The post-war history of cyclical construction booms – wherein the extent and pace of new building runs

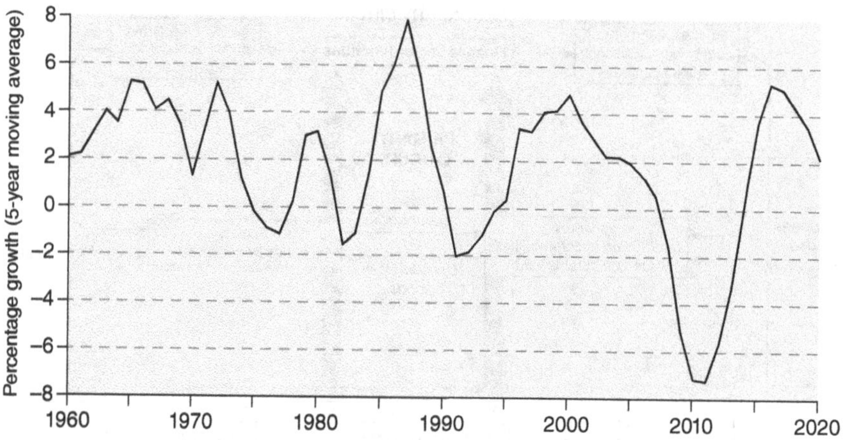

Figure 5.2. Growth in US construction industry real output, 1960–2020.[2]

Source: Bureau of Economic Analysis.

far beyond anything that might be traceable to actual latent demand for occupancy – demonstrates as much. Such booms – for instance, of the kind which occurred in the United States in the 1960s, the early 1970s, the mid-1980s and then again around the turn of millennium (see Figure 5.2) – are, Harvey has insisted, much more to do with supply (of excess capital) than demand (for new physical space). They represent a 'massive movement of capital into long-term investment in the built environment as a kind of last-ditch hope for finding productive uses for rapidly accumulating capital' (1985a: 20). Whereas in the industrial age the production of urban space generated the steam to power capital accumulation, now it enables an over-accumulation-afflicted capitalism to let *off* steam. Urbanisation in the form of city-building, in short, has become an 'internal' spatial fix to capitalism's crisis tendencies, with the result that real-estate bubbles frequently presage the emergence of more generalised crisis conditions.

Inter-place competition

The crisis that engulfed North Atlantic capitalism from the early 1970s, and which to all intents and purposes lasted for the whole decade, seeded a wholesale renewal of the political economy of the United States, the United Kingdom and a host of other Western nations. Having held for the best part of three decades, the post-war Keynesian compromise finally disintegrated and gave way to neoliberalism. In Chapter 4, we examined the core of Harvey's understanding of this shift and its implications: of how neoliberalism generated conditions of over-accumulation which in turn led to the ill-fated rise of finance.

But the shift in question, Harvey argues, also had a range of more explicitly geographical consequences, not least for cities. In his landmark article about urban entrepreneurialism, which we introduced in Chapter 2, Harvey (1989c) spelled these out. His immediate focus in the paper – the subsequent influence of which is reflected in the fact that it's been cited more than any of his other scholarly articles, with only a handful of his books garnering more citations – was on urban governance, which is to say, the question of how and to what ends actors with the power to control urban social and economic life exercise that power. But if governance was the immediate object of enquiry, at a more fundamental level the paper represented a significant contribution to Harvey's theorisation of the geographies of late capitalism. For, in shifting regimes of governance, Harvey also detected shifting relations *between* cities and ultimately new patterns of uneven geographical development.

Harvey maintained that the corollary of national-level Keynesianism in the 1950s through mid-1970s was a distinctively 'managerial' approach to urban governance. Such governance was bureaucratic and the preserve more-or-less exclusively of publicly elected local governments, which generally enjoyed the necessary authority and resources to provide services, facilities and benefits to the local population, with the principal goal being the 'amelioration of conditions within a particular territory' (1989c: 8). But the crisis of the 1970s – '[d]eindustrialisation, widespread and seemingly "structural" unemployment, fiscal austerity at both the national and local levels, all coupled with a rising tide of neo-conservatism and much stronger appeal (though often more in theory than in practice) to market rationality and privatisation' (1989c: 5) – ushered in a very different urban-governance regime. In Harvey's view, this new regime was (and still is) at once both a local manifestation *and* a crucial constitutive element of neoliberalism more broadly.

Harvey labelled this new regime 'entrepreneurial'. Stimulating local economic development and thus maximising local growth increasingly substituted for the improvement of local social conditions and resolving collective needs as the primary objective of governance. What's more, elected local governments were increasingly expected to work with local business elites towards these new ends: the proliferation from the early 1980s of a range of urban public-private partnerships of various forms was a testament to this shift. In other words, what changed was not only the objectives of governance but the identity of those doing the governing. Cities and those in charge of them could use various different entrepreneurial strategies to try to generate growth. They could try to stimulate the local primary circuit (i.e. the production of goods and services), for example through financial incentives for commodity producers such as tax breaks; they could try to boost local consumption expenditures, for instance by subsidising the construction of shopping centres or facilities for sports and cultural events; they could try to acquire 'key control and command functions in high finance, government, or information gathering and processing' (1989c: 9), which was what the 'global cities' studied by Saskia Sassen (1981) often did, using investment in advanced transport and communication infrastructures; and, finally, they could invest in infrastructure with a view to attracting activities funded by national-government expenditures, most prominently in the health, education, and military and defence sectors.

The significance of the shift from managerial to entrepreneurial urban governance has been multiform. Not least among the implications has been the fact that cities – and those governing them – have become increasingly competitive with one another, vying for investment within a 'spatial division of labour'. The opportunities that can be exploited to boost the local economy are inherently limited: there are only so many producers to be attracted to town, only so many central-government tax dollars allocated to higher education institutions. Cities are therefore trapped within what Harvey (1989c: 5) described as 'a framework of zero-sum inter-urban competition for resources, jobs, and capital'. Competition thus disciplines cities in much the same way that Marx, in *Capital*, envisioned it disciplining capitalists – competition becomes, said Harvey (citing Marx), 'an "external coercive power" over individual cities to bring them closer into line with the discipline and logic of capitalist development' (1989c: 10). Urban governance is reduced to the undignified spectacle of 'place promotion', whereby local officials proclaim a 'good business climate' and offer 'all sorts of lures to bring capital into town' (1989c: 11). Witness, for instance, various Canadian and US cities bidding in recent years to host Amazon's new corporate headquarters (HQ2) and distribution hubs (Figure 5.3). The reduction in spatial barriers brought about by ongoing advances in communication and transportation technologies intensifies all of this inasmuch as it makes capital more mobile and hence better able to exploit the relative advantages offered by different locations. For all the talk of 'the end of geography', place in fact becomes *more* important. 'Small differences in labour supply (quantities and qualities), in infrastructures and resources, in government regulation and taxation', Harvey asserted, 'assume much greater significance than was the case when high transport costs created "natural" monopolies for local production in local markets' (1989c: 11). Competition based upon those 'small differences' accordingly becomes ever more acute.

Figure 5.3. Housing now, Amazon later. Protestors have claimed cities like New York are more interested in trying to lure corporations to town than in fixing local social problems.

The overall result is restless transformation across the wider economic-geographic landscape. Cities 'get ahead' one moment by luring mobile capital, only to fall behind once firms have exploited the inducements on offer and subsequently moved on to greener pastures. After all, a tax break of 20 per cent can be trumped by a tax break of 30 per cent; and it is always possible to build a shinier shopping mall, a bigger sports stadium, a faster local broadband network. Investments made in one place are imitated and bettered elsewhere, 'thus rendering any competitive advantage within a system of cities ephemeral' (1989c: 12). As Neil Smith put it in his germinal book *Uneven Development* (1984), capital oscillates or 'seesaws' geographically from relatively developed localities to less developed localities, and then back again, creating a ceaseless and unstable dynamic of uneven geographical development. Harvey saw exactly this emergent dynamic at work in the US urban system as the 1970s segued into the neoliberal 1980s. 'Houston, Dallas and Denver, boom towns in the 1970s, suddenly dissolved after 1980 into morasses of excess capital investment bringing a host of financial institutions to the brink of, if not in actual bankruptcy', he wrote (1989c: 13). And, as capital fled those particular cities, it returned to cities it had previously shunned: 'New York, on the edge of bankruptcy in 1975, rebounded in the 1980s with the immense vitality of its financial services and command functions'. Such is the seesawing dynamic of capital circulation and inter-urban competition under conditions of enhanced capital mobility and the logic of urban entrepreneurialism.

Rent and the market for land

Insofar as all buildings are erected on land, land is clearly pivotal to Harvey's 'secondary circuit' and the urbanisation of capital. Land under capitalism is a commodity with a price, one which is intrinsically geographical inasmuch as it reflects both absolute location (the quality of the site, however 'quality' might be measured) and relative location (nearness for instance to relevant amenities, infrastructures and so on). 'Rent', of course, is the name of the payment that a tenant on a piece of land pays to the landowner. It occupies a crucial role in economists' understanding of land because land's price is usually conceptualised as the value in present terms of future rents – that is, the value that buyers and sellers place in the present on all rents that the land could in future generate if it were to be leased. Land trades in land markets, the operation of which in most countries is modulated in various ways by the state and its powers of land-use regulation and planning. Representing the locus of exchange in future rents, land markets in a very real sense underpin capitalism. They are based on delimiting parcels of land (historically, land was a 'commons', open to all) and assigning ownership rights to these parcels.

Although Marx did discuss land and land rent (he called the latter 'ground rent', as does Harvey), they represented something of a quandary for him. Ultimately, he could not bring himself to assign more than a relatively minor role to the landowner. A landed-property class having a significant role in society and economy was something that Marx associated with feudalism, a historic hang-over. In the brave new world of industrial capitalism, by contrast, the landowner was what Marx once dismissed derisively as a 'useless superfetation', serving – so far as Marx could see – no good purpose. As a class with genuine power, he expected landed property to soon pass quietly into the night. It was a socioeconomic relic of the past.

But time would prove Marx's expectations on this score to be fundamentally flawed. Landowners not only retained their importance as capitalism developed but, arguably, grew in significance. 'Capitalism has taken possession of the land', Henri Lefebvre observed in the mid-1970s, 'and mobilised it to the point where this sector is fast becoming central' (Lefebvre, 1991: 335). Yet, many political economists indebted to Marx have continued – both before Lefebvre and after him – to treat land, landowners and the land market much as Marx did, which is to say, inadequately. 'The power of land and resource owners has been much under-estimated', Harvey (2010a: 182) has observed, 'as has the role of land and resource asset values and rents in relation to the overall circulation and accumulation of capital'.

No such under-estimation, however, characterises Harvey's own work. Just as he has given exchange relations more attention than many other Marxist scholars (Chapter 4), so too his preoccupation with cities has crystallised a longstanding interest in land markets, in the process of which he has demonstrated just how pivotal land and land rent are to contemporary capitalism, and particularly urbanised capitalism. Land and the money to be made from owning, developing and letting it – money which flows in astronomical proportions in dense global cities like Hong Kong, London and New York – today shapes more general processes of capital accumulation and corresponding transformations of class relations in profound ways.

Indeed, in the context of the wider concerns of the present chapter, Harvey has pressed the case further still. As noted at the outset of the chapter, Harvey is adamant that to understand capitalism one must understand its geography. Thus, political economy – the study of capitalism – must be 'spatialised'. But how? Precisely by focussing on land and land rent. The power of the landowner is, Harvey maintains (and it's quite a claim), the 'singular principal power [lurking behind] all the contingencies and the uncertainties involved in the perpetual making and remaking of capitalism's geography' (Harvey, 2010a: 180). It follows that 'rent and land value are the theoretical categories whereby political economy integrates geography, space and the relation to nature into the understanding of capitalism' (2010a: 183). Without theorising the land market, in short, one cannot spatialise political economy – or, therefore, comprehend its object of analysis. Land parcels frame capitalism and its geography economically and legally, as much as they do physically.

For this reason, Harvey's theorisation of rent and the market for land is a cornerstone of his wider theorisation of capitalist spatiality, and it's the final building-block in our extended examination of the latter. He began with one of the questions about private landownership under capitalism that Marx had himself pondered: why, with the rise of industrial capitalism, did the newly ascendant class of industrial capitalists leave land in the hands of a largely separate 'landed property' class? After all, this required capitalists to share some of the surplus value created in production with the landowners from whom they leased land: the payment of land rent directly diminished profits. Marx thought it would have made much more sense *from capital's perspective* to turn privately owned land into a form of common property of the capitalist class at large.

Harvey thinks that the most compelling of several possible answers to this question is that private landownership, and in particular private land's circulation as a commodity in land markets, performs a vital 'coordinating' function for capitalism: in his own words, a 'positive role in co-ordinating the flow of capital on to and through the land in ways broadly supportive of further accumulation' (1982a: 361). This coordinating role works, as in theory it does in all capitalist markets, through allocative efficiency; rent, like other market prices, sends 'signals' to market actors that help coordinate their respective movements and investments. Consider a situation, Harvey says, in which, thanks to the locational advantages of the land she leases, one capitalist producer is able to generate 'excess' profits. What does the rational landlord do? Increase the rent at that location, of course. By thus 'taxing away' the excess, 'the landlord operates to equalise rates of profit between competing producers'. She facilitates the process of inter-capitalist competition. Is this good for capitalism, in the sense of good for 'further accumulation'? Absolutely it is: 'When the unfair advantages are eliminated, competition forces producers into further development of the productive forces and further rationalisation of production' (1982a: 361). Markets, price signals, efficiency, coordination, rationalisation – Harvey, it would appear, is something of a mainstream, orthodox economist.

And yet of course he is not – and the reason, at least where landownership and land markets are concerned, is that, as Harvey went on to say, capitalism does not only get the 'good', the positive elements of rent-facilitated coordination and rationalisation. Capitalism, for Harvey as for Marx, is as we know always about contradiction, and thus with the 'good' it gets the associated 'bad' – it necessarily gets elements of disorder into the bargain. Rent, and the system of land privatisation and commodification underlying it, is a source not only of coordination but also, Harvey wrote, of 'contradiction, confusion and irrationality' (1982a: 362).

How so? This is where Harvey's argument becomes dense – but bear with us, because it repays close consideration. It emerges out of two vital insights. The first is that capitalist land markets (and landowners) can only properly fulfil their coordinating role if market actors are free to invest in land solely with a view to maximising rents – which is to say, if exchange value is privileged over use value. This insight is the foundation of Harvey's influential claim that under capitalism, land is increasingly treated like a financial asset (in other words, as an asset with only exchange value) – rent representing the effective 'interest' on the money used to purchase land,

and the land market therefore becoming part of the wider arena for the circulation of yield-seeking capital. The freer yield-seeking capital is to 'roam the land looking for titles to future ground-rents to appropriate', Harvey (1982a: 369) argued, 'the better it can fulfil its co-ordinating role'. What he was saying, in short, is that capitalism *requires* land speculation. For land markets and rental yields to coordinate productive allocations of land according to the mainstream economic model, it has to be possible to buy and sell land strictly according to expected rents – to speculate on it.

The other key insight is that while under capitalism land can be traded like any other commodity, it is in fact not like any other commodity. Specifically, *monopoly inheres in it*. All land is non-replicable; and every piece of land is unique. 'Monopoly power over the use of land', Harvey (1982a: 348–349) noted, 'can never be entirely stripped of its monopolistic aspects, because land is variegated in terms of its qualities of fertility, location, etc.'. Or, as none other than the former British Prime Minister Winston Churchill (1909) famously put it: 'Land monopoly is not the only monopoly, but it is by far the greatest of monopolies – it is a perpetual monopoly, and it is the mother of all other forms of monopoly' (quoted in Christophers, 2018: 61).

Combine these two qualities – the necessity of speculation in land and the endemic nature of monopoly control over it – and you have, Harvey has concluded, a recipe for trouble. As we have seen, effective coordination of capitalist production through the land market requires landowners to charge market-clearing rents: these discipline commodity producers to be competitive, and therefore help keep productive forces in balance. As Harvey (1982a: 362) said, however, 'there is no way to ensure that the appropriators of rent take their due and only their due'. The way in which markets typically ensure that market participants only take 'their due' – the amount designed to keep the system as a whole in balance – is through competition. But competition, as noted, is always circumscribed in land markets because monopoly control is, in Harvey's words, 'chronic and unavoidable' (1982a: 349). This monopoly power, he continued, 'creates all kinds of opportunities for the appropriation of rent which do not arise in the case of other kinds of financial asset except under special circumstances'. There is, in other words, nothing to stop landowners from charging excessive rents, which is anything but system-stabilising behaviour: 'individual landholders, acting in their own immediate self-interest and seeking to maximise the ground-rent they can appropriate, may force allocations of capital to land in ways that make no sense from the standpoint of the overall requirements of accumulation' (1982a: 370).

Furthermore, if the system, as it must, allows speculation in future ground rents, then it also by extension allows speculation in something else:

future capital gains. One of the most notable features of land investment in early-twenty-first-century capitalism is individuals and institutions widely investing in property not for proprietary occupation or productive use – and not for letting to tenants either – but rather in the hope and expectation of value appreciation and the possibility of resale at a higher price. We see this, for example, in the form of empty, high-end housing in cities like Hong Kong, London, New York and Sydney. If, with speculation in future ground rents, we get, after Harvey, both 'good' (coordination) and 'bad' (disorder), with speculation in future capital gains we arguably get *only* the latter. It does not contribute in any way to allocative efficiency.

We know only too well today, just as Marx himself knew, that financial markets are fertile fields of speculative excess; in volume three of *Capital*, Marx envisioned such markets as a kind of warped doppelgänger of 'real' capitalism, representing its 'height of distortion' and the locus of its most 'insane forms'. But where speculative frenzies are concerned, financial markets, Harvey has suggested, are almost as nothing compared to land markets. And the allure of monopoly rents, undisciplined by competitive pressures, is a big part of the reason for this: 'The "insane forms" of speculation and the "height of distortion" achieved within the credit system stand' – precisely in view of monopoly control in land – 'to be greatly magnified in the case of speculation in future rents' (1982a: 349).

Of course, the very openness of the land market, the free play of speculation within it, only serves to exacerbate all of this. So, while yield-seeking capital must be free to speculate on rental yield in order to perform a positive coordinating role, the same conditions contain within them the very seeds of disorder, for 'the more open the land market is, the more recklessly can surplus money capital build pyramids of debt claims and seek to realise its excessive hopes' (1982a: 369). This is capitalist contradiction writ large: insofar as the positive 'co-ordinating functions' of rental appropriation 'are bought at the cost of permitting insane forms of land speculation', the land market 'necessarily internalises all the fundamental contradictions of the capitalist mode of production' and 'thereby imposes those contradictions upon the very physical landscape of capitalism itself' (1982a: 372). In other words, the contradictions are always ultimately lived and experienced contradictions in a deeply grounded geographical sense. The economic disorder generated by speculative land markets is at once, and necessarily, a disorder that is geographical and developmental, playing out in the built environment and in the field of land use. It is overbuilding booms. It is vacant offices. It is home foreclosures. 'Speculation in land may be necessary to capitalism', Harvey thundered, 'but speculative orgies periodically become a quagmire of destruction for capital itself' (1982a: 370).

And if ever this phenomenon was in evidence, it was in 2007–2009, in the global financial crisis – which, as we know by now, was triggered precisely by unchecked forms of speculation in markets for housing – read: land – and out of which a quagmire of destruction for capital itself was averted only by massive state intervention. If any market indubitably refutes the neoclassical conceit that private markets produce efficient and stable outcomes, then the land market is surely it.

Putting geography into Marxism (and Marxism into geography)

There can be little doubt that Harvey himself regards his work on the multifaceted and contradictory material geographies of capitalism as his most original and significant contribution to scholarly advancement. As we noted in Chapter 2, he has always said that *The Limits to Capital* (1982a) is – and will forever remain – his most important book. And he's often said that the second half of the book – where he laid out the financial-temporal and, in particular, spatial dimensions of capitalism and its crisis tendencies – is where he genuinely advanced Marxist thought. Indeed, it was to 'better ground' his understanding of urbanisation, Harvey has admitted, that he wrote *The Limits* in the first place (Harvey, 2002a: 177). Moreover, the publication in 1985 of the two-volume 'Studies in the History and Theory of Capitalist Urbanization' (1985a, 1985b) 'would seem' on Harvey's own reckoning 'to mark a high point' in his career (2002a: 178).

Helpfully, Harvey summarised his overall take on capitalism's geographies in a chapter entitled 'Space: a keyword' (Harvey, 2006a). Elaborating on an insight first ventured briefly in *Social Justice and the City*, he there suggested that we need to study material space as *simultaneously* 'absolute', 'relative' and 'relational' (Table 5.1). *Absolute space* refers to the particular qualities of material arrangements in unique locations; *relative space* refers to how material connections between particular absolute locations affect those locations; and *relational space* refers to the sum total of these connections, such that all absolute spaces are, in the end, shaped by the totality of their material ties to numerous places and regions. Figuratively, use value, exchange value and value map on to each of the three renderings of space. 'So is space absolute, relative or relational?', Harvey asked. 'I simply don't know if there is an ontological answer to that question', he continued, but '[i]n my own work I think of it as being all three' (2006a: 275).[3] Knowledge of geography, then, has to be kaleidoscopic, capturing a

Table 5.1: The dimensions of space according to David Harvey

	Qualities of space
Absolute space	Particular material forms and functions operative at specific scales (e.g. roads, airports, houses)
Relative space	Specific material connections between absolute spaces influencing those spaces' fortunes (e.g. railways, migration flows, levels of foreign direct investment)
Relational space	Abstract material connections that shape and are shaped by absolute spaces and their specific connections to other absolute spaces (e.g. exchange rate fluctuations; interest rate shifts)

Source: Adapted from Harvey (2006a).

churning 'difference-in-unity' from the level of a single neighbourhood or farm to global flows of money and migrants (Harvey, 2009a).[4]

However, despite such didactic summary explanations on Harvey's part, academic Marxist thought has remained either (i) stubbornly aspatial or (ii) reliant on an older, simpler sense of geography as 'where things occur'. To Harvey's 'surprise and disappointment', *The Limits* was neither widely read nor influential apart from with 'those specifically interested in geographical and urban questions' (2002a: 176) – which did not, and still generally does not, include many Marxist scholars despite *The Limits* being republished more than once. Also, the likelihood is high that most such scholars are not even aware of the towering 1985 brace of urban 'Studies…' (Harvey, 1985a, 1985b), let alone have read them. Harvey could well be the most famous Marxist intellectual in the world today, but oddly the work that he – and we – regard as his pivotal contribution to Marxist thought (and indeed to social science more generally) has not had a major impact within Marxism as an academic constellation.[5]

Nor has it really had a major impact within 'public' Marxism, which is where Harvey's profile has in recent decades become so prominent (see Chapter 9). To the educated, radical but non-academic Left, Harvey is indisputably best known as a general interpreter of Marx – via his internet-based lectures and his *Companions* to *Capital* – and as a critic of neoliberalism, imperialism, and postmodernity, not as a Marxist geographer or geographically minded Marxist. Certain spatially resonant concepts such as the 'right to the city' (which he borrowed from Henri Lefebvre) have cut through to an extent, but they don't begin to get at Harvey's own original, complex and multi-layered conceptualisation of capitalism's historical geography that we have sought to flesh out in this chapter. Again, the likelihood is high that very few among the thousands who have watched Harvey's online lectures could give a passable explanation of the spatial fix (one significant geographical concept of Harvey's that has successfully permeated wider consciousness), let alone of the tension between fixity and motion, the dynamics of capital switching or the operation of land markets.

For this, there are likely several reasons. A general dismissal of geographical knowledge in public as much as in social-scientific thought is probably one. As Harvey noted in his book *Cosmopolitanism and the Geographies of Freedom* (2009a: ix), 'I have long been used to the somewhat lowly status of the discipline [of Geography] in the academic pecking order of prestige'. Another, certainly, is the fact that Harvey's writing on capitalism's geographies is just, well, difficult. Substantially all Harvey's essential arguments vis-à-vis capitalism's space economy were published before he restyled his writing for a more public audience around the turn of the millennium. This is not to say that he doesn't emphasise the importance of geography in his more recent, accessible, books. He often does: witness, for instance, the chapter on 'The Space and Time of Value' in 2017's *Marx, Capital and the Madness of Economic Reason*. But such chapters barely scrape the surface of his longstanding geographic theorising. And for one reason or another, they don't appear to be the parts that 'stick' with readers. For chapter and verse on capitalism's historical geography as Harvey theorises it, one needs to go back to the extraordinary publications of the early and mid-1980s. Without exception, these, as this chapter has made plain, are dense, difficult texts. And the *really* difficult and exacting concepts – such as the differences between 'absolute', 'monopoly' and two forms of 'differential' ground-rent – have generally been left to one side in our rehearsal.

Where Harvey has had much more success is in getting those within his own home discipline to take Marxism seriously: 'It was, it turned out, far easier to bring Marxism into geography than to take geographical perspectives back into Marxism' (2002a: 176). Traditionally, economic geography – the sub-field of geography concerned with economic study – had been a dry, descriptive discipline, categorising geographic regions by their economic 'characteristics' (a corn-growing region here, a tourist region there etc.) but making little effort to theorise those characteristics or indeed much else besides. The 'spatial science' of the 1960s sought to put economic geography on a very different (positivistic, quantitative, modelling-based) track, but by the 1970s this was largely a busted flush, and not only because of Harvey's own attacks on the enterprise. Economic geography was, in short, crying out for a rigorous and relevant theoretical framework.

Marxism seemed to many practitioners (the likes of Doreen Massey, Ray Hudson, David Rigby, Eric Sheppard and Mike Webber) to provide it.

Over the past half-century, Marxism has been enormously influential within economic geography (and indeed human geography more broadly). To be sure, 'Marxism' as it has influenced economic-geographic understanding is not synonymous with 'David Harvey'. But it is indisputable that Harvey and the theories adumbrated in this chapter have long been a principal conduit whereby the currents of Marxism have flowed into and coloured the diffuse body of economic-geographic thought. Furthermore, Harvey's influence has been exerted indirectly as well as directly. Some of the most creative and impactful economic – not to mention urban – geographers in their own right of the past few decades have been close colleagues of Harvey much influenced by him (e.g. Erica Schoenberger) or his graduate students (e.g. Andy Merrifield, Neil Smith, Erik Swyngedouw, Dick Walker and Melissa W. Wright).

Of course, one shouldn't overstate the success with which Harvey (and others) have brought Marxism into the discipline of geography. Only a minority of urban or economic geographers today would likely categorise their theoretical inclinations as being explicitly Marxian (and fewer still are card-carrying Marxists *politically*). And plenty of very compelling and influential economic geographers have consistently tilted against Marxism, even if in several cases they were more sympathetic to Marxist theories early in their careers. Names such as Ash Amin, Nigel Thrift and Michael Storper can be listed in this regard.

Nevertheless, the extent to which some of the most basic ideas of Marxism have essentially become baked into the cake, so to speak, of economic geography really is nothing short of remarkable. That capitalism is conflictual, contradictory and crisis-ridden – a whole world away from the smooth equilibria of mainstream economics – is more-or-less universally accepted in contemporary economic geography, even if some of those who hold to such a view are not necessarily aware of the historic role of Marxism in progressively cementing such orthodoxy. In addition, many of Harvey's strongest critics within economic geography, such as J. K. Gibson-Graham and Massey, have criticised him not for his Marxism *per se* but for the particular brand of classical Marxism to which he cleaves. Gibson-Graham's work, for instance, is 'post-Marxist' in the sense of adding to and reformulating Marxism rather than leaving it behind.

We'll close this final section of the chapter with a much more mundane but nonetheless telling marker of Marxism's (and Harvey's) impact within geography. In an essay in the *London Review of Books* from 2016, the British journalist and novelist John Lanchester recalled a conversation with

Danny Dorling, holder of the Halford Mackinder geography professorship in Oxford that Harvey once held, and a high-profile commentator on social issues. Lanchester (2016) asked Dorling to resolve something that had been puzzling him, asking 'why, when I was at school, geography was about the shapes of rivers, but now all the best-known geographers seem to be Marxists'? Dorling's answer was as illuminating as Lanchester's question. He (no Marxist) conceded that 'when you look at a map and see that the people on one side of some line are rich and healthy and long-lived and the people on the other side are poor and sick and die young, you start to wonder why, and that turns you towards deep-causal explanations, which then lead in the direction of Marxism'.

Conclusion

In this chapter, we've shown how Harvey theorises capitalist political economy as something that's intrinsically geographical. This does not just mean that capitalist development 'takes place' somewhere – a correct but banal observation. Much more than that, it means that the production of new spatial configurations – new geographical patterns of trade, new regional distributions of labour power, new arrangements of the built environment, new production clusters and so on – is *essential* to such development. Another way of saying this is that capitalism does not and could not evolve in the way it does were it not for the geographies that are part-and-parcel of its remaking. 'Space' – in all its myriad forms – allows capitalism to innovate, change and grow; but it also presents obstacles to such evolution. Capitalism is a spatially differentiated, expansionary, uneven yet geographically integrated system.

It's for these reasons that Harvey has long preferred the concept of 'historical-geographical materialism' to Marx's 'historical materialism'. The latter concept posits that capitalism's material conditions – the forces and relations of production, and especially the contradictions internal to them – drive its development through (socially constituted) time. Harvey concurs, and, as we saw in Chapter 4, argues that at the heart of this historical development are forms of long-term investment that manage to defer crisis tendencies to a later point in time – a kind of 'temporal fix' to underlying contradictions. But capital's 'fixes', imperfect as they are, are not just temporal; they're also spatial. Managing crisis tendencies involves 'buying time' *and* making space. Though, for reasons of explanatory expediency, we've examined Harvey's understanding of these temporal and spatial dynamics largely separately, in Chapters 4 and 5, respectively, it's crucial to emphasise that they are *not* separate, either in reality or in Harvey's thinking. Capitalism's 'fixes' are generally not temporal *or* spatial; they are, Harvey says (e.g. Harvey, 2003a), *spatio-temporal*. And, rooted in its own distinctive material contradictions, capitalism's development is always necessarily historical-geographical. The political economist's task is thus to understand the punctiform times and spaces of capitalism together, relationally (see Table 5.2).

That, essentially, is what Harvey, at his best, does. Nowhere, perhaps, is his relational historical-geographical materialism more vividly realised and to such powerful effect than in his work on the capitalist city in general, and nineteenth-century Paris in particular. Reflecting on how capital's attempts

Table 5.2: A matrix of capitalist space-time

	Qualities of space-time
Absolute space-time	For example a parcel of fertile agricultural land produces barley and wheat for ten years before being sold for housing development
Relative space-time	For example a rural village that becomes 'closer' to a city forty kilometres away because of a new motorway that allows more people to live there and commute to work; the motorway allows some local farmers to expand their vegetable production, supplying households in the city with direct delivery vegetable boxes; home owners and farmers take out various bank loans to be repaid over 15–25-year terms which lock in certain land uses for the foreseeable future
Relational space-time	For example rural property and land values increase after a new motorway is built, with monetary loans against present and future value calculated by banks in light of interest rates, national risk assessments and so on, with specific property and land assets 'tranched' into abstract asset classes that are priced and sold on money markets; the performance of these markets can rebound on the absolute space-times being valued

Source: Inspired by Harvey, 2006a.

to resolve its 'self-dissolving contradictions' wreaked decades of creative destruction on the French capital and its inhabitants, Harvey invoked a striking metaphor. 'It is rather as if the strings within the monetary, temporal, and spatial nets that frame social life are pulled taut in the face of an accumulation process that demands their rapid adaptation and reorganisation', he wrote (1989b: 193), as if grasping for the basic tenets of historical-geographical materialism in one sentence. 'Simultaneously tightened and stretched, the nets distort and snap, only to be hastily repaired into a patchwork quilt of new possibilities'. These possibilities, as we will now explain, involve capitalism growing dramatically in scope.

Further reading

Castree, N. (2009). The spatio-temporality of capitalism. *Time & Society*, 18(1), 26–61.

Harvey, D. (1985b). Money, time, space, and the city. In *Consciousness and the Urban Experience* (pp. 1–35). Blackwell.

Harvey, D. (1985c). The geopolitics of capitalism. In D. Gregory & J. Urry (Eds.), *Social Relations and Spatial Structures* (pp. 128–163). Macmillan.

Harvey, D. (1989c). From managerialism to entrepreneurialism: The transformation of urban governance in late capitalism. *Geografiska Annaler*, 71B, 3–17.

Harvey, D. (2009a). Space-time and the world. In *Cosmopolitanism and the Geographies of Freedom* (pp. 133–165). Columbia University Press.

Harvey, D. (2017) The space and time of value. In *Marx, Capital and the Madness of Economic Reason*. Profile Books.

Jessop, B. (2006). Spatial fixes, temporal fixes and spatio-temporal fixes. In N. Castree & D. Gregory (Eds.), *David Harvey: A Critical Reader* (pp. 142–166). Blackwell.

Notes

1. Even, we would argue, in the essay 'Notes towards a theory of uneven geographical development' (in Harvey, 2005b), the title of which is apt: what he offers are indeed *notes towards* such a theory, not a theory of uneven development as such. For this reason, we say little about Harvey's notion of 'development' in this book since there is just too little to base this discussion on.
2. This is shown as a five-year moving average to smooth the trend.
3. In his 'Keyword' chapter, Harvey linked the three meanings of space to the other trio we flagged at the start of this chapter (material space; representations of space; spaces of representation). He also made a pitch for understanding space in a more-than-capitalist sense, as much as a purely capitalist one, using this six-way matrix. Throughout, Harvey is really talking about space-*time*, not

space on its own. For instance, material space is absolute in the sense that its characteristics are static and given at any specific moment in time; but such characteristics are relative insofar as structured not only by ongoing practices geared to twenty-four-hour clock time, but other socially shared temporal systems near or far; and they are relational in that a globally dominant clock time, and the forces of 'socially necessary labour time, and 'socially necessary turnover time', exert endless pressure on absolute spaces to restructure. Aside from Harvey (2006a), the other major statement about absolute, relative and relational space-time is to be found in Chapter 7 of *Cosmopolitanism and the Geographies of Freedom* (2009a). Some readers may struggle to understand relational space-time (we ourselves do sometimes), whereas absolute and relative space-time are far easier to grasp. Harvey offers a relatively clear and brief treatment of the 'matrix' in *Marx, Capitalism and the Madness of Economic Reason* (2017a: Chapter 7).

4. Several human geographers have made significant attempts to elucidate what it means to research specific places – in their own right and comparatively – in a world that's now so integrated. We give a shout-out here to Gillian Hart, Cindi Katz, the late Doreen Massey, and Jennifer Robinson whose empirical and conceptual work has done much to operationalise the kaleidoscopic geography Harvey wishes us to pay close attention to.
5. It is perhaps telling that, in the chapter about 'Space' in a new multi-volume handbook of Marxism, the author gives more attention to Henri Lefebvre and Raymond Williams than to Harvey's work (Goonewardena, 2022). Likewise, in this same book the chapter on 'The urban' makes scant mention of Harvey's work (Holgersen, 2022).

Capital unbound

The commodification of everything

6

Using theory to make sense of history; Time-space compression and the 'globalisation' of capital; The manipulation of new wants, needs and desires; Environmental change under conditions of financialisation; Neoliberalism's contradictions; The geopolitics of capital; What Harvey chooses to see; Conclusion

Harvey published *The Condition of Postmodernity* in 1989, the same year as the Berlin Wall came down. It was an inauspicious moment to assert the superiority of Marxism over postmodernism – a relatively new aesthetic and intellectual movement that Harvey (1989a: 44) derided for its celebration of 'ephemerality, fragmentation, discontinuity and the chaotic' in modern society. The fall of the Wall, and with it the collapse of the Soviet economic system and Communist Party-rule in Central and Eastern Europe, seemingly represented 'the last nail in the coffin of any sort of Marxist credibility', as Harvey was to recount a decade later (2000a: 5). 'To pretend there was anything interesting about Marx after 1989', he recollected, 'was to sound more and more like an all-but extinct dinosaur whimpering its own last rites'. The world had allegedly reached the 'end of History' (Fukuyama, 1992). Free-market capitalism was the only game in town. In this context, who would listen to, let alone *commit to*, a Marxist analytical and political project?

To his credit, Harvey refused to acknowledge any kind of defeat after 1989. He remained convinced that, if anything, these seismic political events and cultural shifts lent even more urgency to the Marxist cause. As he has recently recalled, the 'changing material transformations of capitalism … were making Marx's analysis in Volume 1 of *Capital* more rather

DOI: 10.4324/9780429028120-6

than less relevant during those years' (Harvey, 2022a: 18). In the thirty-plus years that followed the publication of *The Condition*, Harvey would persist in his efforts to alert readers to what he thought was at stake in the expansion of capital's reach and power across the globe. Against the free-market apologists and the postmodernists who celebrated the passing of Marxist 'grand narratives' about capitalism and its evils, Harvey would consistently advocate Marxism as the only theoretical resource capable of fully illuminating the totalising and destructive power of capital.

In this chapter, we move down a level of abstraction from the previous two and review Harvey's analysis of the unfolding historical geography of 'real-world' capitalism over four decades. By piecing-together a narrative distilled from his books published from 1989, the main thematic we develop is that of capital's relentless expansion beyond prevailing limits since the 1970s – its mission to commodify more-or-less everything, thus subsuming populations, cultures, 'ways of being' and the material environment to the needs of its own expanded reproduction. Along the way, we'll encounter several more of Harvey's most well-known and impactful conceptual innovations, such as 'time-space compression' and 'accumulation by dispossession'.

Using theory to make sense of history

Before we begin, it's worth noting how Harvey approaches the task of putting theory to work to make sense of the 'real world':

> When trying to interpret, understand, and analyse the daily flow of news, I tend to locate what is happening against the background of two distinctive but intersecting models of how capitalism works. The first level is a mapping of the internal contradictions of the circulation and accumulation of capital as money value flows in search of profit through the different 'moments' (as Marx calls them) of production, realisation (consumption), distribution, and reinvestment. This is a model of the capitalist economy as a spiral of endless expansion and growth.
>
> [...I] envision this model as embedded, however, in a broader context ... This second model constitutes, as it were, my working understanding of global capitalism as a distinctive social formation, whereas the first is about the contradictions within the economic engine that powers this social formation along certain pathways of its historical and geographical evolution.
>
> (Harvey, 2020a: 179–180)

Harvey's *modus operandi* plainly draws a conscious analytical distinction between *capital* and *capitalism*, two closely related but sufficiently distinctive objects of inquiry. Much of the theoretical contribution he had made by the late 1980s concerned the former, since when Harvey has been tenacious in deploying this model of capital in making sense of ongoing world-historical events and processes. It's this focus on capital as the 'economic engine of capitalism' (Harvey, 2014a: 7–8) that frames much of what we'll cover in this chapter, as we identify the systemic drivers of global capitalism's post-1970s evolution as a 'social formation along certain pathways'.

Harvey has represented his 'model' of the circulation and accumulation of capital in the form of a schematic diagram, reproduced in Figure 6.1. It shows a dynamic 'ecosystemic totality' that, at any given time, comprises various tendencies and tensions operating between multiple forces of motion and potential sources of disruption. At the level of theory, then, Harvey's model allows for a good deal of variegation in the concrete forms taken by multiple national and regional social formations (or different, connected 'capital*isms*') at any given time, as well as diverse evolutionary

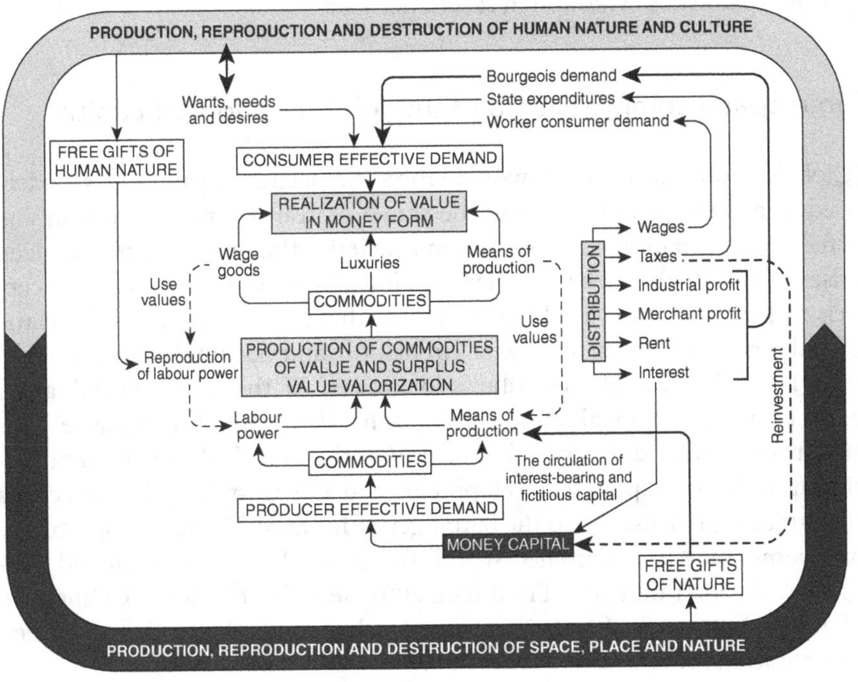

Figure 6.1. The paths of value in motion.

Source: Modified from Harvey (2014a: 6).

outcomes in the historical geography of global capitalism as a totality. The model does not claim to predict the course of capitalism's 'real' historical evolution. We should recognise that only careful and reflexive consideration of what is happening 'out there' in the 'real world' will enlighten us as to how capital encounters both opportunities for – but also barriers to – its expansion and growth. Reasoned analytical choices must be made about the *forces and contradictions that matter* at any given conjuncture.

The model reflects the importance Harvey has attached to three primary forces of motion at work in capital accumulation. We examined the process of *value production* in Chapter 3, and in Chapter 4 we highlighted the dynamics of the *realisation of value* after commodities go to market. We also paid close attention to the ways in which *financial intensification* feeds the progressive accumulation of capital, but how, in the process, it compels creditors and debtors alike to engage in all manner of behaviours that accentuate the most self-destructive tendencies of capital, inviting the possibility of systemic crises. From *The Condition* onwards, Harvey has attached explanatory importance to all three forces of motion of capital, and perhaps especially the machinations of finance capital, in fashioning global capitalism's evolution in recent decades.

Time-space compression and the 'globalisation' of capital

'Globalisation' became a key word in the social sciences by the 1990s, widely used as a short-hand to capture the range of transformations within and across various national economies and societies that ensued after the deep crises of the 1970s. It's a term Harvey himself often treats with some scepticism, however. For one thing, he insists there is nothing new about the global-territorial reach of capital circulation and accumulation (he often cites 1492, the year of Columbus's 'discovery' of the 'New World', as an early example of globalisation). Second, he also wanted to distance himself from popular discourses that prioritise 'the global' above all other particular scales of capitalist development, and not least liberal perspectives that greeted globalisation as the harbinger of harmony, fairness, opportunity and democracy in a 'flattened world' freed of arbitrary political and geographical constraints (e.g. Friedman, 2005; see Harvey, 2009a: Chapter 3). Harvey's own work after 1989 is very much a corrective to that one-sided globalisation literature.[1]

In *The Condition*, Harvey argued that capital's turn to globalisation as a response to the crises of the 1970s (see Chapter 4) led to a renewed phase of *time-space compression*. This term refers to a propensity for the forces of capital accumulation to speed up the pace of economic activity, and indeed of everyday life more broadly, in the process of seeking to overcome spatial barriers to the mobility of capital and of facilitating a faster turnover time of capital accumulation. It is widely experienced whenever capitalists simultaneously act to overhaul and remake the spatial and temporal conditions of accumulation (usually in moments of deep-rooted crisis). At the heart of Harvey's work post-*The Condition* is the argument that the succession of crisis events and political interventions in the period 1973–1982 led to precisely this kind of system-wide restructuring of capitalism, resulting in a 'radical readjustment in time and space in economic, political and cultural life' (Harvey, 1989a: 26).

Harvey's work identifies four essential and inter-related drivers of global political and economic transformation and time-space compression since the 1970s:

1. First and foremost are *financial deregulation and the removal of capital controls* following the collapse of the Bretton Woods system (Chapter 4). Initiated within the crisis economies of the North Atlantic, processes of deregulation proliferated around the world in the 1980s and 1990s, creating 'a global system that was more decentralised, coordinated through the market, and [which] made the financial conditions of capitalism far more volatile' (Harvey, 2000a: 61). The removal of capital controls meant that money in its various forms could be moved around the world far more freely that had hitherto been possible, more rapidly, and on an essentially unlimited scale. The freeing of money-capital from the fetters placed upon it via Bretton Woods after the Second World War was both the leading-edge of, and a vital pre-condition for, the 'globalisation' of capital accumulation and the spread of free-market capitalism across the world. This development was part of a broader process of what many commentators, Harvey included, term the 'financialisation' of the world economy, meaning the heightened importance of financial institutions, financial markets, and financial methods of accumulation.
2. The second driver of time-space compression is *technological change*. This is, of course, always fundamental to capitalism's evolution, but what distinguishes the post-1970s period is the accelerated rate of the transferral and imitation of technological innovations on an amplified scale around the world, including for example widely implemented advancements in the automation of manufacturing processes.
3. The third driver is the so-called *information revolution* and the effects of technoscientific advancements in communications and information processing. These have engendered rapid and widespread change in

'relations between working and living, within the workplace, [and] in cultural forms' (Harvey, 2000a: 62): think, here, of the relatively recent impacts of Web 2.0, new social media and online platforms.[2]

4. Fourth is a general *diminution in the costs (and timeframes) of moving goods and people around the world*, aided not only by the aforementioned technological innovations but also by a multiplicity of free trade agreements since the 1980s, including the creation of the WTO in 1995. This has contributed to the contemporary intensification of what Marx referred to as capital's impetus towards the 'annihilation of space by time'.

These processes have, in turn, paved the way for several more 'derivative' transformations in the historical geographies of global capitalism (Harvey, 2000a: 63). Of prime significance here is the global restructuring of the production of capital itself. To cut a long and complicated story short, this has entailed – on the one hand – the diffusion of supply-chain capitalism and processes of labour exploitation in 'value chains' now spanning the entire world (e.g. Tricontinental, 2019). On the other, it has driven processes of deindustrialisation in some parts of the world, and with it the internal transformation of distinct national 'models' of capitalism. This has posed various challenges for public policy since the 1980s, not least that of equipping future generations for work and changing labour market conditions. The expansion of university education under New Labour governments in the United Kingdom (1997–2010), for instance, was seen by many to be a response to the challenge of the employability of young people in a more 'knowledge intensive' economy: one in which you are more likely to be more geographically mobile and have a 'career portfolio' of successive, perhaps fixed-term service-sector or retail jobs (unlike much of the post-war 'baby boomer' generation who worked the same job, in the same factory, in the same town or city, for decades).

These transformations have been accompanied by others integral to the evolution of capitalist production on a world scale. To highlight just a few: Harvey (2000a: 41–42) has drawn attention to how the period 1966–1995 saw the doubling of the size of the global working class and at an exponential rate after the collapse of the Soviet Union. Crucially, this expansion comprised the drawing-in of millions of women into the world's labour markets, greatly facilitating the possibilities for capital to profit from the exploitation of low-wage labour. Inward migration has also played a key role in the transformation of labour markets within 'advanced' capitalist economies, providing capital with fresh (and very often racialised) sources of cheap labour-power, and a means of driving down the wages and conditions of workers in general while at the same time undermining working-class solidarity by fomenting social divisions between different communities (Harvey, 2010a: 14–15). Harvey has also drawn a link between the transformations in production and corollary processes of urbanisation and even 'hyper-urbanisation', as perhaps most visibly demonstrated in twenty-first century China (Harvey, 2005a: 127, 2010a: 172–173, 2016b).

Finance capital has played a pivotal role in facilitating all these latter-day global transformations. Indeed, Harvey (2017a: 170–171) asserted that '[t]he liberation of finance capital from many constraints after the 1970s ... along with the long-standing attempts to reduce barriers to cross-border trade both by tariff reductions and lower transport costs, has changed the whole spatial dynamic of capital accumulation'. The implications of these deep-rooted structural transformations for national states and governments of all political persuasions were also evident to Harvey from an early stage. On the one hand, they have engendered a tendency towards 'geopolitical democratisation' (Harvey, 1996a: 423), insofar as more and more national states were drawn into an open and competitive playing-field for the attraction of international investment, and in a game in which the same rules of free-market capitalism would appear to apply to all players irrespective of size and status. This geopolitical democratisation, however, has come at considerable cost to individual national states who may lack a competitive edge, as well as to the wider system of accumulation insofar as it intensifies and magnifies the crisis tendencies of capitalism on an international scale (Harvey, 2000a: 178–179).

This contradictory turn of events has tipped the balance of structural power towards finance capital and away from national states. Having been 'servant' of the 'real economy' under the Bretton Woods order (Helleiner, 1993), finance increasingly became the 'master'. Meanwhile, national states became preoccupied more with their status as attractive sites or nodal points within global flows of 'butterfly forms' of world money (Harvey, 2020a: 83) than with questions of egalitarianism and social justice within their borders. One of the main ways in which capital has compelled national states to engage in economic restructuring over the last four decades has been through the process of creative destruction brought on by financial crises and 'capital flight'. As Harvey (2005a: 94–98) has shown, recent history is rife with examples of attacks by private financial interests such as hedge funds against national currencies deemed to be mis-priced, often prompting states to respond to capital flight by taking emergency measures: raising interest rates, depleting national currency reserves, devaluing the national currency and exposing themselves to the risk of a sovereign debt crisis. Crises of this sort have occurred with greater frequency and synchronicity across the world since the 1980s. Harvey described the global crisis of 2007–2009 as being 'undoubtedly, the mother of all crises', but underlined that 'it must also be seen as the culmination of a pattern of financial crises that had become more frequent and deeper over the years since … the 1970s and early 1980s' (2010a: 6). In all the many cases he's discussed, Harvey emphasises how the destructive effects of these crises and the structural adjustment programs that invariably ensue are most acutely felt by low-income and disadvantaged populations. 'Foot loose' money comes to have very geographically and socially specific impacts on the ground.

The manipulation of new wants, needs and desires

As discussed in Chapter 4, the need to realise value is, for Harvey, one of the motors of capital accumulation that propel capitalism down its evolutionary paths. And, in periods when capitalism's evolution is increasingly shaped by the question of how to profitably invest vast quantities of surplus capital in the shortest turnover time possible, there is a powerful imperative for capital to rapidly expand the range and magnitude of what can be consumed at a price (Harvey, 2020a: 186). It is no accident, then, that the period since the 1970s has witnessed various developments favourable to the manipulation of new wants, needs and desires in capitalist societies, and Harvey has listed the commodification of 'sexuality, culture, history, heritage; of nature as spectacle or as rest cure; the extraction of monopoly rents from originality, authenticity, and uniqueness (of works of art, for example) – these all amount to putting a price on things that were never actually produced as commodities' (Harvey, 2005a: 167).

Harvey has used several terms to identify the different ways by which capital has looked to secure its realisation since the 1970s: terms like 'expanded consumption', 'instantaneous consumption', and 'compensatory consumption'. The first term refers to the inherent propensity for capital to perpetually create new wants, needs and desires on the part of consumers. The sphere of realisation expands along with the circulation and accumulation of capital in general. Just reflect, as Harvey occasionally does, on the sheer diversity of consumer goods and services on offer at any one time in any one locality (even in just one supermarket) within today's 'globalised' system of production and trade (Harvey, 1989a: 301, 2017a: 160). The range of 'consumer choice' compared with that of the post-war era is staggering.

'Instantaneous consumption' refers to how, as the repertoire of what can be manufactured, commodified and consumed within capitalism has expanded and proliferated over time, so too has the speed and transiency with which acts of final consumption take place *in* time. If the period 1945–1973 was an era characterised by the mass production of consumer goods with relatively substantial lifetimes (like stainless steel knives and forks), the last forty years or so have been characterised by the production of new products that become useless or outmoded in a very short timeframe indeed. Manufacturers today deliberately engage in a policy of 'planned obsolescence', and many of the most in-demand consumer goods are simply not made to last: 'we need a new computer every three or four years and a new mobile phone every two' (Harvey, 2020a: 164). This logic is taken to the extreme in the form of instantaneously consumed events or 'spectacles' with potentially global reach (Harvey, 1989a: 156). Harvey was here mindful of mega-events like the Olympics or the FIFA World Cup finals, but he's also pointed to more everyday forms of consumption like watching a newly released series on a TV streaming platform. Vast sums are spent (and earned) on a single act of consumption that is over in a flash.

The third term, 'compensatory consumption', signals how capital often creates and manipulates new wants, needs and desires to mollify consumers; to distract them from the feelings of exhaustion and alienation they otherwise feel as subjects in capitalism. Capital has historically manipulated consumer demand to secure its own realisation in just such a way: Harvey has pointed to how capital accumulation in the United States from the 1950s comprised 'the development of a whole new suburban lifestyle along with all sorts of propaganda for the "American Dream" of individualised home ownership' (2017a: 185). This was the era of affordable new homes, cars and 'labour-saving' modern conveniences for many working-class families. In the current era, the compensatory effects of consumption have become even more conspicuous and have combined with forms of instantaneous consumption. Of late, Harvey has been especially vexed by what he calls the 'Netflix economy' (see Harvey, 2017a: 198–199). Millions of dollars are invested in making a single episode of a series which can be consumed instantaneously by an unlimited number of people all around the world. The effectiveness of such spectacles for capital is palpable in the profits and stock market valuation of a company like Netflix, but perhaps even more so in the *affective* impact on the consumer: 'You watch a Netflix episode in an hour and that's it, it's done, and that's your consumption, and then you turn to the next hour. Binge-watching consumerism takes over' (2020a: 164).

Harvey's overarching argument as regards consumption, then, is that the sphere of the realisation of capital has been just as subjected to the pressure of time-space compression as the productive and financial spheres. Capital's injunction is: 'consume more, consume faster!' Harvey is interested in documenting this as a politico-economic phenomenon, but he's also mindful (and scornful) of the damaging effects of this tendency upon human cultures: 'because capitalism is expansionary and imperialistic', he warned in *The Condition*, 'cultural life in more and more areas gets brought within the grasp of the cash nexus and the logic of capital circulation' (Harvey, 1989a: 344). Harvey often discusses how capital has narrowed the possible range and variety of different 'ways of being'.

Take for example, how the production of new-built spaces for everyday cultural interaction has been dominated by large-scale real-estate developments incorporating shopping malls, retail parks and entertainment complexes with cinemas, bowling alleys and chain restaurants – spaces of crass and unfulfilling consumerism. Harvey's fierce disdain for the Canary Wharf development in London's Docklands (Figure 6.2), in a piece published more than twenty-five years ago, still resonates, alongside his more recent criticisms of the Hudson Yards development in New York City (Figure 6.3), the first phase of which was completed in 2019 (Harvey, 1994, 2020a: 106–109). Today, China is the world's most prolific producer of shopping malls, most of which closely resemble any mall you may find in the West. Harvey has seen such developments as being products of, and monuments to, 'the universal and homogenising uniformity of money power without even a trace of guilt' (Harvey, 1994: 420). To Harvey, their homogeneity as produced spaces is both striking and depressing. Hordes of retail and office workers daily enter and leave these sites, experiencing an

Figure 6.2. The Canary Wharf development in London's Docklands.

Figure 6.3. The Hudson Yards development in New York City. Built three decades apart, the strikingly similar Canary Wharf and Hudson Yards developments have both been criticised by Harvey.

affective sense of 'loss' and 'nothingness'. These spaces symbolise 'the death of public place and of the street as a site of heterogeneity and difference' (1994: 420). They epitomise soulless and unliveable capitalist urbanisation, inscribing alienation, inequality and exclusion into urban space: 'there's no space to sit down unless you go into one of the coffee bars, restaurants or whatever' (Harvey, 2020a: 106).

Often being integral to entrepreneurial projects and strategies to attract inward investment into cities and regions by providing opportunities for the capture of monopoly rents (see Chapter 5), these incisions in the physical landscape of capitalism can therefore entail dramatic transformations in the everyday lives of workers and consumers. Harvey has periodically commented on the city of Barcelona as an example. The construction of shopping malls, entertainment complexes, hotels and large conference spaces has been integral to that city's strategy of attracting mass leisure and business tourism, and of using mega-sports events and spectacles to spur urban redevelopment geared mainly towards capturing revenues from mass consumption (Harvey, 2002b; Harvey and Robles-Duran, 2011). While the economic rewards of such a strategy are high for the relevant investors, developers, hotel chains and local elites, there are huge costs in the form of rampant real-estate speculation and associated rent inflation, displacement of traditional residents due to gentrification, the loss of authentic cultural markers of distinction (or 'Disneylandification') and the manifold social and ecological problems associated with over-tourism.

What's notable about Harvey's critique is that it extends beyond the hedonistic and wasteful consumption of luxury goods and services by the mega-rich, and the shopping habits of comfortable middle classes who can afford to engage in moderate forms of conspicuous consumption in shopping malls. Capital, he insists, has penetrated the everyday lives of people and households across the world, irrespective of status, nationality or ethnicity, and in very insidious ways. Take, for instance, a necessary and intimate ritual such as preparing the family's evening meal. Harvey recently noted that whereas only a couple of decades ago food preparation was, by and large, done in the privacy of the home using various ingredients bought separately at the store or supermarket, today it is now more commonly the case that pre-prepared takeaways are ordered in from outside the home, relying therefore on a capitalist labour process, and increasingly upon on-demand food-delivery platforms like Uber Eats or Grubhub. Harvey (2020a: 134) points out that this practice has today become so widespread and normalised that Chinese takeout is more popular than it has ever been ... in China! From a certain point of view, this may have its benefits: it relieves time pressures in everyday life and reduces the burden of domestic labour on women especially. But it also amounts to giving yet another aspect of our private lives and of our kinship over to circuits of capital, including the platform 'gig economy', with all the exploitation of labour that implies.

Environmental change under conditions of financialisation

Harvey's model of the paths of value in motion acknowledges how capital benefits from certain 'free gifts of nature' in the form of raw materials, as well as 'free gifts of human nature' such as the reproductive labour that goes into homemaking and raising children as future sellers of labour-power. Value-producing processes have always consumed such free gifts, transforming the 'external' environment and producing new forms of capital's 'second nature' in the process (Harvey, 1996a: 185–186; Smith, 1984: 65–69). One of the most damaging by-products of capital's expanded consumption of energy in productive processes is, of course, greater levels of atmospheric carbon dioxide (CO_2). Just a superficial glance at how

CO_2 levels have increased over the last few decades would suggest that there is certainly a coincidence between globalisation and climate change (Figure 6.4), while many, like Harvey, would accept that there is in fact a direct causality.

Over the last decade, Harvey has become especially concerned with how compound economic growth and 'endless capital accumulation' necessarily produces, among other contradictions, a range of environmental crises. In recent decades, we have seen capital consume ever-greater quantities of raw materials, especially as hyper-urbanisation in places like China has stimulated enormous demand for finite resources such as copper, lithium and iron ore that must be extracted from the earth. In the sphere of the realisation of capital, expanded consumption among populations has generated unprecedented levels of excess waste and pollution. And as with the fall-out of financial crises, we know that global warming and the rising incidence of 'climate events' (drought, floods and so forth) impact most adversely upon the poorest populations of the world, and not just in 'developing' countries – witness for instance the devastating, disproportionate impact of Hurricane Katrina upon the low-income Black population of New Orleans in 2005.

Harvey's take on capital and Nature has been controversial on the Left.[4] He's long expressed his scepticism towards environmentalist arguments

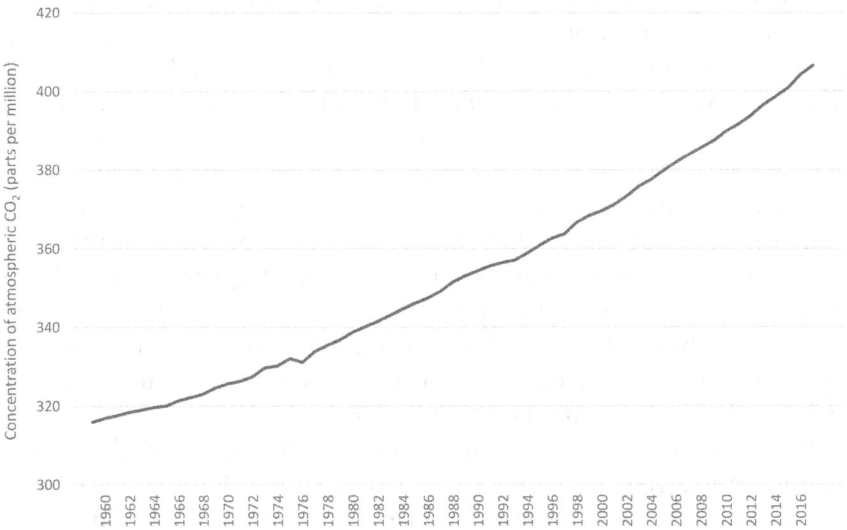

Figure 6.4. Concentration of atmospheric CO_2, yearly average 1959–2017.

Source: Global Monitoring Laboratory.[3]

that see Nature as something to be 'managed', and ecological movements that overly romanticise Nature and which fail, in his view, to recognise that Nature and society stand in a two-way symbiotic (or dialectical) relation. He writes: 'Capital modifies the environmental conditions of its own reproduction but does so in a context of unintended consequences (like climate change) and against the background of autonomous and independent evolutionary forces that are perpetually re-shaping environmental conditions. There is, from this standpoint, no such thing as a truly natural disaster' (Harvey, 2020a: 180). Nonetheless, for Harvey, as with many other critics of capitalism's relationship with Nature, the idea that the prevailing liberal-capitalist paradigm of endless economic growth can be reconciled with climate-change mitigation is fantasy. Leaving aside the impossibility of such reconciliation in theory, there is, he points out, the pragmatic political question of convincing finance capital to depart from business-as-usual in its patterns of investment of the world's surplus capital: 'The prospect of using the huge mass of investment moneys to address the two key questions of environmental degradation and social inequality without the interventions of a world government or at least strong coordination amongst the world's disparate governments is', Harvey (2020a: 10) estimates, 'close to zero'.

Yet such fantasies abound today; many powerful figures champion capital itself as the solution to climate change. Some, like the billionaire founder of Microsoft, Bill Gates, argue that the development of climate-change solutions could present significant opportunities for corporations and investors to profit from new technological innovations and remedies. They also point to market-based solutions that can be deployed by institutions of global climate governance to incentivise states, corporations and consumers to off-set or reduce their use of fossil fuels. So, in this framing, while climate change may well present a challenge to globalisation in its existing form, the former is potentially resolvable without breaching the underlying logic of the latter. *More* globalisation – configured around 'greener' technologies, or new initiatives that capture atmospheric CO_2 – could, it is said, be the answer, together with modest political commitments to control emissions, invest in a Green New Deal transition and to help mitigate the costs of the so-called green premium on manufacturing.

This, in short, is the degree to which today capital has achieved hegemony over mainstream environmental imaginaries, proving the oft-repeated adage among Marxists that 'it is easier to imagine the end of the world than the end of capitalism'. Harvey argues that, ultimately and perversely, the stakes of environmental degradation or catastrophe are simply not high enough for capital to deviate from its own 'nature':

> Capital … can continue to prevail as a social relation and as a mode of accumulation even in the face of the direct and most unwanted forms of environmental transformation that it produces. The problem is not that capital cannot possibly survive but that the social, economic, political, and material conditions of that survival would be devastating for large swathes of the world's population while the ultra-rich would probably happily continue their elite and sheltered way of life.
>
> (Harvey, 2022a: 20)

To avoid this – that is, to switch epic amounts of capital into 'green investment' – would require coordinated government intervention at a global scale, likely accompanied by social revolutions. In the end, to make the Earth liveable it is necessary, after Harvey, to alter the basic logic of valuation that capitalism imposes on the material world. But he has long insisted that any future social order will not be determined by absolute environmental constraints. Instead, societies have degrees of freedom about the ways they value and use the non-human world.

Neoliberalism's contradictions

The structural transformations of global capitalism adumbrated in the preceding sections are only one part of the story Harvey's work tells of the last forty years. Capital's seemingly boundless expansion has been greatly facilitated by the construction of a world-spanning 'institutional structure encouraging individual institutive and personal responsibility, [and] comprising free markets, strong private property rights and free trade' (Harvey, in Primrose, 2013: 5–6). That structure is usually labelled 'neoliberal': we need, then, to expand upon our brief earlier discussion of neoliberalism and of the role of specific class actors and institutions in aiding and abetting the empowerment of finance capital since the 1970s.

In Chapter 4, we discussed how, by the 1980s, governments like Margaret Thatcher's in the United Kingdom and Ronald Reagan's in the United States were at the vanguard of this new political-ideological movement that championed 'free enterprise' and the retrenchment of the welfare state. Harvey has had much to say about neoliberalism as such a 'mental conception of the world', and indeed about 'neoliberalisation' as a contested and uneven process of imposing free-market economics upon societies, with profoundly deleterious consequences (see Chapter 7). But the point on which Harvey has been most insistent is that we need to comprehend the last forty years of the transformation of global capitalism as both a product of the underlying and evolving dynamics and crisis tendencies of capital, as outlined in preceding sections of this chapter, *and* as a product of an opportunistic offensive on the part of certain economic elites to seize their moment, disempower labour and maximise their own capacity to go on accumulating unassailable wealth and private power into the future. *That*, for Harvey, is what is truly distinctive about the 'neoliberal' era.

He argues that progress on the latter front has been engineered by what he terms the '*state-finance nexus*', most visibly represented today by the alliance between state treasury departments and (formally 'independent') central banks. 'This state-finance nexus is not subject to democratic or popular control', Harvey (2017a: 203) has written. 'It has for its mandate the regulation and control of the private banking system for the benefit of capital as a whole'. It has secured 'the national and then international deregulation of financial operations, the liberation of debt-financing, the opening of the world to heightened international competition and the repositioning of the state apparatus with respect to social provision' (Harvey, 2010a: 131). Harvey (2017a: 205) has even gone so far as to suggest that 'the only mode of capital's survival is through the coherence and fusion achieved through the state-finance nexus'. The degree of entanglement between the state and finance capital is particularly plain to see in the United States, where 'Goldman Sachs has provided the Secretary of the Treasury ... since around the 1990s' (Harvey, 2020a: 37). The bank bailouts across the Global North during the 2007–2009 crisis fully exposed the reality that, in Harvey's words, 'state and capital are more tightly intertwined than ever, both institutionally and personally. The ruling class, rather than the political class that acts as its surrogate, is now actually seen to rule' (2020a: 218–219; see also Harvey, 2003a: 135–136).

The effects have been felt far beyond the Global North. As Western societies leaned further towards a culture of free markets and 'possessive individualism' from the 1980s, many countries across the Global South were experiencing economic crises that seemed to express the very real limitations of debt-fuelled and hyper-inflationary state-led developmentalism. The response of the IMF and a wider network of international and national cadre institutions was to impose on such countries various forms of 'structural adjustment'. In signing-up (often far from voluntarily) to this program of economic policy reforms, later dubbed the 'Washington Consensus', government after government – at first in crisis-stricken Latin America in the mid-1980s but increasingly elsewhere too – committed to programs of restructuring precisely along the lines prescribed by neoliberalism. With the end of the Cold War, several notable 'transition economies' in Central and

Eastern Europe even adopted neoliberal reforms on an almost instantaneous basis, in what became known as 'shock therapy'. These programs comprised the privatisation of state-owned or -managed enterprises; the removal of barriers to foreign direct investment and to free trade; a commitment to 'fiscal discipline' that oft necessitated draconian cuts in public spending; and, of course, the abolishment of capital controls and the deregulation of financial markets. Once initiated, these reforms would bind the future fortunes of the countries in question to the growth path (and volatility) of a globally integrated system of free-flowing investment, finance and trade: in a word, with 'globalisation'. To a significant degree, then, processes of globalisation and of neoliberalisation have gone hand in hand.

For proof that the objective of neoliberalisation always was to restore class power, Harvey invites us merely to take stock of its results. Notwithstanding its uneven impact across the globe, it has generally served to undermine and disempower organised labour and trade unions. It has led to the normalisation of precarious work, as with an ever-greater reliance on fixed-term and zero-hour contracts across the Global North in recent years. Meanwhile, it has enhanced the prosperity and power of actors with 'a certain accordance of interests' (Harvey, 2005a: 36): financiers, CEOs and majority stockholders of leading corporations, and entrepreneurs in key technoscientific, industrial and service sectors (Harvey, 2000a: 36). For all the talk of 'free' markets, neoliberalisation has created huge monopolies in big tech, energy, the media, pharmaceuticals, transportation and even in retailing (e.g. Walmart) (Harvey, 2005a: 38). In so doing, it has generated enormous inequalities of both income and wealth. By the close of 2021, the highest earning 1 per cent of adults in the United States earned an average of $1.6 million per year, while the bottom 50 per cent earned on average only $18,000. The average total worth of the wealthiest 1 per cent of individuals amounted to $18.9 million, compared to just $7,900 for the bottom half of the wealth distribution. Seventy-one per cent of total wealth in the United States is today held by just 10 per cent of the population – in a country where 37 million people live in poverty (US Census Bureau, 2021) and where 40 per cent of the population would struggle to raise $400 in cash for an unexpected bill (Federal Reserve, 2018). The disparity between the top one and bottom 50 per cent of the population in wealth terms has widened markedly since the Reagan era: from a ratio of around 23:1 in 1980 to circa 36:1 in 2021.[5]

These data should also be placed within a global context. By 2022, the world's ten richest billionaires (all white men, nine of whom are from the United States, and eight of whom made their fortunes in the tech sector) owned six times more wealth than the poorest 3.1 billion people on the planet combined (Oxfam International, 2022: 2–3). Moreover, income inequality within the majority of 'developing' countries and in several major middle-income countries (including China and India) has increased since 1990 (United Nations, 2020: 3).

In Harvey's view, understanding how the contemporary state-finance nexus has succeeded in concentrating ever greater magnitudes of wealth in fewer and fewer hands requires Marxists once again to think more broadly than the process of commodity production and the primary circuit of capital (Chapter 3). To be sure, capital is today capturing surplus value on a prolific scale courtesy of intensified rates of exploitation of labour power. But there are, Harvey claims, also all manner of other – and often much more overt and remunerative – forms of exploitation at work. In various texts beginning with *The New Imperialism* (2003a), Harvey has collectively referred to these processes in terms of what he calls *accumulation by dispossession*. This is Harvey's reversioning of the classical notion of 'primitive accumulation', which Marx coined in *Capital* to foreground the violent origins of industrial capitalism. Harvey uses this refashioned concept to signal the various means by which 'already accumulated wealth is being appropriated or stolen away by certain sectors of capital without any regard for investing in production' (Harvey, 2020a: 121; see also, 2005a: 159–165). Though the specific forms taken by accumulation by dispossession vary considerably – 'a privatisation here, an environmental degradation there, a financial crisis of indebtedness somewhere else' (2005a: 178) – their invariable effect is to redistribute wealth from the many to the few, leaving expropriated populations, households and individuals to pick up the pieces. Just take, Harvey says, the 'spectacular example' of 'the foreclosure on more than seven million households in the US after the 2007-8 mortgage crisis and the loss of more than 70 per cent of the asset values held by low-income black populations' to financial institutions (Harvey, 2019a). Homeowners across Spain saw something similar.

Perhaps above all else, what repeatedly strikes Harvey about neoliberalism is its contradictions. His sweeping appraisal of the past forty years reveals a fundamental tension between on the one hand the explicit utopianism of neoliberalism as a 'mental conception' in which individual liberty and prosperity for all prevail, and on the other its actual crystallisation as a political program oriented to the restoration of the power of economic elites in the aftermath of the crises of the 1970s. 'The evidence suggests', Harvey (2005a: 19) has concluded, 'that when neoliberal principles clash with the need to restore or sustain elite power, then the principles are either abandoned or become so twisted as to be unrecognisable'. This is the nub of Harvey's arraignment against neoliberalism: it simply has not delivered on any of its own promises. In place of the beneficence of the 'invisible hand' of the market and the 'trickle down' of wealth and well-being to all, neoliberalisation has only enriched a tiny proportion of the world's population and has driven down incomes and living standards for the vast majority. Instead of reconciling political and economic freedoms, it has served to perpetuate and exacerbate fundamental contradictions at the heart of 'globalised' capitalism.

Managing the contradictions of neoliberalism

Neoliberalisation has fractured societies, fomented political protest, and undermined governments. Harvey has reeled-off a list of key contradictions: between the facilitation of the free flow of capital and labour across borders, and the need to guarantee the coherence of (an 'imagined') national community; between the 'rights' of capital to private property and profit, and the 'rights' of workers and citizens to jobs and homes; between the supposed virtues of free competition, and the real tendency towards economic monopoly and 'rentier capitalism'; and between social cohesion and the proliferation of anti-social behaviours (Harvey, 2005a: 79–81).

He has suggested that states have attempted to manage these contradictions in several ways. First, 'politics has been depoliticised and commodified' (2010a: 218). Efforts have been made to insulate policymaking from popular contestation and 'discretionary' government through reforms such as central bank independence (see Burnham, 2001).[6] Underpinning such formal depoliticisation has been the ongoing inculcation among populations of a sense of individual personal responsibility for one's material failures (as much as for one's successes): *it's not politicians' fault, it's mine*. Harvey (2005a: 23) quoted Thatcher herself on this psychological dimension of neoliberalism: '"Economics is the method", she said, "but the object is to change the soul"'. He has further suggested (2005a, 169, 2020a: 111) that the promotion of the idea that 'you are your own human capital', together with the expansion of compensatory consumerism in recent years, have gone some way towards reinforcing this project to normalise the core principles of neoliberalism and to neutralise the scope for mass dissent in many societies.

The most insidious and effective means of entangling individuals in the net of neoliberal capitalism, and of distracting them from its contradictions, has been to normalise *indebtedness* among populations (Harvey, 2020a: 23).[7] Harvey has been increasingly preoccupied by a widespread condition of 'debt peonage', and the foreclosure of the future that it implies for younger generations in particular (2017a: 79–80, 93, 2018c). If a culture of consumerism 'limits and imprisons rather than liberates the horizons of personal fulfilment' (Harvey, 2017a: 198), then the rising levels of indebtedness required to sustain expanded consumption only engender deeper feelings of impotence, resignation, and passivity among populations (Harvey, 2019b: 138). Today, debt peonage is, for Harvey, 'capital's favoured means to impose its own slavery' (2017a: 205).[8] The affective impact of all this is witnessed in 'increasing individual isolation, anxiety, short-termism and neurosis' (2010a: 176): a condition Harvey labels 'universal alienation' (Harvey, 2018c).

Last but not least, and given succour by precisely such alienation, political elites in several countries have resorted to authoritarianism and populist appeals to nationalism to manage the contradictions of neoliberalism and to thereby perpetuate their own power and the power of capital more generally. For some time now, many people in many different societies have felt as though the world is speeding up and getting smaller, that the pace of these changes is accelerating all the time and that there is little refuge from the vicissitudes and pressures of the highly competitive, debt-fuelled, predatory and alienating neoliberal social order.[9] In sustained periods of time-space compression, when everything seems chaotic, ephemeral and beyond one's control, people frequently look for something safe, reassuring and familiar to cling to (Harvey, 1989a: 292, 339). Voters become susceptible to nostalgia. They crave a return to a safer, less changeable (and, frankly, mythologised) past. Politicians and elites can use this to their advantage. They can foster paranoia and suspicion of 'external threats', fomenting religious fundamentalism, nationalism and xenophobia in the process. One place the world (and Harvey) saw this happen from the early twenty-first century was in the United States, creating support for highly destructive – but also highly lucrative – overseas geopolitical conquest and accumulation by dispossession on the part of the United States and its allies.

The geopolitics of capital

On 11th September 2001, terrorists used hijacked commercial airplanes to attack four sites in the United States, destroying the twin towers of the World Trade Center in New York City, striking the Pentagon building, and killing some 3,000 people. A few months later, Harvey and several of his colleagues at CUNY published an op-ed piece that condemned these acts of 'sheer horror and insanity' in the strongest terms (Harvey et al., 2001). They warned, however, that these attacks should not be used by the George W. Bush administration to 'justify the continuation, let alone intensification of erroneous policies and practices', citing a litany of global malpractice on the part of US governments and their financial and commercial allies in recent decades. Calling for 'serious reflection' on how to make 'real democracy work everywhere', and 'how to make freedom mean something more than freedom of the market', they denounced the 'sabre rattling' and threats of a US-led military response in the Middle East. By the time the piece was published, however, the US military was already at war on Afghan soil, on the pretext of defeating global terrorism and protecting 'freedom'. Iraq was subsequently invaded in March 2003, on the same pretext plus that of negating the threat of 'weapons of mass destruction' (WMDs). 'Regime change' was achieved in both cases.

US troops eventually withdrew completely from Iraq in 2011. The last remaining soldiers left Afghanistan in late 2021, almost twenty years after the invasion began. Researchers at Brown University estimate that the total budgetary cost of the post-9/11 wars by the United States, including future obligations on such things as injured veterans' care, has been some $8 trillion (Crawford, 2021). Over 7,000 American soldiers were killed in these wars, and thousands more non-military contractors lost their lives. The estimate of the total 'direct' death toll of the wars in Afghanistan and Iraq (including police personnel, other allied troops, journalists, humanitarian aid workers, and, of course, civilians) stands at between 451,000 and 482,000 people (Crawford and Lutz, 2021). Was it worth it? WMDs were never found in Iraq. As we write, the country is mired in economic crisis and is facing renewed 'political instability' and 'growing social unrest' (World Bank, 2020: 1). And in Afghanistan, the despotic Taliban have returned to power, two decades after their 'defeat' by US-led forces.

Why did the United States commit to such costly, protracted, and seemingly futile wars? Many critics on the Left condemned the actions of the United States and its Western allies as acts of blatant imperialism. To Harvey, however, the classical theories of inter-state imperialism and colonialism that were often invoked by these critics were inadequate to the task of understanding what was going on in the early 2000s (Harvey, 2017b). He argued in *The New Imperialism* (2003a) that the roots of the invasions of Afghanistan and Iraq lay in the contradictory 'inner dialectic' of American civil society under the fissuring pressures of financialisation and neoliberalisation, and in the compulsion on the part of the US state-finance nexus to secure new means of accumulating wealth beyond its borders just as the country's edge in terms of global economic competitiveness was waning. By the 1990s, American society was, he surmised, 'fragmenting and flying apart at an alarming rate. It seemed … in the process of collapsing back into the aimless, senseless chaos of private interests' (2003a: 17). The Bush Jr. administration seized advantage of this societal malaise and the 9/11 attacks to push ahead with a geopolitical project initially hatched, Harvey suggested, by neo-conservative political elites concerned with the potential emergence of a rival Eurasian geopolitical power bloc. In exacting retribution upon terrorists and their sponsors, in promoting 'freedom' abroad, and in wresting control of the 'global oil spigot' in the Middle East (Harvey, 2003a: 19, 2010a: 210), the US government could at once boost legitimacy at home but also secure another half-century of effective control over the global economy (Harvey, 2003a: 75, 198–199).

Harvey's critique of US foreign interventionism in the early 2000s was commensurate with his *modus operandi* of beginning with his model of capital circulation and accumulation; and it fitted seamlessly with his narrative of the transformation of global capitalism since the 1970s. The roots of the post-9/11 interventions lay in the contradictions of globalisation and financialisation, of neoliberalisation and of the increasing fragility of the US' own status as the fulcrum of international processes of capital accumulation (which it had enjoyed since 1945). The hallmark of the power of the United States had long been that it rests upon 'imperialism without colonies', as most clearly exemplified in its track record of using debt relations to extract wealth from Latin American countries since the 1980s (Harvey, 2005a: 27). For Harvey, the post-9/11 wars likewise had more to do with this practice and 'the struggle for hegemony – financial hegemony in particular ... rather than struggles for direct control over territory' (2010a: 212).

Geopolitical tensions, Harvey argues, today arise from the contradictory intertwining of two 'logics' that the unleashing of finance capital and the corollary processes of 'globalisation' since the 1970s have served to make more discordant and difficult for all states to manage (see Harvey, 1996a: 247). On the one hand, as we have seen above, states must do all they can to facilitate the accumulation of capital by attracting the 'butterfly form' of world money into their borders. This is what Harvey (2003a: 108, 2017b: 171) has termed the 'molecular logic of capital flow'. This logic, however, contradicts the 'logic of state interests', of national economic stability, political integrity and legitimacy. As each individual state or alliance of states seeks to manage this contradiction under conditions of financialisaton and volatility, the outcome is

> Increasingly fierce international competition as multiple dynamic centres of capital accumulation compete on the world stage in the face of strong currents of over-accumulation ... [This can be] converted via the territorial logic of power into confrontations between states in the

> form of trade wars and currency wars, with the ever-present danger of military confrontations.
>
> (Harvey, 2003a: 124)

From this general observation, Harvey deduces why and how the United States – compelled by the contradictions of capital and state interest – took such a 'high risk' strategy to maintain a strong competitive footing within the global economy by engaging in aggressive forms of geopolitical expansion after 9/11.[10]

Note, again, that, for Harvey, this was not principally about competition over control of processes of production of value and surplus value. Rather, this was accumulation by dispossession via acts of direct force of expropriation. To this degree, Harvey has argued, the 'new imperialism' visited upon the Middle East from the early 2000s was symptomatic of a more general systemic trend towards profit-making by means of the direct appropriation of wealth from populations, households and individuals. It's a counterpart to the 'secondary forms of exploitation' (Harvey, 2012a: 128) widely exercised today across both Global North and South through for instance predatory creditor-debtor relations, housing repossessions and the reneging on pension rights by investment funds (Harvey, 2020a: 122–127).

On the transformation of China and geopolitical tensions to come

Harvey's recent commentaries on the transformation and rise of China go some way towards affirming the explanatory power of his theory of geopolitics, touching also upon the theoretical ideas and constructs discussed in preceding sections of this chapter.

It's safe to say that Harvey is mesmerised by China, as his 2016 book *Abstract from the Concrete* attests. His work since *A Brief History* has traced China's transformation from being predominantly rural and unindustrialised at the founding of the People's Republic in 1949 to becoming the second largest economy in the world today. Since 1978, China has averaged an annual economic growth rate of 10 per cent thanks in large part, Harvey has argued, to a project of 'neoliberalisation and the reconstitution of class power, albeit with "distinctly Chinese characteristics"' (Harvey, 2005a: 151).

The gist of Harvey's account goes something like this: China's transformation began in earnest with a massive industrialisation drive in the 1980s that was tantamount to 'a classic case of primitive accumulation of the sort that Marx describes back in the seventeenth and eighteenth centuries' (Harvey, 2020a: 119). Along with rapid industrialisation came accelerated urbanisation comprising massive infrastructural development and the proliferation of mega-cities (places that were mere villages in the 1950s are now cities concentrating up to 10 million people, see Figure 6.5) (Harvey, 2017a: 172–173). A mobilisation of labour power on a scale and at a rate never previously seen in one country propelled Chinese economic development in the 1980s and 1990s, cementing its status as the 'world's factory' by the early twenty-first century. This rapid path of capitalist development was rife with contradiction, however. As a new middle class emerged and consumption expanded – heralded by the multiplication of shopping malls, entertainment complexes, gated communities and golf courses – hordes of migrant workers from the countryside crammed into the urban dormitories hastily constructed by corporations like Foxconn, which assembled products for the world market using low-cost, overworked labour. All of this occurred with the blessing and indeed active support of the Chinese Communist Party; many of the largest Chinese corporations, financial and non-financial alike, remain state-owned and controlled.

When the global crisis of 2007–2009 erupted, China was faced with the prospect of a slump in demand, an economic slowdown, rising

Figure 6.5. Hyper-urbanisation in China. A fishing village in the 1970s, Shenzhen is now one of China's largest cities and home to 12 million people.

joblessness and social unrest. The state therefore seized the moment to step up its urbanisation drive. Hyper-urbanisation in China sustained huge demand for raw materials, in the process insulating mineral-exporting countries like Australia from the worst impact of the global crisis. One of Harvey's oft-cited statistics is that 'between 2011 and 2013, China consumed 6,500 million tons of cement. In three years, the Chinese used around 40 per cent more cement than the United States had in the whole of the preceding century' (Harvey, 2016b: 9, 2019b: 126). The truly staggering scale of hyper-urbanisation in China begs worrying questions not just about the environmental impact of its development, but also about the sustainability of a property boom that – not unlike those that have punctuated the history of urbanisation in the West (Chapter 5) – has been increasingly financed by debt. The now sizable Chinese private banking system, which had not even existed prior to 1979, was encouraged by the state to provide new lines of credit to developers and consumers alike. The result, noted Harvey (2017a: 183), was that 'the country's debt quadrupled between 2007 and 2015. By 2016 the formal debt stood at 250 per cent of GDP'. The proverbial chickens came home to roost in 2021 when the Evergrande Group, one of the country's (and world's) largest property developers, ran into severe financial difficulties and missed several debt payments. At the time of writing, the crisis is ongoing and the Chinese government is reportedly working to restructure the group to provide resolution.

Notwithstanding China's unique character as a huge and nominally Communist country, it is today as subject to the competitive pressures and contradictions of capital accumulation in a 'globalised' world as any other national state. As it tussles with its own problems of overheated property markets and pockets of social unrest, the Chinese state is presently looking to steer another phase of the transformation of the economy away from labour-intensive manufacturing and speculative urbanisation and towards capital-intensive, high-tech innovation. At the same time, it is pursuing new spatial fixes by investing billions of dollars in sub-Saharan Africa as well as, most notably, in the Belt and Road Initiative to construct vast new trade-route infrastructures across Central Asia (Harvey, 2017a: 191, 2020a: 92) (see Figure 6.6). Harvey (2020a: 70–73) has warned that this, together with China's enthusiasm to create its own versions of Silicon Valley and to gain global superiority in the development of 5G communication technologies, portends the intensification of competitive geopolitical struggles for hegemony between rival national economies. The geopolitics of this, he argues, are already evident in the US-China trade war that escalated during Donald Trump's tenure as US President (Harvey, 2020a: 152). It's clear to Harvey that China will play a pivotal role in the future evolution

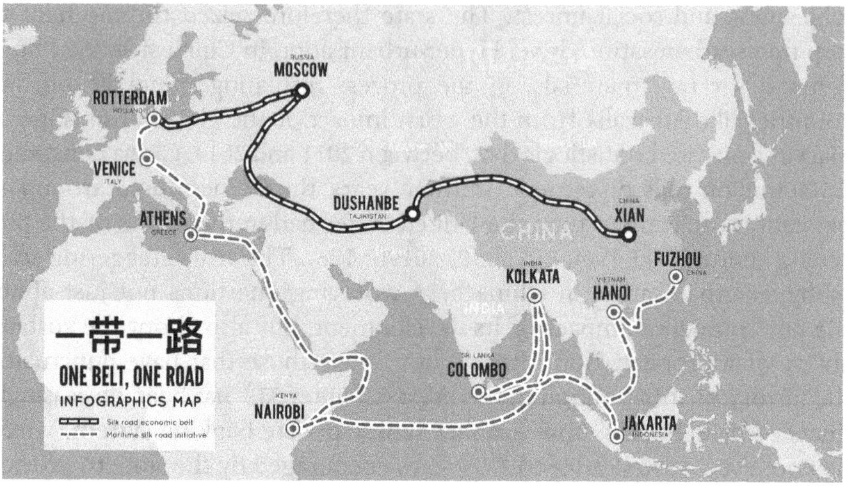

Figure 6.6. A new Eurasian spatial fix? China's 'One Belt, One Road' initiative.

of global capitalism and geopolitics. Its 'contradictions … are rampant and bear watching closely' (Harvey, 2022a: 23).

What Harvey chooses to see

Few commentators today can rival Harvey's status as a widely read critic of globalisation, financialisation, neoliberalism and destructive geopolitics. Since his initial observation in 1989 that the 'widening and deepening of capitalist social relations with time is, surely, one of the most singular and indisputable facts of recent historical geography' (1989a: 344), he's gone on to produce a strikingly consistent body of work that shows why and how, under conditions of the expanded accumulation of capital on a world scale, 'the contradictory laws of motion that [Marx] identifies solely advantage a capitalist class and its acolytes, while reducing whole populations to exploitation of their living labour in production, to paltry possibilities in their daily life and debt servitude in their social relations' (Harvey, 2017a: 175).

But this endeavour has not been without its detractors. From many critical engagements with Harvey's work post-1989, we can distil three principal recurring themes of contention – all of which take issue in some way with Harvey's drawing of a conscious distinction between 'capital' and 'capitalism' and his 'choice' (following Marx) to focus analytically upon the former.

The first accusation is that Harvey's focus on capital is outmoded and unhelpful. Society has moved on since Marx and so too has critical thought.

Post-structuralists and scholars influenced by thinkers like Michel Foucault (1926–1984) have argued that the kind of meta- or grand narrative about 'capital' that Harvey and Marx propose as a model for understanding the world cannot grasp the complex and multifaceted micro-political dimensions of power which operate irrespectively of capital's doing. For example, Pierre Dardot and Christian Laval (2013: 7–12) derided Harvey for his 'decidedly unoriginal' take on neoliberalism and took issue with his extension of Marx's theory to explain 'the pitiless commodification of society in its entirety'. They argued against Harvey's purported reduction of neoliberalism to an economic logic and to a set of ideas or policies redounding to the exclusive benefit of a 'bourgeoisie' that, in their view, no longer even exists to any meaningful degree. Following Foucault, Dardot and Laval maintained that neoliberalism has created an entirely *different* society altogether – one that Harvey's grand theory of capital is incapable of even recognising, let alone explaining.

Second, and in contrast to this line of criticism, 'fellow travellers' in the Marxist tradition have taken issue with Harvey's reluctance to draw upon a rich tradition of historical materialism *after Marx*. Bob Jessop (2004), for instance, has asked why Harvey has failed to elaborate a theory of how different institutional forms of the state have shaped processes of capitalist transformation, given that fecund resources for doing exactly that exist in the writings of Marxists such as Antonio Gramsci and Nicos Poulantzas. Others have questioned why Harvey is so dismissive of historical-materialist theories of imperialism. Sam Ashman and Alex Callinicos (2006), for instance, drew upon this tradition to challenge Harvey's take on geopolitics, arguing that capital is still predominantly more interested in generating profit through labour exploitation than through predatory financialisation and other forms of accumulation by dispossession. More recently, John Smith (2018) has offered a still more trenchant Marxist-Leninist condemnation of Harvey's wilful 'denial' of the essentially imperialistic character of neoliberalism: 'he obfuscates, sows confusion, and pretends to be agnostic on this question of questions'.

A third allegation, levelled even by critics who to some degree accept the significance of his contribution, is that Harvey's 'capital-first' *modus operandi* diminishes the significance of social structures and relations other than class to the broader social formation that is capital*ism*. Upon publication of *The Condition* in 1989, feminist critics were quick to rebuke Harvey for not properly acknowledging the insights and relevance of feminist critique. Depicting him as an unreconstructed Marxist, art historian Rosalyn Deutsche, for example, exclaimed that Harvey 'may not consider feminism worth knowing about, but feminism, although it hardly knows everything, knows something about him' (1991: 29). Though not always so hostile, feminist scholars have repeatedly raised concerns about Harvey's work (e.g. Young, 1998; Wright, 2006), suggesting for example that the scope afforded by his theorisation of capital comes at the cost of paying sufficient and necessary attention to the 'fleshy, messy, and indeterminate stuff of everyday life' (Katz, 2001: 711). While the distinction Harvey draws between capital and capitalism may well make the work of 'big picture' critique more tractable and forceful, it would be difficult to deny that identities and forms of oppression that exist in capitalism but which are not obviously reducible to 'capital' often don't get the attention they deserve from Marxists, Harvey included. Where, for instance, does the reproduction of capital end and the reproduction of, say, patriarchy begin in any given contemporary society? Many a critical theorist of gender relations and of heteronormativity would argue that the two processes are inextricably interwoven. The same applies to questions of capital and racialisation. For David Roediger, Harvey's position on the degree to which 'race sits outside the logic of capital' is not only 'quite wrong' but also puzzling insofar as plenty of other Marx-inspired theorists are much more willing to view capital and race in terms of a co-constitutive dynamic of oppression (Roediger, 2017: 1–4, 19–27). Finally, what of the co-constitutive relation between capital and Nature, which Harvey theorises at the level of highly general and abstract discussions of 'free gifts' but which, according to Jason Moore (2014: 289), 'falls by the wayside in his narratives of neoliberalism'? Once again, does a laser-like focus on capital exclude essential pieces of the analytical and political puzzle?

Harvey's responses to these criticisms have ranged from partial acceptance (albeit sometimes grudging) to fierce dismissal. On the one hand, after considerable initial defensiveness, he has softened somewhat in his acknowledgement that capitalist social formations are multiform and always 'more-than-capitalist' in their constitution. He has endorsed the contribution of feminist Social Reproduction Theory to anti-capitalist critique and has confronted questions of anti-Black racial oppression in the US head-on in his *Anti-Capitalist Chronicles* podcasts. This softening has come partly out of the apparent recognition that many of his critics were essentially sympathetic and were trying to help and to make his Marxism more, not less, robust. Increasingly, Harvey has listened and has changed some of his approaches and claims. As Melissa W. Wright has observed, this greater openness 'laid the groundwork for his tremendous relevance in the 2000s and beyond the Anglophone realm. He could not have reached the youth of Latin America as he has without some of these changes'.[11]

On the other hand, Harvey persists in his recalcitrance towards certain currents of critical thought. He has maintained that, too often these days, '[f]ollowing Foucault, we become sceptics of all meta-theories ... [we] ignore the power of meta-theory on principle rather than as a convenient practice in certain research situations' (Harvey, 2019b: 127). He has scorned the 'needlessly mocking polemics' against his arguments about geopolitics on the part of his 'rigid' and idealist Marxist-Leninist critics (Harvey, 2018d). He has also rejected what he regards as 'misrepresentations' of his work and of his supposedly dogmatic privileging of working-class politics above all else (see Harvey, 2017c). And, for all his growing recognition of the cleavages of race and gender in contemporary *capitalism*, he continues to argue that *capital* – the 'engine' of capitalism – is a distinctively class-based relation and should be theorised as such.

In short, Harvey shows no sign of giving up faith in the *explanatory power* of his capital-first approach: it is 'myopic, if not dangerous and ridiculous', he insists, to not adopt some kind of 'capitalo-centric' framework for understanding how capital accumulation dominates contemporary social life (Harvey, 2014a: 10).

Conclusion

For many, thinking with David Harvey about capitalism is a stimulating and rewarding experience. For those of us who are familiar with and convinced by the explanatory power of his work, making sense of the daily news just feels somehow easier: you can discern longer term historical-geographical tendencies and underlying contradictions within global capitalism that give rise to economic, ecological and geopolitical crises; you can join the dots between apparently disparate events and processes across the globe. You can be certain that capital lurks behind much of what is wrong with our world today. And you can, therefore, entertain the notion of getting on board with a socialist project, after all.

Thinking with David Harvey is plainly not for everyone, however. Some find his 'big picture', 'capitalo-centric' approach just too unwieldy, too susceptible to falling back on singular and one-dimensional explanations for complex and multi-faceted problems: *it's all capital's fault!*. As Nigel Thrift (1987: 405) once put it: 'Harvey's vision of social theory seems to be of a searchlight flooding every nook and cranny of society with light'. Such an approach to social theory, Thrift contended, ignored questions of individual human consciousness and subjectivity and relegated essential non-capitalist dimensions of social life to minor footnotes. In Thrift's view, Harvey offers a theory that 'over-totalises' society, and which therefore cannot possibly command the explanatory power it professes to have. Many, like Thrift, prefer theories of a more epistemologically modest variety, ones that focus on the myriad 'smaller' and more contingent sources of social change across a plethora of diverse spaces – theories which, they argue, are better able to account for multiple and diverse kinds of agency operating in a more-than-capitalist world. But does a penchant for torches lose sight of the promiscuous system Harvey seeks to illuminate and hold in focus? And can these torches illuminate the parameters that govern the room for manoeuvre – the social agency – that all sorts of otherwise different people are able to utilise to make a life for themselves in the twenty-first century? It's to the question of agency that we now turn.

Further reading

Harvey, D. (2000a). Contemporary globalisation. In *Spaces of Hope* (pp. 53–72). Edinburgh University Press.

Harvey, D. (2004a). The new imperialism: Accumulation by dispossession. In L. Panitch & C. Leys (Eds.), *Socialist Register 2004: The New Imperial Challenge* (pp. 63–87). Merlin Press.

Harvey, D. (2006b). Neoliberalism and the restoration of class power. In *Spaces of Global Capitalism: Towards a Theory of Uneven Geographical Development* (pp. 7–68). Verso.

Harvey, D. (2014a). Capital's relation to nature. In *Seventeen Contradictions and the End of Capitalism* (pp. 246–263). Profile Books.

Katz, C. (2006). Messing with 'the Project'. In N. Castree & D. Gregory (Eds.), *David Harvey: A Critical Reader* (pp. 235–246). Blackwell.

Notes

1. Part 1 of Harvey's *Spaces of Hope* was dedicated to demystifying contemporary 'globalisation' in explicitly Marxian terms. Harvey warned against (mis) interpretations of Marx's work that portray capitalism as a once-purely-European phenomenon that subsequently 'diffused' outwards. He then unpacked how 'the bourgeoisie both creates and destroys the geographical foundations – ecological, spatial, and cultural – of its own activities, building a world in its own image … via both internal and external geographical transformations', arguing that 'globalisation' denotes 'a new phase of exactly this same underlying process of the capitalist production of space' (2000a: 23–24, 54).
2. Dan Schiller's (1999, 2014) work on the evolution of 'digital capitalism' draws upon Harvey for much of its theoretical grounding.
3. Measured at the Mauna Loa Observatory, Hawaii.

4. Harvey refutes a good deal of radical-ecological thought for its catastrophism, for considering what we call 'Nature' to be outside of society and subjected to human domination, for not recognising that environmental management is susceptible to co-optation by capital, and for failing to realise that environmental destruction is not necessarily a problem for capital itself (there are perhaps no 'natural' limits to capitalism per se). An earlier, extensive discussion of his position can be found in Part II of *JNGD* (1996a) and is more recently summarised in Chapter 16 of *Seventeen Contradictions* (2014a). For a noteworthy critical engagement with Harvey's position, see Foster (1998).
5. All of these data are available at the Realtime Inequality website: realtimeinequality.org (and are adjusted to account for price inflation).
6. As Japhy Wilson and Erik Swyngedouw affirm (2014: 6), the hallmark of contemporary 'democratic' governance under neoliberalism is that 'political contradictions are reduced to policy problems to be managed by experts and legitimated through participatory processes in which the scope of possible outcomes is narrowly defined in advance. "The people" – as a potentially disruptive political collective – is replaced by the population … Citizens become consumers, and elections are framed as just another "choice", in which individuals privately select their preferred managers of the conditions of economic necessity'.
7. Much of this will be familiar to any British or American undergraduate student. The 'transferable skills' agenda underpins many a curriculum whose 'value' is measured by its contribution to learners' 'employability' after graduation. Meanwhile, the marketisation of higher education saddles students in England with an average debt of £45,060 upon graduation (Hall, 2021), and their American college counterparts with an average debt of $30,000 (Kerr and Wood, 2021).
8. Susanne Soederberg's (2014) work on 'debtfare states' drew inspiration from Harvey and demonstrated just how reliant low-income populations across the globe are upon expensive forms of consumer credit.
9. A large-scale focus group study by the Pew Research Center conducted in 2019 reported that many US and British participants felt both 'left behind' and 'swept up' by the forces of globalisation, leading to a sense of 'alienation and loss' (Silver et al., 2020). The sociologist William Davies (2016) attributed support for Brexit in post-industrial regions of the United Kingdom to the impact of Thatcherism and the lack thereafter of any new 'spatial fix' upon which to base future growth and job creation.
10. The post-9/11 wars have proven to be incredibly lucrative for some. Researchers suggest that just five corporations earned $2.1 trillion in Pentagon contracts over two decades (Hartung, 2021), while a subsidiary of Halliburton (of which Dick Cheney, Bush Jnr's Secretary of Defence, was formerly CEO) profited from $50 billion in US military contracts between 2001 and 2019.
11. Personal communication, February 2022.

From structure to agency 7

The tangled human geographies of difference, inequality, solidarity and protest

Cities, towns and their internal socio-spatial differentiation; Inter-local rivalry at the national and international scales: from the defence and promotion of place to international political solidarity; Political universals, uneven development, scale and the right to geographical difference; Making sense of Harvey on agency: a conclusion

Karl Marx famously observed that 'Men make history, but they do not make it as they please; they do not make it under self-selected circumstances, but under circumstances existing already, given and transmitted from the past' (Marx, 1852). In the parlance of sociologists, he was referring to how people exercise 'agency' within the limits prescribed by existing 'structures'. We use the word structures here in a broad sense to encompass the many things that confront individuals as variously constraining and enabling – for instance, institutions, ethical norms, professional standards, temporal measures, social processes, infrastructures and legal rules existing at various scales. Structures are generally enduring and difficult to change – they form our 'operating environment', even if we are only dimly aware of many of them (as with the hidden network of pipes that supply clean water to our homes). Structures not only influence human action but also our sense of who we are as people. Marx focussed largely on the structures specific to capitalism, such as the class relationships between owners of the means of production and those they employ. His mission, of course, was to understand how these structures could be rendered less intransigent so that better ones could be created.

DOI: 10.4324/9780429028120-7

Clearly, Harvey believes these structures are globally prevalent and powerful, and that their geography matters. We have focussed on the specific nature and impacts of those structures in the previous three chapters. But, equally clearly, these structures intersect with a plethora of other ones that are irreducible to capitalism – for instance, the norms and institutions associated with organised religion, with national belonging or with liberal democracy as a particular form of political life. It is the ensemble of structures, as experienced by people with different degrees of agency relative to them, that shape our senses of self and other, as well as our material circumstances throughout the course of life.

In this chapter, we elucidate Harvey's understanding of human agency in a world dominated by capitalism. Agency is a major theme in his work, unsurprisingly for someone committed to progressive political change. To grasp it requires reading across a great many of Harvey's publications spanning over forty years – the agency question runs like a red thread through them. Harvey focusses both on everyday agency (geared to people sustaining themselves over time) and political agency (exercised more occasionally and geared to challenging and changing prevailing conditions). Compared to the previous three chapters, we look at the other side of the proverbial coin, having only glimpsed it now and then so far. We ask: how do the globalised, multifaceted structures of capital accumulation govern the terrain of agency for billions of people? And how do all sorts of people reckon with these structures, over which most of them have little-to-no control?

These questions have been central to Harvey's Marxism since the publication of *Social Justice and the City* (1973) (though he doesn't use the terms 'structure' and 'agency' with the frequency or conceptual precision of someone like influential British sociologist Anthony Giddens).[1] Harvey's interest in these questions arises not only because the reproduction of capitalism depends on certain degrees and forms of human agency being prevalent – for instance, the 'freedom' of workers to sell their labour-power and of consumers to purchase a range of commodities. It also arises because efforts to supersede (or at least 'civilise') capitalism depend on forms of collective agency that are structured – that is, inhibited or enabled – by the very system they seek to overthrow or reform. (We focus on what can serve to *motivate* agency, politically, in Chapter 8.) Fundamentally, Harvey believes that capitalism – for all the various types of progress it's delivered to humankind – does not allow a rich form of human flourishing to occur around the globe. It diminishes agency and future possibilities for far too many individuals and groups. The aim is not to eliminate all structures (we need them) but to ensure we create just structures that enjoy democratic legitimacy.

Though we accent ordinary people's agency in the pages below, we also follow Harvey in showing how political decision-makers and even the wealthiest capitalists are together forced to respond to 'invariant' capitalist structures, such as inter-firm competition and the need to ceaselessly invest monetary surpluses. Crises, for example, see a general contraction of agency for millions of people in many walks of life (see Chapter 4). Central to the exercise of this 'constrained freedom', in both normal and crisis periods, are *socio-spatial differentiations* of numerous kinds. Forged out of spatial *connectivities* of varying length and duration, some of the spatial differentiations are micro-scale (sub-local), while others are inter-place, inter-regional or international; and they both condition and are expressed by manifold, intersectional social differentiations, of which the 'primary' class relationship between wage-workers and those who employ them is but one. These socio-geographical differentiations, as Harvey sees it, are both formative for people yet – insofar as relations 'internal' to capital intersect with other modalities of association, identification and belonging – produce fragmentations and constraints which tend to stymie forms of combined agency that might, if not vanquish capitalism, at least tame its worst consequences.

As we write in 2022, many of Harvey's insights over the years about agency may not now seem terribly novel to those versed in Marxism and critical theory more broadly – after all, he ventured some of them half a century ago. Critics would also argue that when Harvey has ventured onto the terrain of agency, subjectivity and intersectional coalitions, he's been less sure-footed than when discussing say finance capital or land markets. This, we would suggest, is true enough: if Harvey struggles anywhere in his work, it is here. But is this a weakness? On the contrary, in taking on something that doesn't come as easily to him and that (arguably) he doesn't do as well, and in doing so increasingly in acknowledgement of criticisms of his work of the type discussed in Chapter 6, Harvey has demonstrated precisely his courage and dynamism as a thinker; and his work has certainly gained even more relevance and accessibility as a result. As we hope to show in this chapter, Harvey's insights are of enduring importance and interest for those seeking to comprehend people's room for manoeuvre – their means and ends – in our thoroughly capitalist world. The history and geography we can collectively make matters to us, to our children, and to the fate of the non-human world. It's essential to know what it means to act within, and beyond, the parameters set by the capitalist mode of production.

Cities, towns and their internal socio-spatial differentiation

We begin at the smallest geographical scale, that of a district or neighbourhood. Our major sources here are Harvey's many articles, chapters and books about urbanisation: notably *Social Justice and the City* (1973), the mid-1980s books (*The Urbanization of Capital* and *Consciousness and the Urban Experience*) and Harvey's first 'greatest hits' book *The Urban Experience* (1989b). These works (mostly drafted in the 1970s) provide a rich mix of conceptual and empirical insight, the latter arising most especially from Harvey's investigations in Baltimore and Paris. To understand Harvey's reasoning, we need first to recount (in rather abstract and decidedly non-spatial terms) the 'primary' and 'secondary' social relations that, in capitalism, (i) specify the roles that people play and (ii) define the scope of their possible and 'rational' agency. We then attend to the micro-geographies of agency. We do this without detailed reference to Harvey's voluminous writings on these matters (quotations, citations etc.), deliberately glossing in order to remain relatively succinct.[2]

A schema of capitalist class relations

The class relationship between those who own the means of commodity production and those they employ is fundamental. In part, it's a relationship of power: owners ultimately decide how many workers to employ, how much to pay them, what they will be employed to do, when, for low long each day etc., subject to certain constraints (e.g. labour laws or prevailing morality). It is also a relationship based on the concept of private property: workers sell their personal 'labour power' (their capability and time) in return for a salary, usually on a voluntary basis; conversely, owners 'sell' job opportunities. Furthermore, it's a relationship that obliges employees to work so as to purchase the many things they need but cannot produce themselves – things like nutritious food, a bed, electricity, clothing, a cooker, a laptop computer or a house. This means that all wage workers are also commodity consumers, using money they've earned to enter markets for various goods and services. The same applies to owners of capitalist firms: they must not only 'consume' commodities in order to produce new ones within their businesses, but privately they must also spend some of their often sizeable income to enjoy holidays, cars, watches, speed boats, jacuzzis etc. In short, though they encounter each other in the processes of commodity production and sale, both capitalists and their workers use privately purchased commodities in the process of reproducing themselves outside the workplace and the shop (e.g. in the home).

However, for this primary class relationship to be sustained over time, other relationships necessarily arise that still have a class (socio-economic) character. Harvey on occasion has called them 'secondary' or 'derivative'. We've already touched upon many of these in Chapters 3–6. One is the relationship between financiers (e.g. retail banks) and those people – business owners and workers – to whom they lend money. Financiers make profits principally in the form of interest (i.e. money begetting money). Harvey, after Marx, sees interest payments as ultimately parasitic on the creation of surplus value arising out of capitalism's primary class relationship. Capitalists and workers need money lenders, but money lenders cannot accrue profits, in the end, without growth in the 'real economy'. Another cardinal relationship arises between owners of land, property and other valuable assets and the people who pay to use them for periods of time. These multifarious owners make profits in the form of rent (money captured from loaning use values), and again Harvey sees this as derivative of surplus value generated in the 'primary circuit' of capital. He's described interest and rent as 'revenues' captured from elsewhere (the same applies to taxes and wages too).

Overall, financiers and property owners enter into contracts with various borrowers and users, just as business owners contract people to work for them (the exceptions being various weakly- and unregulated markets). As with the primary class relation, Harvey has argued that interest and rent payments are predicated as much on legal and monetary power as on the 'free play' of competitive markets involving myriad buyers and sellers. Note that none of this is to imply that capitalists, financiers or rentiers each act as a unified class locally, nationally or globally. Instead, the class dynamics are exceedingly complex, involving competition, cooperation, differentiation and fragmentation at different times and levels. Fostering 'class consciousness' at any scale, let alone intra- or cross-class collaboration in a practical sense, takes considerable time and effort.

Even using this simple (and far from complete) depiction of capitalist class relationships, it's immediately clear that the aims and scope of various people's agency is multifarious within specific social limits. Pretty much everyone has a vested interest in private ownership of goods and services, as well as the command of money to enable this. But capitalists, financiers and rentiers are all profit-driven, whereas consumers of commodities usually seek out use values at a price that seems cheap or at least fair. Likewise, capitalists, financiers and rentiers must vie with their rivals for market share (unless monopoly conditions apply), while workers employed in the primary circuit, in the financial industry or in rent-based businesses compete for jobs to a greater or lesser extent. The roles of owner, worker and consumer, arising from and reproducing capitalist social relations, set up an intricate and contradictory play of actions and reactions among all those involved.

Importantly, the billions of actors performing in this ongoing drama have sharply divergent degrees and kinds of agency. For instance, the young, single, female Indonesian sweat-shop worker has barely any agency in the labour market compared to the middle-aged, Harvard University-educated, male management consultant who's spent fifteen years working for McKinsey and has his own portfolio of rented apartments in Boston. Relatively speaking, the wealthy enjoy far more freedom than the poor, their money being exchangeable for a vast array of commodities that can enhance their lives. Marxists and others have exerted considerable effort over the years analysing the within- and between class differentiations of wealth, symbolic status and other things that serve to 'slice and dice' people within the capitalist order (e.g. see Erik Olin Wright's book *Classes*, 1985).[3]

Social relations and micro-geographical forms: the socio-spatiality of human agency

Let's now consider how capitalist class relations find geographical expression at a small scale and how, in turn, this rebounds on the agents defined by these same relations. It's self-evidently the case that, during its long history, capitalism has become progressively urbanised: more numerous and larger cities (and towns) are, in various ways, clearly functional to the reproduction of this evolving mode of production. We now have huge metropolitan regions, as well as new agglomerations springing-up virtually overnight (e.g. consider Shenzhen in China, which was but a village in 1985). These concentrations of people, buildings and institutions vary in the detail: for instance, in a number of key respects Santiago (Chile), Seoul (South Korea), Saint Petersburg (Russia) and Solapur (India) are distinctly different. Yet Harvey has long insisted that there are critical commonalities insofar as capitalist class relations have spread their tentacles globally over time.

One commonality is land-use sorting and differentiation: in almost every capitalist town and city, there are multiple, distinct districts. They look different, and people use them in varied ways towards a range of ends, depending on their roles and resources in respect of these districts (see Figure 7.1). The districts, that is, have come to shape the relations they express. As Harvey once put it, the key point is that, at this local scale, differentiation in terms of where people live and work is 'not to be construed as the product of the autonomously arising preferences of people' (1989b: 123), even though the freedoms that many people enjoy are meaningful rather than illusory.

Harvey made the case in numerous writings, starting with his early 1970s research into Baltimore housing markets (e.g. Harvey and Chatterjee, 1974). The gist of his argument has been as follows. In thousands of capitalist towns and cities, we find geographical concentrations of retail spaces (for consumer purchases), of production spaces (factories, offices, workshops etc.), and residential spaces (rented and owned accommodation that permits social reproduction). We also have transportation networks and various public spaces (e.g. Central Park in New York City), with local government usually playing a major role in their provision and maintenance. The residential spaces are typically differentiated according to the size, appearance and cost of accommodation – for instance, in Manchester, Moss Side (close to the city centre) contains much small, relatively low-cost Victorian housing stock (often in poor condition), while Didsbury (on the edge of the city) is very expensive and dominated by professional people earning above average salaries.

Figure 7.1. Land-use differentiation. This is a signature feature of towns and cities across the globe, with capitalist class inequality a key driver of residential and commercial differentiation.

Why does this local-level material differentiation occur, and what effects does it have? Let's consider low-income residential zones (like Moss Side), which in twentieth-century Western cities were typically close to central business districts; and let's do so in the context of primary and secondary class relations. Low-paid workers clearly have limited agency in markets for accommodation – yet they need decent quality housing just as much as any other person. As Harvey discovered in inner-city Baltimore just after the late-1960s riots there, many of these workers were (and still are) obliged to rent properties existing in a state of disrepair, yet which are relatively expensive per square meter. That is, the use value of housing was inadequate to their needs because they possessed insufficient exchange values (money) to afford better accommodation. Accordingly, a family of five might be squeezed into a two-bedroom apartment with improper heating and cooling, and care-worn (even faulty) fixtures, utilities and fittings.

It may sound as if Harvey was saying supply and demand are in equilibrium here, rather as a mainstream economist might. But, of course, Harvey's view is different to this, as we intimated in Chapter 3 in our discussion of counter-revolutionary theory. First, he's noted that there's nothing natural about the 'primitive accumulation' process that historically (and today) has separated workers from the means of production and from the land.[4] Second, he's noted that wages are set not by universal, 'blind' supply-demand dynamics but, in part, by class struggle within and among workplaces in the context of varying rates of unemployment and economic growth. Third, Harvey's further noted that landowners and property owners are preoccupied with costs and income, not the welfare of citizens. They are thus disposed to prioritise exchange value over use value and to find it 'irrational' to improve the quality of inner-city rental accommodation when low-income workers and their families are unlikely to pay more for housing. Indeed, some landowners and landlords find it 'rational' to leave land unused and property derelict for many years.

Fourth, some low-income families presumably have the option to arrange a mortgage and avoid the tenant-landlord relationship entirely. They could become home-owners and upgrade their private living space over time. This then inserts them into a relationship with financiers (e.g. building societies). But, again, because financiers are driven to seek-out profits, and because low-income workers are typically cash-poor and often lack long-term job security, mortgages may be hard to come by. Harvey and Lata Chatterjee (1974) discovered as much in inner-city Baltimore, where many districts were 'red lined' because of high mortgage-default risk (see also Harvey, 1985a: Chapter 3). Fifth, in turn this helps explain why developers of land and property often do not cater to low-income communities.

Instead, they will step in to refurbish old or construct new dwellings only when governments finance them (directly or indirectly) or when a 'rent gap' appears that spurs a gentrification process (on this see Smith, 1987b). For instance, in Moss Side, a fair bit of gentrification has occurred since 2010 as the adjacent University of Manchester campus has been upgraded and expanded. This gentrification threatens to reduce rental stock for local people as better, pricier accommodation gets put on the market for better paid, fairly transient tenants (see Figure 7.2).

This rather stylised discussion of what, in the United States of America, was once called the 'ghetto problem' offers us useful insight into how geographical form at the smallest scale rebounds on the social relations of its construction. The concentration of low-income workers (along with their dependents, the unemployed and often the homeless) necessarily focusses those workers on the quality of their living conditions. Their proximity to each other can create strong community bonds, though the 'possessive individualism' intrinsic to capitalism may encourage many to aspire to exit their neighbourhood and 'move up the housing ladder'. In the case of cities like Baltimore in the 1960s, local-level solidarity was heightened by the racism of the (then) white majority population in the United States towards people of colour (slavery, of course, had been a major feature of

Figure 7.2. Signs of gentrification? A juxtaposition of old and new housing in Moss Side, Manchester.

early US development). This neighbourhood-level sense of community may then inspire local political struggles over consumption and social reproduction, while weakening class solidarity at a city-wide level across the many workplaces in which low-income people are employed.[5] Indeed, Manuel Castells (1983) famously argued that much grassroots politics in capitalist cities was understandably focussed on 'collective consumption' issues, like housing, public transportation and the quality of local schools.

This applies as much to wealthier workers (e.g. living in suburbs like Didsbury), as to medium and low-income ones. Indeed, the expense of housing and the typical length of a mortgage (twenty years or more) tends, as Harvey has often noted, to bind better-off workers to their neighbourhoods. They seek to command private spaces of their own, not least because the institution of the family – something that precedes and is irreducible to capitalist social relations – is anchored in the domestic domain. This command of micro-spaces of privacy, though, must occur via commodity purchases that serve to reproduce capitalism as a whole: not only a house (with a mortgage), but a private motor vehicle (in order to travel to work and shop), furniture, gardening equipment and supplies, and so on. In the end, the fragmentation of towns and cities into thousands of housing units, into wider residential areas and other districts has, Harvey has argued, a clear tendency to splinter the mental, emotional and ultimately political sensibilities of workers and capitalists alike. While people have agency in relation to the built environments they rely upon, these environments are in effect small scale 'structures' that place parameters on how, why and to what ends they exercise their agency at any moment in time. 'Our historical geography is always ours' to make', so Harvey (1989b: 55) once wrote, but – as Marx memorably said – not under conditions of our own choosing.

To conclude this section, Harvey's work on the internal geography of towns and cities shows us that: 'There are immense gains to be had by looking closely at the rich complexity and intricately woven fabric of urban life as the crucible for much that is fundamental to human experience, consciousness formation, and political action' (Harvey, 1989b: 54). Though we cannot summarise it here, Harvey's brilliant chapter on 'Paris, 1850–1870' offered a compelling empirical exploration of this fabric as it was remade in France's capital city across two dramatic decades (Harvey, 1985b: Chapter 3). This essay showed how primary, secondary and pre-capitalist class relations fused with all manner of other things – for instance, religious identity, gender relations and the family – to produce an extraordinary reconfiguration of the streets, residences, workplaces and public spaces of Paris. In turn, the construction of a new urban boulevard system (overseen by Georges-Eugène Haussmann) sparked new dynamics of protest, sociality, conformity and creativity in Parisian society, culminating in the ultimately unsuccessful insurrection led by the Communards in 1870.[6]

Inter-local rivalry at the national and international scales: from the defence and promotion of place to international political solidarity

It's true but trite to say that all human activity must occur somewhere and cannot simultaneously occur somewhere else. As we saw in Chapter 5, capitalism's endless attempts to 'annihilate space by time' can never circumvent the need to 'fix' accumulation in all manner of locations, connected by communication arteries. As we know, many of these locations are extremely large and complex (think Tokyo, Mexico City or Rio de Janeiro). The sorts of micro-scale variations discussed in the previous section are real, but at the scale of a town, city or metropolitan region they somehow hang together functionally (what Harvey, 1985a: 129 once called a 'structured coherence').

Geographical difference and division

At this larger scale, people inevitably have all manner of economic, social and psychological commitments. Their life histories and loyalties become rooted in place, as evidenced when they say they are Athenean, Baltimorean, Bristolean, a Londoner, a Mancunian, Parisian or a New Yorker. The defence and promotion of a particular place – be it Arequipa (Peru), Calgary (Canada), Detroit (USA), Glasgow (Scotland), Kiev (Ukraine), Kolkata (India), Ostrava (Czech Republic), Singapore or Zanzibar (Tanzania) – can become a prime arena for the exercise of peoples' agency. Over the years, Harvey has had an awful lot to say about this (see, for instance, Harvey, 1985a: Chapter 6; Harvey, 1989c).

One key theme has been the logic of what we might call 'conjoint agency', or what Harvey (1985a: 148) has more straightforwardly called 'local cross-class alliances'. As explained in Chapter 5, the spatial fluidity of capital accumulation does not gainsay – and in certain important respects, it actively encourages – enduring investments of various kinds *in place* by workers, capitalists and governments alike. The absolute (material and unique) qualities of different places obviously matter to all who work and reside in those locations. Even large businesses, which may in theory be able to relocate production, have a stake in protecting their sunk costs (e.g. buildings, machinery, a skilled work-force). Meanwhile, because all government is territorially based, politicians have a vested interest in sustaining wealth in the jurisdictions they are responsible for. The stage is therefore set for cooperation at the scale of towns and cities among classes and strata within them, mediated by local government (sometimes with direct national government involvement). The actors involved are not merely place-based but, in important respects, they are place-*bound*.

These locally embedded actors have to be constantly vigilant. After all, uneven geographical development is part of capitalism's DNA (Smith, 1984). Changes in investment patterns, new technological breakthroughs, changing transportation costs, new consumer tastes, reduced labour costs and innovative means of communication can see once prosperous localities lose out to other places (classic US examples are the 'rust-belt' cities of Flint and Detroit). Given the intra-local complexities recounted in the previous section, there's no guarantee of a stable, coherent or inclusive response to external opportunities and threats (Harvey, 1985a: 150). Local politicians typically play a crucial role in brokering and forging agreement among fractions of capital, workers and others (this because all government is by definition fixated on conditions within a defined territorial unit). In general terms, Harvey (1985a: 213–221) sees local cross-class alliances choosing among some mix of four options and devising strategies accordingly:

1. *Attract new investments in commodity production to complement or replace existing industries, or else to spark brand new agglomerations.* An example is the prodigious expansion of Chongqing in China since 1990. Another example is Masdar City in the United Arab Emirates, which aspires to be a 'cleantech' hub in the next twenty-five years.
2. *Attract new investments, with associated image construction and marketing, in the arena of consumption and lifestyle.* An example is Wollongong, Australia. Once a steel and coal production town, since 2015 it has used its beautiful coastal location and proximity to Sydney to attract huge amounts of inward investment in residential property, bars, restaurants, cafes and tourist enterprises (such as sky diving and sea kayaking).
3. *Attract new 'command functions' existing in the commercial or governmental domains.* An example is Salford, adjacent to Manchester. A deeply deindustrialised city by the 1990s, it managed to attract the BBC from London in 2011, since when a 'media city' complex has grown around the old ship canal port area called Salford Quays.
4. *Attract national or supranational government aid and support, such as grants, tax breaks, legal exemptions and the like.* An example is the European Union funding deployed to assist 'lagging regions', and which has benefitted hundreds of towns and cities, such as Košice in Slovakia.

As we saw in Chapter 5, in Harvey's view inter-place competition has intensified in the era of 'neoliberal globalization' that's prevailed since the 1980s. Towns, cities and metropolitan regions have had to become more entrepreneurial, more creative or more willing to make sacrifices in order, variously, to prosper or at least stem economic decline. That is, the agency exercised via place-bound alliances of actors has been geared to creating *geographical differences* – the larger the better – within a much wider and fairly open landscape of capital circulation and accumulation. To be sure, many of these differences are superficial, but others are very real. Accordingly, Jamie Peck and others have long recommended that we substitute the verb 'neoliberalisation' (designating a non-linear process playing out along various pathways) for the singular noun neoliberalism (e.g. Brenner, Peck and Theodore, 2010). Within this uneven and changing landscape, the room for local manoeuvre is considerable. Actors can employ all manner of tactics to attract investment and build a distinctive reputation for their town, city or metropolitan region.[7] But Harvey has consistently urged caution in how we understand the means and ends of these tactics. The big risk, in his view, is that we fixate on the local-to-regional scale analytically and politically as we seek to keep track of the remarkable geographical changes afoot since the Fordist-Keynesian regime of accumulation progressively dissolved after 1973.

An oppositional politics of here and there, now and then, us and you

Analytically, Harvey (1987a, 1990a) noted that there's an understandable, but somewhat problematic, desire among human geographers and other researchers to take an 'empirical turn' designed to capture new forms of micro- and meso-scale difference – especially when economic crises spur major rounds of economic restructuring. The 1980s 'localities debate', to which we referred in Chapter 3, was a key part of this. This 'idiographic' focus threatens to lose sight of the larger structural forces that spur locally based and bound agents to accentuate geographical difference. In other words, it threatens to foreground and even fetishise place (or region) at the expense of wider processes and relationships stretched-out across the expanded space economy of capitalism forged in the last forty to fifty years.[8] Instead, Harvey insists, the right approach is to attend to the dialectical relationships between place and space, near and far, the local and the global. Each town and city is 'the concentration of many determinations'. As Harvey's former doctoral student Erik Swyngedouw is wont to say, our contemporary existence should be regarded as thoroughly 'glocal' (e.g. Swyngedouw, 1997).[9]

This has political implications for understanding the 'proper' locus of agency in a geographically variegated yet tightly interconnected capitalist world. Here, Harvey's experiences in Oxford, and his influential analysis of a factory fire in Hamlet, North Carolina, are especially worth noting. Let's consider each in turn briefly.

As noted in Chapter 2, soon after moving to Oxford in 1987, Harvey became involved in a campaign to protect threatened automobile manufacturing jobs in nearby Cowley. He subsequently co-edited a book about the campaign (Hayter and Harvey, 1993) and reflected on his experience in a much-cited essay about the novels of celebrated Marxist cultural critic Raymond Williams (1921–1988) (Harvey, 1995b; reprinted as Harvey, 1996a: Chapter 1). Though a medieval university city, a(n eventually large) British motor company (Morris) had set up operations in the adjacent district of Cowley over a century ago. By the 1980s, the company and its Cowley operations were part of a national government (publicly) owned company called British Leyland. In the mid-1970s over 20,000 local workers were employed in the Cowley plant. However, overseas competition (especially from Japanese, South Korean and Taiwanese vehicle makers) and assembly line automation saw employment drop to under 5,000 by the mid-1990s.

By then, the Cowley plant had been sold to a company with no historic roots in the area (British Aerospace), which acquired it quite cheaply courtesy of the Margaret Thatcher government in 1988 (one of many post-1979 privatisations of public assets in the United Kingdom). The plant had a long and strong history of worker solidarity and militancy, with the support of national trade unions and successive local Labour governments. But by the mid-1990s trade unions were on the back foot in Britain (Thatcher's governments legislated numerous reductions in their power), and British Aerospace began to consider selling land, buildings, machinery and other assets in Cowley. The remaining workers and their families feared the worst, and the local union was willing to make accommodations (e.g. in pay and working conditions for its members) in order to protect the remaining jobs. Meanwhile, Oxford University had expanded significantly and local land and property prices were very high. Accordingly, local government was promoting the image of Oxford as an educational and research powerhouse, with associated 'clean' industry potential (e.g. in pharmaceuticals, electronics, computation and medical devices).

As a Marxist, it might be thought that Harvey sided with the local campaign to protect jobs in the Cowley plant. But he only did so up to a point. First, he noted the requirement to attend to the needs and wants of the wider local community who had little involvement in the car factory. For instance, the nearby Blackbird Leys council estate contained many people with low skills, limited employment prospects, alcohol and drugs problems, and so on. What, Harvey asked, should be done to improve their situation? But even supposing a joined-up strategy for the plant and wider Cowley community were possible, Harvey then questioned the defence of jobs that involved making polluting motor vehicles for wealthier people in the United Kingdom and beyond (Cowley manufactured Rover cars, a brand that was associated historically with Britain's professional classes). Furthermore, as Harvey saw it, a 'militant particularism' grounded in Cowley essentially reproduced the 'divide-and-rule' logic of neoliberal capitalism with its playing-off of workers in different locations against each other. Harvey's overall political point was that there is a deep tension – even a paradox – involving on the one hand attempts to enact a pro-worker politics locally, and on the other a wider project to improve the lives of all workers. Socialism, he noted, cannot be built one town or city at a time because, in the end, it 'is always about the negation of the material conditions of its own political identity' (1996a: 41). These conditions are, today, thoroughly glocal and deeply capitalist. Class struggle in and around a single workplace can result in real gains for the workers affected, but in the end, it can be counter revolutionary in Harvey's view – *necessary* yet deeply *insufficient*.

At the least, what is needed is inter-place solidarity among working people, the classic goal of national and international trade unions. And since working people are young and old, Black and white, religious and secular, straight and gay etc. then working class political organising is necessarily about *both respecting and transcending forms of both social and geographical difference*. Harvey made this key point in his reflections on a shocking 1991 fire at a chicken-processing factory that occurred in Hamlet, North Carolina. Unable to escape easily, twenty-five workers died and fifty-six were seriously injured out of a workforce of around 200. Yet there was no trade union response, no sustained critique of Imperial Foods (who offered low-paid jobs to Hamlet workers in conditions that were described as unacceptable and illegal) and no public condemnation of state and local government bodies (who were anti-union and had failed to inspect the plant properly for health and safety compliance). 'When it is realised', wrote Harvey (1996a: 338), 'that of the 25 people who died in Hamlet, 18 were women and 12 were African American … [then the] commonality that cuts across race and gender lines in this instance is quite obviously that of class, and it is hard not to see the immediate implication that a simple, traditional form of class politics could have protected the interests of women and minorities as well as those of white males'.[10]

This class politics would have needed to be organised at least at the level of several southern states to prevent small, remote settlements like Hamlet

Figure 7.3. Transnational solidarity for the Liverpool dockers, 1995–1998. Compare this with the Hamlet fire disaster Harvey wrote about: in Liverpool transnational worker solidarity for 350 striking Liverpool dockers allowed the strike to last three years, making it the longest industrial dispute in modern British history.

being used by firms like Imperial Foods to treat their workers with impunity in order to make money. Combined worker agency among places and across axes of social difference here would have made a huge positive difference (see Figure 7.3). Yet the fire occurred at a time when Marxism was under assault (both in academia and the wider world – the 1989–1990 collapse of communism in the USSR and Central and Eastern Europe exacted considerable reputational damage), when trade unions were generally less powerful and popular than in the 1970s, when Left-wing political parties had been neoliberalised, when changing geographies of commodity production had created new and atomised workforces likes those in Hamlet, and when both 'identity politics' and environmental politics had risen up the political agenda worldwide to create a broader but less cohesive Left.

Political universals, uneven development, scale and the right to geographical difference

Let us take stock. By the turn of the millennium, as we've seen, Harvey had crystallised a view of human agency as profoundly structured by capitalism, but also a number of other things (such as patriarchy and racism). For him, the classic Marxist injunction 'workers of the world unite!', had to contend with all manner of socio-geographic differentiations within capitalism as they intersect with myriad 'external' differentiating forces and factors. This 'concentration of many determinations' at many scales poses formidable political challenges to any attempt to reform or topple the capitalist system, especially given the broadly neoliberal conditions prevailing since the early 1990s. It also rightly complicates the goals of any Marxism-inspired politics. Harvey has offered a summary perspective on these challenges and goals in Parts I and II of his book *Spaces of Hope* (2000a), as well as in several later works (e.g. Harvey, 2010a: Chapter 8). Let's consider his key insights by way of a synthesis and further development of this chapter's themes, both as a prelude to some final critical reflections on Harvey's views about human agency and as a precursor to the normative focus of Chapter 8. There are seven things to say.

1. Since the early 1980s, the size of the working class has grown prodigiously, both numerically (it's now well over 4 billion) and geographically (as capitalism has expanded into new territories). Yet while it may be a 'class in itself', it is assuredly not (and is never likely to be) a cohesive 'class for itself'. This is because the differences among working people are manifold and real, not somehow secondary to what 'should' somehow be a 'primary' class identity. As Harvey expressed it in a constructive critique of *The Communist Manifesto* of 1848, 'The central difficulty lies in the presumption that capitalist industry and commodification will lead to a homogenisation of the working population' (2000a: 40). He went on: 'The global proletariat is larger than ever and the imperative for workers of the world to unite is greater than ever. But the barriers to that unity are far more formidable than they were in the already complicated European context of 1848' (2000a: 45).
2. During the era of neoliberal globalisation that persists to this day, wealth inequality has soared, as Harvey reported in *A Brief History of Neoliberalism* and elsewhere, referencing the empirical research of Dumenil and Lévy (2004), among others. Geographically, this redistribution of wealth has been operationalised via new and expanded patterns of uneven development.[11] This poses the questions 'what is development?' and 'what kind of development should we aspire to?'. Though he's never provided detailed answers to these important questions, Harvey has nevertheless supplied some key insights. One is that the globalising, 'molecular' tendencies of capitalism *force* these questions to be considered by more and more otherwise different and far-flung people. After all, the system has profited from, and altered, existing variations in customs, gender

relations, geographic conditions and so on – many of which precede and exceed capitalism proper. It thereby brings all this difference within a common, but far from homogenous, universe of 'development'. The fortunes of the Malaysian sweatshop worker are, indirectly, bound to the fortunes of the Auckland stockbroker and the Kenyan vegetable farmer. Questions of wages, working conditions, costs of living, the price of everyday goods and so on become universal questions for *causal* reasons, not merely reasons of *formal* commonality among wage workers and their dependents. Answering these questions, however, does not require that a single, general, substantive conception of what counts as 'development' be accepted, and Harvey certainly does not suggest this.

3. Since the early 1990s, there has been considerable global discontent with various elements of neoliberal capitalism. For instance, we have witnessed: the Zapatista peasant uprising in southern Mexico; 'reclaim the streets' actions from 1995 onwards; the dramatic anti-free trade protests in Seattle and beyond in 1998; the World Social Forum, founded in 2001; electorates rejecting neoliberalism in Venezuela and Bolivia; the Occupy Movement, which started in New York City in 2011, the same year as the Spanish Indignados movement began; the 2015 Free Pass protests across Brazil; the worldwide school student strikes against climate change (Fridays For A Future), sparked by Greta Thunberg; the French *gilets jaunes* protests from autumn 2018 onwards; various provocative Extinction Rebellion protests in public spaces; and any number of local and national worker strikes against their employers (an example being the 2021 John Deere action by some 10,000 workers in the United States of America). The political slogans of our time include 'another world is possible', 'de-globalisation', 'we are the 99%', 'de-growth', a 'green New Deal', 'a world for the many, not for the few' and 'there is no Planet B'. As Harvey has argued in *The New Imperialism* and elsewhere, the protests have, understandably, been diverse in their political claims, with some being local-cum-regional, and others being more resolutely global in terms of their audiences and ambitions. Broadly, many protests relate to classic issues of production, trade, consumption and social reproduction (the historic focus of Marxist analysis and politics). But many other protests relate to 'accumulation by dispossession' and to forced incorporation into the dynamics of capitalism (e.g. indigenous peoples' struggles to reclaim communal rights to expropriated land and water). The different political inflections reflect the various facets and geographies of a complex, globe-girdling capitalism. As Harvey has noted, the trick is to harness all this political energy rather than simply accept it as it is: 'Ignoring the multifaceted nature of such

struggles under contemporary conditions is tantamount to foregoing the creation of anti-capitalist alliances that can actually do something to check, if not transform, what a predatory capitalism is all about' (2005b: 88). For instance, 'living wage' campaign groups have done precisely this by linking production (workplace issue) and reproductive (home, consumer and community issue) politics (see Harvey, 2000a: Chapter 7, for a Baltimore example).

4. For Harvey, such anti-capitalist alliances need at once to be global, local *and* everything in-between. Here Harvey has quoted the wise words of Raymond Williams in many of his publications: 'The unique and extraordinary character of working-class self-organisation has been that it has tried ... to make real what is at first sight the extraordinary claim that the defence and advancement of certain particular interests, properly brought together, are in fact the general interest' (in Harvey, 1996a: 32). This may sound like 'the particular' begins and ends with 'the local', as far as Harvey is concerned (e.g. Cowley, Hamlet or Baltimore). But since *Spaces of Hope*, if not before, Harvey has rejected this (seemingly obvious) view. This is because social (and environmental) differences are, plainly, organised at other geographical scales too. Historically, the trade union movement has been good at connecting localities to the national scale, and (to a lesser extent) the international level too (the research of geographer Andrew Herod is replete with inspiring examples). Harvey is clear that any anti-capitalist politics today needs to be multi-scalar, both spatially and temporally. While not analysing scale in the depth that his former students Neil Smith and Erik Swyngedouw have famously done, he shares their view that scales are contingent and constructed, not timeless universals. For instance, as noted in the previous section of this chapter, what counts as 'local' for people in places like Chicago, Vancouver and Istanbul has been enlarged over time by greater private vehicle ownership, public transportation investments and improvements in road quality. More widely, there are scalar mismatches between political, economic, cultural and ecological relations, processes and systems. 'The upshot', Harvey has written, 'is to render all ways of thinking that operate only at one scale at least questionable, if not downright misleading. [We need] to work simultaneously with multiplying and volatile geographical differentiations operating at [scales] which are themselves rapidly changing' (2000a: 80). This work is difficult but unavoidable, being chock-full of contradictions and dilemmas. 'A common error', Harvey has noted, is to 'lock ourselves into one and only one scale of thinking, treating differences at that scale as *the* fundamental line of political cleavage' (2000a: 79). Ultimately, the trick is to

match the scale-crossing powers of capital. 'Neoliberalisation', Harvey once opined with sardonic reference to journalist Thomas Friedman (2005), 'has created a flat world for multinational corporations and for the billionaire entrepreneur and investor class, but a rough, jagged and uneven world for everyone else' (2009a: 58).

5. The question then arises as to what motivating reasons and concepts can allow a reformist or more revolutionary anti-capitalist movement to work across socio-geographic differences and connect workerist/trade union politics with the burgeoning civic, social and environmental movement politics of the last half century. We will explore Harvey's normative vision more fully in Chapter 8. For now, though, it's enough to note his prioritisation of arguments about *rights*.[12] Rights discourse, he's argued, is sufficiently established, sufficiently global in purchase and sufficiently elastic to enable articulations among otherwise disparate responses to the ills of a neoliberalising capitalism. Starting in *Spaces of Hope* and evolving through several subsequent texts, the political value of rights talk has become something of a Harvey refrain. This may seem odd for a Marxist, since bourgeois rights (e.g. to legally protected private property) are integral to the maladies caused by capitalism. So why does Harvey commend rights as a galvanising political idea?

   In part, the reason is negative: Harvey is clear that a shared political *identity* is both impossible and undesirable as a foundation for progressive, multi-scalar political agency.[13] For instance, since the 2007–2008 global financial crisis, we've seen much grass-roots political protest but no unified response predicated on subjective similarities between people. More positively, Harvey noted two decades ago that the notion of 'universal human rights' has become usefully established since the inspiring United Nations Declaration of 1948 (Harvey, 2000a: 18). The Declaration posits common rights that rich and poor, straight and gay, old and young, men and women, people of faith, secularists and others all share regardless of location, identity or belief. Harvey noted too that many parts of the New Left since the late 1960s have voiced their agendas in terms of rights, often with great success (e.g. the feminist and transgender movements). The same applies to other political movements, such as the Zapatistas in Mexico or aboriginal peoples in Australia, and to respected global organisations like Amnesty International and Médecins Sans Frontières. These movements and organisations show that collective rights are just as important as individual rights.

   Harvey has further noted the sometimes-overlooked radicalism of the rights concept in all its variety across the domains of the personal, economic, political, cultural and environmental. For instance, Article 25 of the UN Declaration states that 'Everyone has the right to a standard of living adequate for the health and well-being of [themselves] ... including food, clothing, housing, and medical care ...'. As Harvey observed in *Spaces of Hope*, 'Strict enforcement of such rights would entail massive and in some senses revolutionary transformations in the political economy of capitalism' (2000a: 90). The fact that supporters of neoliberal capitalism take very seriously the importance of a certain bundle of rights (primarily economic, personal and legally enforceable) does, at least, mean they may be obliged to listen when other sorts of rights are promoted by those who are losing out despite the 'freedoms' neoliberal capitalism offers. These rights, for those so minded, extend to what we call 'nature' and to future persons. In sum, 'As a matter of practical politics, some notion of rights appears indispensable' (2000a: 94). The challenge is to integrate various rights claims beneath and at a global scale, while avoiding co-optation to the neoliberal rights agenda.[14]

6. Harvey's emphasis on 'rights talk' as a potentially potent means of conjoining diverse political struggles in and against capitalism has led him, since *Justice, Nature and the Geography of Difference*, to propose two important (if general) normative ideas. The first is 'the right to geographical difference', that is the right 'to build different forms of human association characterised by different laws, rules and customs at a variety of scales' (2000a: 93). This right, at some level, adjures general conceptions of 'development', however sophisticated and ecumenical (compare with Escobar, 2008). It extends to rights to determine the balance of public, private and communal spaces; to determine the material and symbolic qualities of the built and natural environments; to shape prevalent social relations, identities, moral norms, theisms and so on. Inevitably, in many situations the forms of human association being claimed as rights could clash with more general rights claims. In Harvey's pithy formulation: 'The right to geographical difference confronts the universality of rights' (2000a: 93). This raises the important question of when does a 'difference' become an inequality that abrogates widely accepted rights? Rephrased more broadly: since all universals are generalised particularities, which universals are acceptable as a basis for judging the validity of particularities that don't achieve such general purchase? However, Harvey has held out hope that this 'thorny problem' can be handled with tolerance and creativity:

> Between the absolutist relativism that says that nothing that happens in, say, Jakarta or Vietnam or even in Boulder and the inner city of Baltimore is a proper subject for my moral or political judgement, and

> the absolutism that rigidly views universality as a matter of total uniformity and equality of judgement and treatment, there is abundant room for negotiation.
>
> (2000a: 93)

The other key rights concept that Harvey has proposed is 'the right to the city' (originally formulated by French Marxist Henri Lefebvre in 1967).[15] This concept is explored in *Rebel Cities* (2012a) and a few other places. It signifies the use of individual and collective agency so as to rebuild and re-create the city as a socialist body politic in a completely different image – one that eradicates poverty and social inequality, and one that heals the wounds of disastrous environmental degradation. For this to happen, the production of the destructive forms of urbanisation that facilitate perpetual capital accumulation has to be stopped (2012a: 138).

For Harvey, this right matters not simply because much anti-capitalist (or at least anti-neoliberal) protest has occurred in cities (e.g. Seattle and El Alto), nor because the majority of humanity is now urbanised (important though that fact undoubtedly is). More than this, for Harvey the right to the city matters because our cities – with all their commonalities and differences – are made *for* people but not *by* the majority of people whose daily environment they constitute. Private enterprise and local government, rentiers and landowners, financiers and entrepreneurs are the 'one per cent' who determine urban function and form for the billions who are then 'free' to work and play in the world's cities. This is profoundly undemocratic. In Harvey's view, a rights politics thus needs to be promoted not merely in cities but, in significant measure, that's *about* them too. It 'has to be construed not as a right to that which already exists, but as a right to rebuild and recreate the city' (2012a: 138), so Harvey wrote.[16] Ultimately, all human activity must occur somewhere and, as Harvey has long insisted, the qualities of the 'somewhere' deeply influence the qualities of human action.

7. Finally, what is the implication of all the above in an organisational-logistical sense? Harvey has never said much about this, and what he has said is very general, though still worth recounting. In *Spaces of Hope* he addressed the need for political leadership and coordination when he asserted that:

> We desperately need a revitalised socialist avant-garde, an international political movement capable of bringing together in an appropriate way the multitudinous discontents that derive from the naked … pursuit of

a utopian neoliberalism. This does not mean an old-style avant-garde party that imposes a singular goal and arrogates to itself such clarity of vision as to exclude all other voices.

(Harvey, 2000a: 49)

This global avant-garde would not only have to wrestle with how to bridge across socio-spatial diversity, using rights or related normative concepts. It would also, Harvey notes, have to wrestle with the reform-revolution tension: after all, there are losses, costs and risks in trying to overhaul, rather than improve, the present state of things (Chapters 4 and 8). The forces of inertia are very real in even the most progressive politics. 'The courage of our minds' (2000a: 255), intoned Harvey, is required to think outside the proverbial boxes, both theoretically and practically.

As for cities – and rights to them – Harvey accents their potential in light of the Left internationalism pioneered in places like Porto Alegre. 'Progressive anti-capitalist forces', he argued somewhat hopefully in *Rebel Cities*, 'can more easily mobilise to leap forward into global coordinations via urban networks that may be hierarchical but not monocentric, corporatist but nevertheless democratic, egalitarian and horizontal, systemically nested and federated, ... internally discordant and contested, but solidarious against capitalist power' (Harvey, 2012a: 153).

In sum, given the political-organisational complexities highlighted in the previous six points, Harvey has obviously been minded to identify the need for a 'new left international' that's somehow both 'vertical' and 'horizontal' in its structures, processes and decision-making.

Making sense of Harvey on agency: a conclusion

After three sections of exposition, what are we to make of Harvey's assorted views on agency within a more-than-capitalist world suffused with the contradictory logics of capitalism? As we've seen, when we read across his many books and articles, a complex picture of human agency emerges. For Harvey, all agency is ineluctably enabled and constrained by various 'structures', key among which are those constitutive of capitalism. These structures, we have also seen, articulate in complex ways and, courtesy of capital's globalising impulses, are ultimately interleaved at numerous scales simultaneously, from the local and present day to the global and longer term. That is, agency affects and is conditioned by absolute, relative and relational geographies and temporalities. The structures create and modify historical-geographical forms, and these forms shape people's consciousness of self and other, as well as what matters to them today and tomorrow (see Table 3.2).

In order to exercise forms of agency that might improve the life conditions of those who are subject to these structures, Harvey's view is that we face both dilemmas of scale and a reform-revolution dilemma as well. In the end, the 'we' of these dilemmas is, of course, no homogenous mass of wageworkers but, rather, a heterogenous 'multitude' whose lives are governed by capital accumulation. Indeed, by the time of *Justice, Nature and the Geography of Difference*, Harvey had moved beyond the traditional productionist notion of class towards a much wider conception:

> Marx appears to define class relationally as command (or noncommand) over the means of production. I prefer to define class as *situatedness or positionality in relation to processes of capital accumulation*. All of us who live under capitalism live out our lives under conditions of embeddedness in such processes. But those processes are often disparate and chaotic, also operating at radically different spatio-temporal scales, so that our individual positionality in relationship to those processes can also be as complicated as it is confused.
>
> (Harvey, 1996a: 359)

This shift reflected Harvey's acknowledgement that Left politics had to pivot on something more generous than an older 'class identity' position. Accordingly, his political mantra these days is 'anti-capitalist struggle' rather than 'class struggle' alone, or even primarily. There are many points of entry into this struggle (see also Skeggs, 2022).

Harvey's insights about human agency are interesting and important – as far as they go. However, it would be remiss of us not to point out the limited analytical attention he gives to several important 'arenas of agency', if we may so call them. That is, Harvey has *acknowledged* these arenas but has largely ignored them in a *substantive* sense. In practice, agency is (or is not) exercised in functionally different arenas organised at various scales in light of diverse pressures, opportunities, interests and goals. Some arenas are mainstream (like purchasing commodities), others created at the societal margins. While capitalism *affects* all of them, it does not *subsume* all of them. Conversely, the non-subsumed arenas can significantly impact capitalism. For instance, in Western-style democracies, civil society and the public sphere are two closely linked arenas, another is the formal political arena (where actual and aspiring governing parties operate), still another is the arena of law and order, and yet another is the arena of insurrection and violence (operating beyond the rule of law, and thus breaking the bounds of 'acceptable' agency). The resourcing, form and consequences of agency exercised in these intersecting arenas matter hugely to the local-to-global trajectory of capitalism at any one moment. The 'logics' animating these arenas are not reducible to profitmaking.

Moreover, people have differential access to these arenas and, again, that makes a difference. For example, most adults are allowed to vote periodically in most countries so as to determine who controls the state apparatus, but most adults and children have very limited agency when it comes to determining news content in the public arena (about which, see Chapter 9). Imagine, though, if the agency granted by free elections and the right to free speech were exercised *en masse* so as to decouple a locality or country from the global economy – say on religious or ethno-cultural grounds. That political potential exists and is not functional for capitalism. Social theorists of various persuasions, such as Anthony Giddens and Jürgen Habermas, are part of a tradition of seeking to properly map-out these arenas of agency, and their associated structures (including forms of social power and injustice).[17]

With the signal exception of his long empirical study of mid-nineteenth-century Paris (2003b), Harvey has not really elucidated how various distinct modalities of agency intersect, preferring to foreground capitalist structures (in an often-general sense) as they define arenas of political-economic agency. Yet, in the end, it is the interleaving of multiple structures that conditions whether and how agents submit to the structural dominance of the capitalist mode of production. For instance, consider the rise of right-wing populism across the globe since 2010. Why have millions chosen to believe in, campaign for and vote for the likes of Donald Trump, Boris Johnson and Jair Bolsonaro? The answer is complicated, requiring a grasp of how economic hardship, representative democracy, international migration, 'multi-culturalism', perceived corruption in elected government and more besides have converged to create collective agency fuelled by anger in search of greater local and national control over peoples' life conditions. Populism cannot be explained without reference to neoliberal capitalism, but it is also irreducible to it. Understanding how to make history and geography differently thus requires a keen grasp of this 'over-determined' situation, conceptually as much as empirically. We need, that is, a 'Marxism-plus' perspective – what Cindi Katz (2006: 245) called 'a more vigorous, supple multiply-fanged oppositional theory': a *post*-Marxism that is not post-*Marxist*. This is different to Nigel Thrift's (1987) call to analytical modesty, flagged at the end of Chapter 6. Instead, it's a call for a mix of high analytical ambition with suitable sophistication.

Further reading

Bohrer, A. J. (2022). Intersectionality. In B. Skeggs, *et al.* (Eds.), *The Sage Handbook of Marxism* (pp. 1047–1066). Sage.

Harvey, D. (1985a). Class structure and the theory of residential differentiation. In *The Urbanization of Capital* (pp. 109–24). Blackwell.

Harvey, D. (1985b). The place of urban politics in the geography of uneven capitalist development. In *The Urbanization of Capital* (pp. 125–164). Blackwell.

Harvey, D. (1996a). Militant particularism and global ambition. In *Justice, Nature and the Geography of Difference* (pp. 19–45), Blackwell.

Harvey, D. (2000a). Uneven geographical developments and universal rights. In *Spaces of Hope* (pp. 73–96). Edinburgh University Press.

Harvey, D. (2014a). Freedom and domination. In *Seventeen Contradictions and the End of Capitalism* (pp. 199–220). Profile Books.

Notes

1. The one place where Harvey uses the term most self-consciously is also one of his most disappointingly abstract contributions (1996a: Chapter 6).
2. We draw especially on Chapters 4 and 5 of *Social Justice and the City* (1973), Chapter 5 of *The Urbanization of Capital* (1985a) and Chapters 2 and 5 of *Consciousness and the Urban Experience* (1985b); some of these chapters are reproduced in *The Urban Experience* (1989b) and other 'greatest hits' edited works compiled by Harvey.
3. The capitalist-worker relationship, itself conditioned by relations of competition and complementarity among capitalist firms, produces variety routinely: differences in products, work processes, technologies etc. emerge and morph ceaselessly. Firms require different kinds of workers, with different skills, and pay them accordingly. Working class struggle within and between workplaces, and via the national and local state, can improve working conditions and rates of pay. But it requires collective organising and tenacity to succeed, especially at the lower end of the labour market hierarchy.
4. There's also nothing natural about the demarcation of work locations and living spaces: again, that's a historical creation led by capitalists in England and elsewhere from the early nineteenth century.
5. The urban riots in the United States in the late 1960s were complex in their causes and were expressions of anger (e.g. about long term unemployment) as much as of coherent political thinking. The same is true of the urban riots in the United Kingdom in the early 1980s in districts like Moss Side (Manchester) and Toxteth (Liverpool). If we look at present day spatial segregation in cities, class-based inequalities intersect with any number of other axes of social discrimination. For instance, in Israel consider how the religious differences between Jews and Muslim Palestinians affect the wages and job prospects of

the latter and how this finds geographical expression in residential differentiation. In recent times, there have been a slew of urban protests worldwide, but class inequality is rarely not a key part of the story.

6. The chapter was later reprinted in *Paris, Capital of Modernity* (Harvey, 2003b).
7. There's a whole industry now geared to advising places how to be strategically and operationally different so as to attract and retain outside investment and labour power, with geographer Richard Florida among the most prominent exponents in his work on 'the creative class' and 'creative cities' (Florida, 2002, 2004).
8. In Harvey's discipline, Geography, there was a turn to place studies during the 1980s and 1990s led by so-called humanistic geographers. They were reacting to the 'anaemic', seemingly place-less geographies depicted in the 1960s by the 'spatial scientists' (Harvey had been one of them, as we explained in Chapter 2) and later by the new Marxist geographers like Harvey who seemed to fixate on the systemic, global qualities of capital accumulation. Indeed, two humanistic geographers in North America (James Duncan and David Ley, 1982) took aim at Harvey for being a supposed 'structuralist', a person both inattentive to agency and to the affective qualities of people's everyday lives. While Harvey, in fact, has for decades fully acknowledged the elemental importance of place and locality for people, he has also long worried that undue localism and inward-looking communitarianism can take hold. In several published works, he has used the thinking of German philosopher Martin Heidegger (1889–1976) as a focus for these worries. His more positive agenda for place and locality is presented in several works, notably Part I of *Cosmopolitanism and the Geographies of Freedom* (2009a).
9. A fine example of this, using Marxist ideas, was provided by another of Harvey's former doctoral students Andy Merrifield (1993) in a study of one part of Baltimore undergoing economic and social change.
10. While Harvey's key point is fairly easy to understand, it's important to note that in practice 'traditional' working class politics in the United States and elsewhere, led by trade unions, was highly masculinist and not a little racist.
11. As we intimated in Chapter 5, while Harvey has used the term uneven development quite frequently during his post-1973 career, he's rarely paused to consider in detail its full ensemble of causes, its range of outcomes or its normative implications. As part of this, he's not engaged closely with existing Marxian texts about uneven development, be they works of pure theory, be they focussed empirically on the 'developed' world or be they focussed on the so-called developing world. His most focussed treatment is a set of 'notes towards a theory of uneven geographical development', Chapter 2 of his short book *Spaces of Neoliberalization* (2005b).
12. The definition and analysis of rights is hugely complex. In broad terms, there are 'rights to' (positive rights) and 'negative rights' (e.g. the right of a person to be free from violence). There are individual rights and shared rights. There are rights that apply in different realms, such as the private realm, the economic

realm and so on. Harvey, alas, has not plumbed the depths of 'rights talk' in any of his many publications since *Spaces of Hope*.

13. In one book, however, he almost flirts with this idea by highlighting one common *experience* of capitalism shared by billions: namely alienation (Harvey, 2014a: Chapter 17; see also Harvey, 2018c). Alienation is a process of experiential separation, underpinned by real processes, from the fruits of one's own activities, from one's own labour and from other people, all of which come to seem external to us.
14. Harvey, in one of the only somewhat detailed normative statements of any kind offered since *Social Justice and the City*, outlined his preferred rights agenda in the final chapter of *Spaces of Hope* (2000a: 248–252).
15. In *La droit à la ville* (published in English in 1995), the gist of Lefebvre's idea was that cities are concentrations of human difference and should be subject to genuinely collective shaping, thereby being cities for the many not for the few. Guy Debord and The Situationists were also advancing related ideas at the time Lefebvre was writing. In the last twenty years, geographer Don Mitchell, urban planner Mark Purcell and the late urban theorist Peter Marcuse have been among those promoting the right to the city idea, along with others who, more specifically, have criticised inner city gentrification (e.g. Neil Smith, Loretta Lees and Tom Slater).
16. As Harvey explained in *The Condition of Postmodernity* (1989a) and elsewhere, this right to make geography encompasses remaking physical environments, dominant representations of the same and the venturing of novel, even radical new representations of possible and desirable new geographies. The dynamics of peoples' geographical experience, perceptions and imaginings, for Harvey, are cross-cut by power, domination, appropriation, protest and struggle.
17. Harvey's own meta-mapping of a 'more-than-capitalist' reality began in earnest in *Justice, Nature and the Geography of Difference*, recurring now and then in later works. But it's a strangely distanced map, composed almost out in space looking back at Earth from afar. For instance, in *Marx, Capital and the Madness of Economic Reason* (2017a: 113) he talks about the 'totality' of life in terms of 'technologies, the relation to nature, social relations, modes of material production, mental conceptions and institutional frameworks'. Such talk, unfortunately, risks being vacuous. It dodges the challenge of abstracting closer to the ground and specifying how various institutions, social relations, technologies etc. enter into contingent, though structured, ensembles. Compare this to Bruno Latour. Though a non-Marxist, his 'inquiry into modes of existence' (2012) offers a more specific, if still abstract, sense of different actualities and possibilities for humans and non-humans.

8

What is to be done? Towards a more just geography for a feasible future

What's wrong with capitalism in our more-than-capitalist world? Piecing together David Harvey's critical perspective; In search of general principles of justice for people and planet in a large, interconnected and differentiated world; Getting real, politically? In pursuit of neo-socialism in a 'post-socialist' era; Conclusion

The point, Marx once famously said, is to change the world – not merely to understand it. But, as Harvey has often noted, instigating political change without properly understanding why, how and to what ends is futile. 'Critical reflection on our understandings', he once said, is 'as important as political and social engagement on the barricades. That is why Marx wrote *Capital*. And that is why the Marxist tradition is so rich in its attachment to writing, theorising and analysing' (1989b: 3). Towards the end of Chapter 7, we began to explore the normative side of Harvey's historical-geographical materialism (focussing on the parameters of political agency). In this chapter, we offer a systematic treatment. We draw together numerous threads of argument, stretching from his early 'liberal' and Marxist views on social justice to his more recent comments about socialism. In effect, we create a rough normative tapestry, replete with bright patches and holes that reflect Harvey's chequered contributions in this area. As we will see, Harvey offers his readers some suggestive insights – especially in the books *Social Justice and the City* (1973) and *Justice, Nature and the Geography of Difference* (*JNGD*, 1996a). But, overall, the normative side of his work is notably underdeveloped (e.g. compared, among many other Left-leaning scholars, with Axel Honneth, 2017 and Thomas Piketty, 2021). It comprises

DOI: 10.4324/9780429028120-8

a mixture of sporadic, abstract and disconnected insights, alongside some wise and sophisticated observations of enduring interest.

In a sense, Harvey has thereby failed to heed Marx's well-known injunction by not creating useable normative knowledge. This is unfortunate. Accordingly, we point to the areas where Harvey might usefully have focussed his attention over the years. Fortunately, others in the Marxian camp have provided normative insights that help us fill some of the gaps in Harvey's thinking. We will, at various points, draw briefly upon their insights in this chapter. As Harvey once sagely noted, 'The political proving ground may be the most difficult of all terrains to work upon. But, in the final analysis, it's the only one that counts' (1989b: 16). That Harvey only offers us a partial map to help us navigate this vital terrain, where argument and action are fused recursively, means we need to alert readers to the locational devices provided by other analysts. More than other elements of his thinking, it seems to us that it's just as useful to *think against* Harvey than to 'think with' him when it comes to normative questions.

Before we proceed, a word about the term 'normative'. So far in this book, we've used the word in its accepted, general meaning: namely, as claims and practices pertaining to what *could* or *should be the case*. As philosopher Onora O'Neill (1996: xi, emphasis added) once nicely expressed it, 'Normativity pervades our lives. We don't merely *have* beliefs: we claim that we and others *ought* to hold certain beliefs. We do not merely *have* desires: we claim that we and others not only *ought* to act on some of them, but not others'. All critique is normative, as is all politics (politics, in the broad sense, being the practical process of determining how people will live together).[1] Normative reasoning provides arguments and guiding values that allow us to find fault in the present – to a greater or lesser extent – and to seek a better future through appropriate action. The ultimate normative question is 'how, and according to what values, should we live?' And, ideally, such a question should be answered collectively and overtly, without the answer being imposed on people absent proper debate or informed consent. Harvey's scattered animadversions about 'ideology', first ventured in the early 1970s, show that he's long been concerned about whose normative arguments and practices get to be hegemonic (and thereby potentially unquestioned). However, we need to disaggregate the large category of the normative and explore its interconnected components in order to do it justice. This will allow us to see exactly where Harvey has had useful things to say, and where he's been relatively silent about key normative issues.

We begin with an attempt to summarise Harvey's immanent critique of capitalism (we ask: what, exactly, is *wrong* with the system?) and ponder how compelling the critique is. Then we consider how Harvey understands one of the modern world's most potent yet most abstract normative concepts, *justice*. Justice is a positive idea, indicating what a person, organisation or society is aspiring to ethically. Harvey's comments here are sometimes insightful but far from adequate, as we show. Finally, we turn our attention to what we call neo-socialism: has Harvey proposed a programme that might deliver at least some of his vision of a more just world? If not, why and at what cost?

What's wrong with capitalism in our more-than-capitalist world? Piecing together David Harvey's critical perspective

The first key element of normative reasoning to consider is *critique*: the act of identifying what, precisely, is *wrong* with a specific phenomenon and why. To say something is a problem is to say it could or should be eliminated, based on defensible values that deserve to be upheld practically. In Chapter 2, we noted that Harvey's critique is immanent because it shows – both conceptually and empirically – that values constitutive of capitalism (like liberty) are routinely and widely abrogated by the self-same system.[2] The benefit of immanent critique is that it holds something to account according to its own declared standards. However, in Chapter 2 we offered no detailed sense of what, exactly, is wrong with capitalism from Harvey's perspective. It is now time to make amends by being somewhat more granular.

It's odd but true to say that Harvey himself – despite being an inveterate critic of capitalism – hasn't really ever summarised its core problems in one place in a way that convinces. Instead, what one sees in his work as a Marxist are all sorts of different critical comments ventured over the decades in myriad publications, with perhaps his fullest (though still rather loose) statements coming in Chapter 14 of his *Seventeen Contradictions* book (2014a) and towards the end of *Marx, Capital and the Madness of Economic Reason* (2017a). We are thus obliged to join the proverbial dots ourselves, as follows:

1. *Class exploitation*: first and most obviously, for Harvey capitalism rests on the collective exploitation of wageworkers by those who own the means of production and, secondarily, by financiers and rentiers. In this he follows Marx. That is, for him working people together create far, far more wealth than they receive in wages and other benefits. This argument is made most graphically, albeit conceptually, in *The Limits to Capital* (1982a). In a more historically specific sense, it reappears in *A Brief History of Neoliberalism* (2005a) and related essays via Harvey's claim about 'the restoration of class power' since the mid-1980s.

2. *Social domination*: second, Harvey has consistently criticised the undue power that capitalism has over people's lives, regardless of who they are. For those 'inside' the system, it confronts them as an 'invisible Leviathan': it may be *made* by humans but the system eludes human *control*, notably during crisis episodes (explored in Chapter 4 of this book). Harvey's focus on domination comes through strongly in *The Limits to Capital*, but also in a book like *The Urban Experience* (1989b). The point is sharpened in *A Brief History of Neoliberalism*, where Harvey objected to plutocracy, oligopoly and the disempowerment of the masses.[3] Later, in *The Enigma of Capital* (2010a) Harvey lamented how the goal of 'compound growth' makes almost everything a mere means to this end. But even as early as *Social Justice*, he averred that 'The capitalist market exchange economy so penetrates every aspect of social and private life that it exerts an almost tyrannical control over the life support system in which use values are embedded' (1973: 190). For the average person, capitalism locks them into a lifetime of work, of paying rent or a mortgage, of looking for each next job and so on. Metaphorically, it's a treadmill that many get thrown-off periodically.
3. *Alienation*: third, closely linked to the first two criticisms is the complaint that people are commonly severed from the very things they produce and which sustain them. This is a classic Marxist theme, elaborated by György Lukács (1885–1971) and many others. In Chapter 17 of *Seventeen Contradictions*, Harvey homes-in on 'universal alienation' as condition of capital accumulation. The implication is that people have the right to collectively and consciously reappropriate what is, in effect, already theirs.
4. *Economic devaluation of countless people, things, places and regions*: clearly, Harvey follows Marx in his insistence that capitalism thrives on constant destruction as much as creation. It routinely and widely produces unemployment, factory closures, home repossessions, bankruptcies, low tax bases for local government and so on. Perfectly useful use values are robbed of economic value and can thereby fall into disuse. Capitalism thus erodes the life conditions of millions of people at any one time. This theme runs through a book like *The Enigma*. For Harvey, what is 'mad' about this is that capitalism creates more than enough wealth to sustain everyone on Earth at a decent standard of living (Harvey, 2017a) – yet it actively creates scarcity and systematically so.
5. *Endless change and lack of stability*: Linked to this last point, although Harvey is not a cultural or political conservative, he's routinely lamented the fact that capitalism erodes ways of life that many people value. This is obvious in *The Condition of Postmodernity* (1989a), among other texts,

where Harvey's critical comments about the 'aestheticisation of politics' revealed his understanding of why people often yearn for some sort of stability in their moral, social and material worlds. Like an acid, capitalism tends to dissolve the struts and beams that lend meaning to many people's geographically grounded lives.

6. *Uneven economic development, wealth disparities and divisive geographies:* sixth, as we have seen at various points in this book, Harvey objects to capitalism's unequal treatment of people, even as he upholds their 'right to geographical difference'. For instance, his published comments about the Cowley car factory campaign in the 1980s or the Hamlet chicken factory fire in 1991 showed him to be dismayed by the low pay, poor working conditions, insecure employment, low-skilled jobs and limited government support on offer to many working people as capital searches for ways to keep costs down and maximise profits. Why, he in effect asks, is this considered acceptable while other people and places simultaneously prosper? As we have also seen in this book, Harvey has objected to the 'fetishisation of place' that capitalism engenders through its competitive logic and which seduces many workers into not making common cause with other workers, be they geographically near or far.
7. *Capitalistic 'colonisation':* In *The New Imperialism* (2003a) and *A Brief History of Neoliberalism*, among other texts, Harvey clearly objects to the expansionary tendencies of capital accumulation (which we discussed in Chapter 6). That is, people and things outside the system get forcibly drawn into it as businesses privatise everything from public land and sub-surface mineral deposits to communal water courses and rights to pollute the atmosphere (aka 'accumulation by dispossession'). But his objection to metaphorical colonisation is not only that capital expands 'outwards'. With the spread of neoliberalism, Harvey has also objected to the reduced protections from, and enhanced exposure to, the logics of accumulation that many of those *within* the system are expected to live with.
8. *Environmental degradation:* finally, since the early 1990s Harvey has been one of many Marxist critics to point to how capitalism undermines its own biophysical pre-conditions, as well as those that ordinary people need in order to live decent lives. We summarised this in Chapter 6. In Chapter 16 of *Seventeen Contradictions* and elsewhere, Harvey – without hypostatising 'nature' as some fixed, asocial domain in need of protection – notes how destructive of terrestrial, atmospheric and marine ecologies capitalism can be because it's typically 'irrational' for businesses to conserve natural resources (conservation can increase direct costs or else lead to opportunity costs in the marketplace). He further notes the drive of capitalism to commodify all aspects of nature in

search of profit, thereby generalising alienation further and squeezing out other modes of valuing the non-human world. The mix of commodification and 'externalities', he has often observed, drives all manner of 'green' political protest.

Taken together, this list of problems with capitalism (summarised in Box 8.1) is fairly confronting, though most have been variously identified by Marxists going back many decades. That none of these are original to Harvey doesn't diminish their combined importance. But, to better understand them, we need to ask two questions. First, in what senses are they immanent problems: that is, ones we recognise *as* problems using established normative ideas? Second, is it possible to refute the notion that they really are 'problems' and, if so, has Harvey sought to strengthen his own critical perspective by refuting the refutations? We address each question in turn.

Box 8.1 The eight ills of capitalism according to Harvey

1. Exploitation of the working class
2. Social domination
3. Alienation of people from their work and wider life conditions
4. Devaluation of people and places
5. Endless change and instability
6. Uneven spatio-temporal development
7. Capitalistic colonisation of non-economic domains
8. Environmental degradation and destruction

Problems 1–7 above are clearly immanent in the sense they contradict – or, for most people, offer an emaciated version of – the values of personal freedom and liberty that, rhetorically, are core to the 'ideology' of capitalism, as Harvey perceives it. The rhetorical dominance of neoliberal values has only sharpened the contradiction. But, as Harvey makes plain in *The New Imperialism* and elsewhere, they also contradict other existing conceptions of freedom and liberty pertaining to whole communities, to minority group rights, to religious identities, to national self-determination and so on. Problem 8 is immanent on rather different grounds, since rarely in capitalist societies is 'Nature' accorded rights of 'freedom' or 'liberty'. The issue here is that the normalisation of profitmaking, as a value, in tandem with a rather 'instrumental' post-Enlightenment concept of Nature, runs up against the fact of deteriorating biophysical conditions. This then imposes costs upon many capitalists, governments, localities and regions. The costs are not only monetary, and this is why activists and communities draw on other values (e.g. the 'existence rights of species') to protest the capitalist remaking of the material environment. In sum, Harvey's multi-pronged critique of capitalism has not been launched from some idealised position outside the system. Instead, it's pivoted on existing values used to justify the system, as well as other extant values in the wider society, in order to find fault with it. As noted in Chapter 7, Harvey has at times proposed an expansive conception of 'rights' – an established, elastic and resonant normative concept – in order to judge capitalism in negative terms.

However, while immanent critique has helped Harvey avoid using (i.e., imposing) utopian values in his assessment of capitalism, how convincing is the critique? That is, how difficult is it to refute Harvey's objections on other normative grounds? In the decade after his Marxist turn in the early 1970s, he flirted with the idea that analysis and critique were so intimately connected that the 'science' of Marxism bridged the supposed 'is'-'ought' gap in our reasoning. For instance, in *Social Justice* he opined that 'the act of observing *is* the act of evaluation' (1973: 15), while in *The Limits* he aspired to 'the unity of rigorous science and politics' (1982a: 37). However, since the late 1980s he's been more reticent about claiming that his Marxist theory somehow *compels* his readers to find serious fault with capitalism.

This reticence is certainly appropriate because, as Harvey has acknowledged – most fulsomely in *JNGD* – there are *multiple* recognised (often divergent) grounds on which to assess the performance of capital accumulation. While Harvey might regard many (most?) as 'ideological', in the end there is simply no objective or power-free means to determine which values ought to trump all others in our assessment of capitalist political economy. For instance, if neoliberal economist Milton Friedman were alive today he might acknowledge poverty, systemic unemployment, low paid work and so on, yet still insist that (i) billions of people benefit profoundly from 'market freedom' as both wage earners and consumers, while (ii) noting that more interventionist governments would infringe unduly on those people's freedom to keep and spend their own money, be entrepreneurial and so on. He might compare the capitalist system favourably with non-capitalist societies past and present. He might claim that those who succeed, on average, deserve to do so because of hard work and talent. He would have much heartfelt support from many people worldwide who favour a neo-Darwinian ethic of 'sink or swim' in life. Alternatively, many deep ecologists might say to Harvey that one of capitalism's key problems is its propensity to make the non-human world a means, rather than end in itself – even when it is profitable to protect Nature. The problem for them is seen as one of disenchantment and desacralisation of the living world, not only (per Harvey) its material destruction.

When it comes to questions of judgement, then, the best we can hope for is to use a mix of rhetoric, persuasion, logic and evidence to convince others that their normative axioms are somehow in need of revision in light of our own criticisms of the world. For if 'observation *is* evaluation', then why are the values informing Harvey's analysis any more or less sacrosanct or superior to anyone else's? The same question can be asked of any critic: there is no scientific proof for the 'superiority' of someone's values. The conclusion we reach is that normative dissonance is an ineliminable part of human existence. There is no once-and-for-all form of reasoning or body of evidence that will ever convince most, let alone all, people to identify certain failings in our present reality. At the time of writing, this fact has become particularly evident in contrasting views towards COVID-19 vaccines.

Even if this 'gap' between analysis and judgement did not exist, we need also to note just how general Harvey's criticisms of capitalism are. Rather like Marx's, they are universal criticisms devoid of detailed content (though potentially applicable to any number of concrete situations). For instance, it's very clear in multiple publications that Harvey compares capitalist 'freedom' unfavourably with a socialist form of freedom that he presumes to be desirable. But by failing to spell-out in any substantive detail his alternative realm of freedom, Harvey makes it hard to fend off the pragmatist's argument that 'better the devil you know' (which implies reforming capitalism is preferable to anything more ambitious or revolutionary). This speaks to the need to articulate feasible and desirable visions of the future, a theme we will turn to later in this chapter when we briefly consider roads to neo-socialism.

In light of the above discussion, we cannot fault Harvey for failing to anchor his critique of political economy in some sort of 'ultimate' normative foundations whose worth would (or somehow should) be universally recognised. We can, though, lament the overly general character of his composite critique of capitalism, even as may we recognise how widespread the eight identified problems are. And, in closing this section, we can also note one further limitation – and Harvey is far from alone among Marxists in this respect: he has barely ever bothered to formally rebut the strongest normative arguments *for* capitalism in general or its current neoliberalised, globalised version.[4] A systematic rebuttal of one's opponents, which is common practice among political theorists and moral philosophers, would make a critique of capitalism (like Harvey's) much more robust. As it stands, Harvey invites his readers to identify with a somewhat underspecified account of capitalism's ills and of his socialist remedy.

In search of general principles of justice for people and planet in a large, interconnected and differentiated world

In the previous section, we identified the sorts of things that David Harvey is against, in a normative sense. Logically, we now need to ask: what is he *for*? This question can be disaggregated into two others. First, what sorts of values should, in Harvey's view, prevail globally as normative benchmarks? Second, what political proposals might draw people to want to actualise those values? In this section, we address the first question by considering the concept of justice and then linking it to Harvey's views about rights (introduced towards the end of Chapter 7). The word justice is, of course, in the title of two of his best-known books, so we can reasonably presume it's a significant value for Harvey. What, then, *is* 'justice' and in what ways does capitalism fail to deliver it, in his eyes?

Wherever and however it's defined, and pursued, justice is a socially constituted standard specifying what is deemed to be an appropriate way to treat people (and/or the non-human world). 'Justice' then becomes a catch-all term whose contents get defined, depending on the specific context, with reference to more particular normative concepts such as needs, rights, entitlements, responsibilities, liabilities, duties, capabilities and so on. Clearly, 'no society can do without a working and workable concept of justice' (1996a: 333). Perhaps aware of the complexities, Harvey has not ventured a specific definition of social justice since his book of that name, where he maintained that 'The principle of social justice ... applies to the division of benefits and the allocation of burdens arising out of the process of undertaking joint labour' (1973: 97). He further noted in that book that justice should apply to both *outcomes* (e.g. a court ruling or a local government planning decision) and the *process of their determination*: 'we are seeking', he said, 'a specification of a just distribution justly arrived at' (1973: 98).[5] Twenty-three years later, by the time of *JNGD*, the definition had altered slightly, though the dual focus remained. We should be aiming, he said, for 'the *just production of just geographical differences*' (1996a: 5). Let's consider how Harvey framed justice in the two books (and in *Spaces of Hope*, via the rights concept) and what, if anything, we can usefully learn all these years later. Table 8.1 flags some of the dimensions of justice that Harvey touches upon.

Redistributive justice and territorial equity

In *Social Justice and City*, the main discussion of justice occurs in the first few chapters. These are Harvey's so-called liberal formulations and are

Table 8.1: The dimensions of justice

Definitions and concepts of justice	Forms of injustice to be addressed	Just outcomes and just processes of reaching them	Scales of justice	Social, geographical and temporal justice	Anthropocentric and ecocentric justice
For example equal rights for all humans	For example racial discrimination versus appropriating a community's land without consent	For example well-functioning courts that uphold the rights of socially marginal people	For example universal justice definitions versus more locally particular ones	For example justice for specific groups of people, versus justice among places, versus justice for future generations	For example justice for unborn children versus justice for threatened rhino species

rejected in the book's second half. Harvey's major focus in these early chapters was on the social and geographical *distribution* of goods, services and 'externalities' (both negative and positive) in urban society. At times, the discussion was highly sophisticated. Harvey's basic normative view was that, within a specific town, city or metropolitan region, it is unfair to permit significant socio-spatial variations in 'benefits and burdens'. He called upon analysts and professional planners to develop a much better grasp of these 'very poorly understood' (1973: 51) variations, which he summarised in an expansive concept of 'real income' (see 1973: Chapter 2). The gist of his argument was that we need to account for all sorts of things (externalities) that experts leave typically un-costed – things that urban residents enjoy or suffer as their localities change over time due to private and public decisions, such as proximity to jobs, transportation costs to get to work, the location of new major investments (like good schools), the incidence of noise pollution, levels of neighbourhood crime and so on. We then need, at least in social democracies, to use local government so as to redistribute real income in 'the urban system', as Harvey called it at the time:

> The real income of any one individual in an urban system is … susceptible to change through the decisions of others. Since these decisions rarely take his welfare into account, there is little or nothing he can do about them except (i) by changing his own location (which will cost him something) to maintain or improve his real income, or (ii) by joining together with others and exercising group or collective pressure to prevent locational decisions which diminish his real income.
>
> (Harvey, 1973: 72)

Harvey concluded that, somehow, the process of determining 'real income' distribution, as well as the actual distribution itself, needs to be more egalitarian.

This raises the question of how socio-spatial 'equity' might be defined and justified so as to reconfigure the means and ends of justice in places like the United Stated of America and United Kingdom, where Harvey has resided during his lifetime. In Chapter 3 of *Social Justice*, Harvey ventured an answer. He proposed three equity criteria (*needs*; *contribution to the common good*; and *merit*) that would guide socio-spatial redistributions to make 'real income' less skewed – noting, though, that: 'There will be enormous difficulties in elaborating them in detail, [let alone …] translating them into concrete situations' (1973: 108). In the second half of this chapter, Harvey inquired into the process of (hopefully) achieving greater territorial social justice at the scale of cities and metropolitan regions. He voiced scepticism about the possibility of redistributive 'justice, justly arrived at' because – by then a proto-Marxist – he came to regard socio-spatial inequality as constitutive of capitalism (rather than an accidental by-product; 1973: 108–116). In this light, he concluded that all attempts at redistributive justice will be superficial because they leave untouched the class relations characteristic of capitalism. Even so, he offered a helpfully clear sense of the parameters of greater territorial social justice:

> 1. The distribution of [real] income should be such that (a) the needs of the population within each territory are met, (b) resources are so allocated to maximise interterritorial multiplier effects and (c) extra resources are allocated to help overcome special difficulties stemming from the physical and social environment.
> 2. The mechanisms (institutional, organisational, political and economic) should be such that the prospects of the least advantaged territory are as great as they can possibly be.
>
> If these conditions are fulfilled, there will be a just distribution justly arrived at.
>
> (Harvey, 1973: 116–117)

The normative detail of Chapter 3 of *Social Justice and the City* remains unsurpassed by almost anything Harvey has published since; it evidenced his keen awareness of the analytical depths involved in normative justification; and it thereby set a standard he himself should perhaps have emulated in his later comments about justice, to be recounted momentarily. In a broad sense, his preoccupation with territorial justice has not dated: after all, we still live in a manifestly unequal world, even if the 'right to geographical difference' means that mitigating it should certainly never result in sameness.[6] Everyone from the United Nations to Bill Gates to Oxfam to the Pope wants to reduce acute material inequality within and between nations. But we should note the unspoken basis of Harvey's advocacy of greater spatial equality in real income fifty years ago. Implicitly, his argument referenced the sub-national and national scales and left the international scale undiscussed. That is, his argument rested on the presumption that people sharing the same political jurisdiction might be disposed to have fellow feeling for their fellow citizens. How, though, does one achieve territorial justice in a world of over 190 sovereign states, a world that's overflowing with distant strangers often ignorant of, and indifferent towards, each other?

Intersectional justice and geographical scale

When Harvey returned to the theme of justice after years of relative silence – in *JNGD* – the reference points had shifted significantly. As we saw in Chapter 2, in *Social Justice and the City* his concern was to challenge the ideological blind spots in 'status quo' theories of urban land use and planning. By contrast, in *JNGD* – so too *Spaces of Hope* – his concern was to defend Marxist analysis and politics against various critics, including many on the Left. This altered context helps us understand key shifts in the way Harvey framed justice amidst the continuities. There are four things to note.

First, where *Social Justice* pivoted on the value of equality, *JNGD* gave equal billing to the values of socio-geographical variety and of liberty (or freedom) in determining what sorts of 'differences' among people and places should be created and sustained. 'I have a certain attachment to the principle of equality', Harvey wrote, but 'this plainly cannot mean the erasure of all forms of geographical difference ... Indeed, the equality principle could just as easily imply the *proliferation of geographical differences* of a certain benign sort' (1996a: 5–6). Crucially, Harvey acknowledged that this commitment to equality, difference and liberty rebounds on the very concept of justice the trio is designed to underpin: 'radically different socio-ecological circumstances imply quite different approaches to what is or is not [considered] just' (1996a: 6).[7] This, then, suggests the need to work with *plural* notions of what counts as an injustice. But, in turn, such work requires some sort of agreed meta-principle that will allow varied (even rival) conceptions of justice to be articulated. As Harvey expressed it, 'The question of justice falls squarely into the middle of the tension between particularity and universalism' (1996a: 332).

Second, insofar as we live in an era of globe-girdling capitalism, Harvey maintained that the one unavoidable universality we have to confront with our claims to justice is our economic system. His discussion of the Hamlet factory fire (in Chapter 12 of *JNGD*), as we saw in the previous chapter, made the point that it was class inequality, hitched to gender and racial inequality, that led to 'preventable accidents' occurring in thousands of places just like Hamlet. Here, different modalities of injustice coalesced, being orchestrated by the capitalist search for profit. The upshot, for Harvey, was that contesting capitalist injustice does not entail ignoring other forms of injustice nor overlooking the sorts of 'differences' these injustices might in some way harm. Indeed, Harvey cited the then influential book by political philosopher Iris Young (1990) called *Justice and the Politics of Difference*.

Young identified *exploitation, marginalisation, powerlessness, cultural imperialism* and *violence* as the 'five faces of oppression'. Harvey's point was that while these injustices often occur independently of the logic of capitalist accumulation, in many other cases tackling exploitation and marginalisation (two very Marxist concerns) *also* involves contesting powerlessness (e.g. of slaves), cultural imperialism (e.g. suffered by First Nations peoples) and violence (e.g. inflicted by abusive men on their female partners). There are political synergies, at least some of the time.

A similar argument was made around the same time by American socialist-feminist Nancy Fraser, in her influential book *Justice Interruptus* (1997). Fraser showed how economic, cultural (and we would now add environmental, even ecological) injustices are variously distinct, intertwined and contradictory, depending on the precise circumstances.[8] Likewise, Harvey went on to claim in *The New Imperialism* (2003a) and elsewhere, that the 'internal' and 'external' injustices capitalism inflicts may have common causal roots but constitute injustices on *other* grounds too. *Conflating* these injustices is problematic, whereas *conjoining* them in a critique of capitalism is necessary.[9]

Third, this returns us to theme of universal human rights, which Harvey first highlighted strongly in the book written after *JNGD*, *Spaces of Hope*. Recall: given the universality of capitalism, Harvey insisted we need a universal normative language to call-out the harms it inflicts on all sort of different places and people. This language needs to be sufficiently compelling to attract widespread support (such as the notion of housing as a universal right, see Figures 8.1 and 8.2), but open enough to allow 'for contestation within and between differences, rather than suppressing them' (1996a: 433).[10] Though he doesn't quite say it, note that since the late 1990s 'rights' has been, for Harvey, the 'basement' concept of social justice upon which all others necessarily sit. It includes the right to some sort of equality among humans *and* the right to be dissimilar to other people and places. Even so, Harvey noted the risk of imposing rights definitions on others who may reject their universal applicability. His view of such a rejectionist stance was, though, both compelling and withering: 'the repudiation of [universal] standards of evaluation undermines judgements of equal worth as much as it undermines judgements of inferior worth. It is therefore destructive of the very goals that arguments of respect for particularity are supposed to support' (1996a: 351).

Finally, the question arises as to what ontological soil might make universal rights claims a compelling normative flag for otherwise different people to rally around in the twenty-first century. Harvey's answer, in our view, is not wholly convincing, even as we understand his rationale for

Figure 8.1. Housing as a universal right, I. Demonstrators in Los Angeles in protest over rent controls in 2021.

Figure 8.2. Housing as a universal right, II. Demonstrators in Spain protest against evictions in 2021.

proposing it. In *Spaces of Hope* and various publications since, he's anchored his universal rights claims in our biological, psychological and social 'species being'. In the face of all manner of contingent and shifting differences in peoples' identities, preferences, experiences, locations and so on, he reverts to a secular humanism that accords all people equal value *prima facie* and which highlights their shared capacities and potentials. The problem is that his humanism is necessarily abstract, to the point of being bloodless and scarcely human at all. For instance, at one point he notes that 'we have some species-specific capacities and powers, arguably the most important of which are our ability to alter and adapt our forms of social organization ..., to build a long historical memory through language, and ... to build all sorts of adjuncts ... to improve our capacities to see, hear and feel beyond the physiological limitations given by our own bodily constitution' (2000a: 207–208).

Claims like this may be true, but they verge on being trite and can scarcely serve to galvanise a global movement in favour of a more just world. They form thin glue to unite people who may be divided by custom, religion, identity, morality, language, history and so on. Solidarity among people, so as to promote a mix of socio-geographic equality and liberty, requires stronger bonds than a general sense of our shared humanity. One alternative would have been for Harvey to work with a 'thick' concept of universal human *capabilities*, following the Indian economic philosopher Amaryta Sen. He could then, perhaps, have followed Nancy Fraser's lead and undertaken a systemic presentation of how both capitalist and non-capitalist forms of injustice together diminish the capabilities of otherwise different people occupying various locations across the globe. The general 'right to geographical difference' and the specific 'right to the city', both framed by the wider concept of universal human rights, could then have been shown to be all about enhancing human capabilities through a judicious mix of equality and freedom (including local-to-global redistributions of the sought Harvey explored fifty years ago).[11]

Taking stock

We conclude this section by doing what Harvey has not himself done: namely, pull together the threads of his critique of capitalism (covered in the previous section) with his positive agenda for justice. There are, we suggested above, eight widespread ills of capitalism if one reads across Harvey's work. They are recognised as 'ills', we suggested, because they contravene established definitions of key normative concepts like needs, wants, deserts, freedom, fairness and (Harvey's favoured notion) rights. But Harvey wishes to radicalise some of these concepts, not rest content with, say, neoliberal definitions of them. In this light, his concern with 'redistributive territorial justice' in Part I of *Social Justice and the City* is, by his own estimation in Part II of that book, merely 'reformist'. At best, it would ameliorate some, but by no means all, of the problems with capitalism adumbrated by Harvey since 1973 (and by us in Chapter 6). It would also leave untouched other forms of injustice irreducible to, if contingently connected with, the dynamics of accumulation.

This is why Harvey has called for a broader, more ambitious commitment to justice. In the final chapter of *Spaces of Hope*, beyond the geographical rights already mentioned, he suggests nine other universal rights that all people should enjoy, regardless of their differences (Harvey, 2000a: 248–252). They include 'the right to life chances' (e.g. access to sufficient, nutritious food), the 'right to political association', 'the right to a decent and healthy living environment' and 'the rights of labourers in the process of economic production'. Though he offered no real detail, presumably to uphold these universal rights in a just manner would require the elimination of the capitalist system, the cause of the eight earlier itemised ills. That is, these problems are signs of systematic injustice as judged in light of Harvey's list of rights.

Ending the rule of capital is, perhaps, a laughably challenging proposition – yet in his publications since *JNGD* Harvey has talked frequently of the need to do exactly that. This raises a set of very practical questions, such as 'is capitalism today in effect too large and complex to be superseded?' And 'what concrete measures would a more just political economy seek to operationalise?'. The early communist activist-intellectuals, like Lenin and Trotsky, were very preoccupied with these important questions of political organising and political programme. Harvey himself once wisely noted that

> a global anti-capitalist movement is unlikely to emerge without some animating vision of what is to be done and why. A double blockage exists: the lack of an alternative vision prevents the formation of an oppositional movement, while the absence of such a movement precludes the articulation of an alternative.
>
> (Harvey, 2010a: 227)

Yet as we'll now see, and somewhat curiously perhaps, Harvey hasn't had much to say about the creation or content of a new form of socialism. What are we to make of this oversight?

Getting real, politically? In pursuit of neo-socialism in a 'post-socialist' era

While the term socialism is not wholly synonymous with Marxism, in a normative sense Marxism is usually identified with socialism and, more particularly, with that variant called communism. The words signify political programmes that seek to operationalise justly universal values that capitalism routinely fails to uphold. These programmes would instantiate a new 'operating space' for human agency, institute new social relationships, progressively remake the material world and, in the end, foster new modes of self, other and world among humans. Of course, socialism and communism have largely fallen into disrepute, not least because of the serious political and economic failings of the former USSR and Eastern Bloc countries like Bulgaria prior to the fall of Communist governments in 1989–1991. China is still nominally 'Communist', but substantively it's now capitalist in a number of profound ways (see Chapter 6). Meanwhile, other countries that have – or recently had – socialist or communist leadership (e.g. Cuba, North Korea or Venezuela) are rarely seen as role models by the rest of the world.

In short, we live in 'post-socialist' times where talk of a radically new political economy is not taken seriously in most (especially the wealthiest) countries. That former US Presidential candidate Bernie Sanders used the word 'socialism' during his election campaigns was, perhaps, the exception that proves the rule. Indeed, were one to ask the average person alive today what the words socialism or communism mean, they would almost certainly be unable able to give you a sensible answer. The challenge for Marxists and fellow travellers, then, is to infuse one or both terms with new, compelling meaning and to popularise the associated political programmes. That way, capitalist nostrums may see their legitimacy seriously eroded. Since the term 'communism' seems to us irredeemably tainted after the twentieth-century horrors of Stalinism and the Khmer Rouge, the term socialism is the better candidate for renewal – perhaps updated as 'neo-socialism' or by giving existing couplets such as 'liberal socialism' or 'democratic socialism' a new lease on life.

A hazy vision of the future?

Unsurprisingly, Harvey has used the term 'socialism' repeatedly since 1973 and the term 'communism' to a lesser extent. What is surprising, though, is his failure to properly define the words in all but one instance. He seems to have assumed that their meaning is self-evident, sometimes implying that they're synonyms (e.g.: 'The only way to resist capitalism and transform society towards *socialism* is through a global struggle ... [T]he task of the *communist* movement is to find ways, against all odds, to bring together various highly differentiated and often local movements into some kind of commonality of purpose', Harvey, 2000a: 39–40, emphasis added). We can deduce from his comments about justice that socialism/communism, for Harvey, would forge a suitable mix of equality, solidarity and liberty all framed by arrangements that allow much greater collective control over 'structures' that might otherwise unduly dominate peoples' lives. But such general deductions are not too helpful, for obvious reasons. Luckily, though, we do have one thing to fasten on to. Secreted in the final chapter of *The Enigma of Capital* is a definition of socialism in contradistinction to communism. 'Socialism', Harvey wrote,

> aims to democratically *manage* and regulate capitalism in ways that calm its excesses and redistribute its benefits for the common good. It is about spreading the wealth around ... while basic needs – such as education, health care and even housing – are provided by the state out of reach of market forces ...
>
> Communism, on the other hand, seeks to *displace* capitalism.
>
> (Harvey, 2010a: 224–225, emphasis added)

In light of this, because Harvey so frequently advocates the supersession of capitalism, he is by his own lights a communist rather than a socialist. What, then, would a twenty-first-century communist world look like? Again, as with his reticence to define key political terms, Harvey has also been shy about detailing an alternative future. There have been two all-too-brief exceptions. First, near the end of *The Enigma*, Harvey identified some 'general guiding norms' for a post-capitalist world, including 'respect for nature, radical egalitarianism in social relations, institutional arrangements based in some sense of common interests, democratic administrative procedures (as opposed to the monetised shams that now exist), labour processes organised by the direct producers, daily life as the free exploration of new kinds of social relations and living arrangements, ... [and] self-realisation in service to others' (2010a: 230–231). Second, the assiduous reader of Harvey will eventually discover the three-page Epilogue to *Seventeen Contradictions and the End of Capitalism*, where he goes a bit further. However, perhaps keen not to alienate readers who might see them as 'old school', he does not describe his seventeen 'mandates' as socialist, let alone communist. They are simply 'post-capitalist'. We reproduce them in Box 8.2.

Box 8.2 Ideas for political praxis

'We should strive for a world in which …'

1. Direct provision of basic goods takes precedence over profit-maximisation
2. A new means of exchange (i.e. money) is created that cannot afford certain people private power
3. The state stops protecting private property and instead the commons are managed by popular assemblies
4. The appropriation of social power by private individuals is denounced as pathological behaviour
5. Class is abolished – associated producers will decide together what, how and when to produce, and for what common needs
6. Daily life is slowed down – there is more free time
7. Associated populations communicate their needs – thereby regulating production
8. New technologies liberate social labour from unnecessary work, freeing up time and diminishing the ecological footprint of human activities
9. Residual technical divisions of labour are disassociated from social divisions of labour; administrative and policing functions are rotated; we end the rule of experts
10. Means of production are handed to popular associations
11. There is the greatest possible diversification of ways of living and of being, and the free and orderly movement of people across and within territories is guaranteed
12. Inequalities in material provision are abolished, other than those consistent with the principle 'from each according to their capacities, to each according to their need'
13. There is no distinction between work for others and reproductive work; social labour is embedded in the household and in the commune
14. There is equal entitlement to education, health care, housing, food security, basic goods and transport
15. The global economy converges on zero growth
16. There is maximum regard for the protection of ecosystems; we recycle nutrients, energy and physical matter; we become re-enchanted with the natural world
17. The end of alienation, a new sense of collective well-being, empathy for different ways of living, recognition that everyone is equally worthy of dignity and respect

Source: Adapted from Harvey (2014a: 294–297).

The thing to note is that the mandates address the eight principal ills associated with capitalism and (if we parse them) call for the institutionalisation of (i) equality of opportunity and liberty of the person (placing a ceiling on permissible levels of inequality and limiting the exercise of private power), (ii) greater political and economic democracy, (iii) use of science and technology for wide public benefit, including more free time for all, (iv) a low growth economy that does not inflict rapid change on society and environment, (v) respect for and encouragement of socio-cultural 'difference', without undue conflict among individuals or groups and (vi) a concern to protect the non-human world so that it's not subordinated to production imperatives. Though he doesn't do it in the Epilogue, all these things can be phrased as entailing 'positive' (freedom to) and 'negative' (freedom from) rights.

There's no doubt that many people would find these six 'baskets' of proposed rights-based changes very appealing. As suggested above, we might use the term 'neo-socialism' to badge them. But equally, those currently possessed of considerable economic wealth, political power and high cultural status almost certainly would oppose at least half of them, without a second thought.[12] Harvey has frequently acknowledged the inertia exerted by existing structures, norms, practices and identities. For instance, near the end of *JNGD*, he noted that

> A political program which successfully combats any form of oppression has to face up to the real difficulty of a loss of identity on the part of those who have been victims of that oppression … [T]here are subtle ways in which identity, once acquired, can, by precisely virtue of its relative durability, seek out the conditions (including the oppressions) necessary for its own sustenance.
>
> (Harvey, 1996a: 364)

So, the inertia is two-fold: not only do the powerful have much to lose, so too do some of those who might otherwise have good reason to challenge capitalism and the other injustices it feeds off. Given Harvey's recognition of both sources of inertia, it's all the stranger he's had little time for the practicalities of political strategy. A stepwise, concrete roadmap is how one seeks to push beyond any status quo. Harvey's one paper about a specific political measure (housing rent control) was a critique of 'liberal formulations' (Harvey, 1981b), set within his wider caution about academics working through the capitalist state to inform public policy (Harvey, 1974b). Let us now point briefly to the hard but necessary political thinking about 'real utopias' (Wright, 2010) Harvey might usefully have done by way of some of those who've sought to do it.

Thinking through the practicalities of creating a more just world: in search of real utopias

Real utopias comprise goals and strategies that can direct us from a troubled present into a brighter future.[13] They are, in the felicitous words of political historian Ira Katznelson (2020: 534), 'not abstractions but, rather, specific institutional designs, bundles of incentives and disincentives, with normative purpose'. The Marxist sociologist Erik Wright coined the term 'real utopias' over a decade ago. Towards the end of his life, Wright sought to flesh-out the parameters for, and some of the content of, these achievable dreams – notably in his big book *Envisioning Real Utopias* (2010) and his luminous, pithy, posthumous work *How to be an Anti-Capitalist in the Twenty-First Century* (2019). We now highlight some of the advantages of his real utopias project.

Wright mapped-out possible modes of political response to the maladies caused by capitalism, using the very apt analogy of a game. Citing soccer and rugby, Wright suggested we 'think of society as a game: social conflicts can occur over what game to play, over the variable rules of the game or over what moves within a specific set of rules' (2019: 54). This three-level approach is captured in Table 8.2. Wright then identified five ideal-typical political stances towards capitalism. 'Smashing' is the logic of revolutionaries; 'dismantling' is equally radical, but aims for a 'long revolution' by using the capitalist state to introduce and normalise elements of socialism over time; 'taming' also uses the capitalist state, but is reformist in the Keynesian 'welfare democracy' sense and all about managing problems; 'resisting' seeks to affect capitalists and governments through voluble protest, rather

Table 8.2: A matrix of political forms and goals within and against the 'game' of capitalism

Game metaphor	Form of political conflict	Stakes in the conflict	Logic of transformation
What game to play	Revolutionary versus counter-revolutionary	Capitalism versus socialism	Ruptural
Rules of the game	Reformist versus reactionary	Varieties of capitalism	Symbiotic
Moves in the game	Interest group politics	Immediate economic concerns	Interstitial

Source: Reproduced from Wright (2019: 55).

Table 8.3: A matrix of political modalities within and against the 'game' of capitalism

		Objective of struggle	
		Neutralising harms	**Transcending structures**
Level of the system	**The game itself**		Smashing
	Rules of the game	Taming	Dismantling
	Moves in the game	Resisting	Escaping

Source: Reproduced from Wright (2019: 55).

than trying to capture state power; and 'escaping' involves decoupling from capitalism as much as possible through initiatives of self-provisioning and self-governing. The five political stances are mapped-onto Wright's game analogy in Table 8.3.

Wright's typology of stances can perhaps help us understand why Harvey has had so little to say about political strategy. It seems to us that the die was largely cast fifty years ago. By the end of *Social Justice*, Harvey had essentially abandoned 'reform' measures as mere sticking plasters and opted instead for revolution. He was, in Wright's terms, a 'smasher'. Over the years, Harvey has called overtly for revolution several times: most strikingly in 2011 in a UK broadsheet newspaper (*The Independent*), no less (Harvey, 2011a). The bright-line reform-revolution distinction is a longstanding feature of Harvey's work. Unfortunately, it appears to have blinded him to two things: (i) possible *synergies* between incremental and more transformative kinds of political change and (ii) close consideration of the difference between what might seem politically *desirable* versus what is practically *possible*. As geographer Philip Cooke once expressed it, perhaps too harshly, Harvey's rather underspecified focus on a post-capitalist *future* released him from the need to do hard political thinking in the *present*: 'from the heights of Olympus', Cooke (1987: 412) noted sarcastically, 'it may seem wise to put-off doing the merely difficult while the near-impossible is sitting there waiting to be accomplished'.[14] In the very recent past, Harvey has cooled on the idea of 'smashing' capitalism, noting in *The Anti-Capitalist Chronicles* (Harvey, 2020a) that a sudden, revolutionary 'exit' from capitalism would in fact be disastrous because the majority of the world's population relies on successful capital circulation to survive. But Harvey's eleventh-hour shift to (after Wright) a stance of 'dismantling' – and make no mistake, Harvey still wants capitalism gone – has not been accompanied by explicit political strategising.

Wright's key insight meanwhile was that to get to the point of 'smashing' capitalism, realistically one should aim to 'erode' it via the other four strategic stances in a learning process. He noted that what we call 'capitalism' can never be 'pure' and endlessly hybridises with other things, while having the capacity for much internal variety (e.g. property rights in land or stocks can be commanded not only by profit-driven individuals but by ethically minded *groups*). This, Wright argued, always leaves space for political manoeuvre, a space explored brilliantly by Julie Graham and Kathy Gibson in multiple works after their ground-breaking book *The End of Capitalism (As We Knew It)* (1996). To quote Wright:

> Social systems, in general, are better thought of as *ecosystems* or loosely connected interacting parts than as *organisms* in which all the parts serve a function. In such an ecosystem, it is possible to introduce an alien species of fish not found 'naturally' in the lake. Some alien species will instantly get gobbled-up. Others may survive in some small niche … But occasionally an alien species may thrive and eventually replace the dominant species. The strategic vision of eroding capitalism imagines introducing the most vigorous varieties of emancipatory species of noncapitalist economic activity into the ecosystem of capitalism … and figuring out ways of expanding their habitats.
>
> (Wright, 2019: 60–61, emphasis added)[15]

One such 'emancipatory species', which bridges between 'dismantling' and 'taming', is a proposed unconditional basic income (UBI) for all people (or at least all adults). The UBI guarantees a minimum income without compelling people to enter the labour market, though they would be free to work, invest, be entrepreneurial etc. as they wish. A UBI would be funded through general taxation, would seek to eliminate poverty and would give people the choice to work less or undertake more meaningful forms of work (including voluntary/unpaid work). Clearly, the UBI is a redistributive proposal predicated on the values of equality and solidarity so as to uphold, via the national state, people's right to a minimum material standard of living. It equalises for the bad luck, mishaps and injustices many people would (and do) otherwise suffer in the world of paid work.[16] It tackles economic inequality to a degree, and also the status inequities certain groups suffer via the labour market. In theory, the UBI could be applied globally, with income adjusted to local costs and definitions of 'material need', and with richer nations paying into a world UBI fund to assist the poorest countries. The UBI idea illustrates the sort of appealing thinking that might shunt societies in a post-capitalist direction over time (see Wright, 2010: 217–222, 2019: 73–75, 108–109).[17]

As noted, Harvey hasn't burrowed into specific policy ideas like the UBI. But if, like Wright and others, he had done during his career, there's a further challenge: positing *desirable* proposals likely to inspire millions does not guarantee the *feasibility* of those proposals. Here, the insights of another analyst critical of 'unreal utopias', British geographer-cum-sociologist Andrew Sayer, are instructive. In his brilliant book *Radical Political Economy: A Critique* (1995), Sayer offered a guide to 'thinking realistically' about making significant, deliberate changes to capitalism. He advocated the use of decompositional logic, thought-experiments and counter-factual reasoning to anticipate two potential barriers to feasible change: (i) negative unintended consequences and (ii) countervailing forces triggered by one set of changes that inhibit intended outcomes. Decompositional logic, for Sayer, avoids elisions: for instance, he asked if radically expanding collective ownership of the means of commodity production would eliminate the need for the coordinating function of market exchange or significantly reduce technical and social divisions of labour. For him, clinical abstraction is essential: 'If economies are not seamless wholes of internally related parts, then parts of capitalist society may operate in similar fashion in post-capitalist societies, and we can analyse such possibilities' (1995: 26). Thought experiments and counter-factual scenarios allow a conceptual testing of political programmes prior to attempts to actually implement them. They take the form of 'If we remove *this*, and substitute for *that*, then what is likely to happen?'.[18] In Sayer's view, which still seems valid to us, too few Left political economists seriously test their ideas in these ways. This can lull them into what Friedrich Hayek (1988) famously called 'the fatal conceit' of presuming (naively) a problem-free future. At the least – and this indicates the sheer complexity of the challenge – Marxists like Harvey would need to follow Sayer's advice in respect of how proposed changes to the economy, modes of political participation, modes of government at all scales, the private realm, the size of the military, the scope of individual liberties, institutions of civil society and the news media might intersect. This would provide a realistic, wide-angle view on the three 'game levels' in Wright's matrix so as to show people a 'better game' without too much wishful thinking.

In closing, we should note that Harvey has, at times, made much of the power of imaginative thought about future possibilities. But his version has lacked the rigour and focus advocated by Sayer and Wright. The best example is part three of *Spaces of Hope*, where Harvey explored the potential of utopian thought, casting himself as an 'insurgent architect' (2000a: 133–197, also the Appendix 'Edilia', a short work of fiction, pp. 257–281). Despite the analogy, the reader is not provided with a plan of how one removes (or renovates) the existing 'house' and erects a new one on old ground. Instead,

Harvey engaged in a long and abstract discussion of the tension between a 'utopianism of process' versus a 'utopianism of spatial form'. His point was that the geographical expression of any progressive aspirations must not entirely freeze the social relations characteristic of a post-capitalist order. A spatio-temporal utopia of tomorrow, he argued, must somehow preserve space for liberty, change and variety without undermining agreed standards of justice. The point is well-taken. But it's a long way from helping us see how an 'optimism of the intellect' can translate into Wright's 'real utopias' or Sayer's 'radical realism'.

Conclusion

With this chapter, we have now concluded our presentation and assessment of the substantive content of David Harvey's version of Marxism. We've explored normative issues under three headings: *problem identification* (critique), *evaluative standards* (the quest for justice) and *future alternatives* (a feasible and appealing political programme). If much of Harvey's career has involved filling 'empty boxes' in Marx's thinking, then it's clear that he's left many normative boxes relatively content-free. His strength has been explanatory-diagnostic more than anticipatory-utopian or political-programmatic. As he rightly noted in *Social Justice and the City*: 'The intellectual task is to identify real choices as they are immanent in an existing situation and to devise ways of validating or invalidating these choices through action' (1973: 149). Yet, in his voluminous work since that book, we've seen that Harvey's given us little sense of what these choices might be or what strategic goals might orientate them, though he's offered glimpses of what values will underpin them. No thinker can do it all, of course – but we might nonetheless wonder why Harvey has not been more of a 'restless analyst' when it comes to normative issues so as to robustly extend the house of Marxist analysis and practice. This said, some of his critics will no doubt be grateful he's chosen not to be even more 'meta' in his intellectual ambitions during his long career.

In the next and final substantive chapter of this book, we offer a different angle of vision on David Harvey. We shift focus from the content of his Marxism towards his post-2007 decision to communicate his ideas outside the academy. Harvey's public turn, if we can call it that, raises important questions – extending beyond his work – about the means and ends of communicating radical Leftist thought in the 2020s. However incisive or potentially compelling such thought might be, how does the present context affect the way radical ideas are received in the wider world?

Further reading

Harvey, D. (1973). Social justice and spatial systems. In *Social Justice and the City* (pp. 96–116). Johns Hopkins.

Harvey, D. (1996a). Class relations, social justice and the political geography of difference. In *Justice, Nature and the Geography of Difference* (pp. 334–365). Blackwell.

Harvey, D. (2000a). Appendix: Edilia, or 'make of it what you will'. In *Spaces of Hope* (pp. 252–281). Edinburgh University Press.

Harvey, D. (2017a). The madness of economic reason. In *Marx, Capital and the Madness of Economic Reason* (pp. 172–206). Profile Books.

Wright, E. O. (2019). *How to Be an Anti-Capitalist in the Twenty-First Century*. Verso.

Notes

1. As political theorists have argued for decades, the elemental political questions pertain to (i) how to make collective decisions in a society about shared values and goals, (ii) how to achieve social order, (iii) how to ensure the legitimacy of any achieved political order and (iv) what forms of power and even coercion will be deemed necessary to institute an acceptable political dispensation. Broadly, democratic politics are comfortable with questioning the answers to all four questions over time, while more autocratic politics tend to fix the parameters for political thought and action so that change is more difficult to achieve. In practice, of course, most democracies are too large and complex to be deliberative in character, with elections being the periodic means of holding those who wield political power to account. A mixture of low voter turnouts and ill-informed citizens bombarded by political soundbites and 'infotainment' indicate widespread problems with representative democracies today. Many have claimed we now live in largely 'post-political' times, in which thin publics and a 'wild' public domain prevail (see Chapter 9). It is doubtful, though, there was ever a golden era of 'deep democracy' we can use as a historical benchmark.
2. In this chapter, we are using the term 'value' in its conventional sense as a moral or ethical standard that some people agree to observe in their behaviour as opposed to the technical Marxist definition of value summarised in Chapter 3 of this book.
3. For instance, even today – a period when China is supposedly on the rise and the United States of America in decline – it turns out that US-based transnational corporations dominate most products and industries, including search engines (Google); web browsers (Google Chrome); smartphone and tablet operating systems (Google Android, Apple iOS); online advertising (Facebook, Google); desktop and laptop operating systems (Microsoft Windows, macOS); office software (Microsoft Office, Google Workspace); cloud infrastructure and

services (Amazon, Microsoft, Google, IBM); social media platforms (Facebook, Twitter, Snapchat); transportation (Uber, Lyft); business networking (Microsoft); streaming video (Google, Netflix, Hulu); streaming audio (Google, YouTube, Apple); and computer chips (Intel, Nvidia, AMD) – among other products and services. This allows a social and geographical concentration of wealth and power that other countries have to fight extremely hard to dislodge.

4. Such arguments are made at the level of capitalism in general (regardless of its specific forms of operation) and at the level of certain varieties of it. For instance, neoliberals like Milton Friedman argued that a properly competitive capitalist system offers people ample choice in the market at affordable prices, with the corresponding 'night watchman' state giving people space to exercise considerable personal liberty. Meanwhile, Keynesians argue that a robustly regulated capitalism allows technical and social progress to occur via the market, but with governments protecting citizens from the negative externalities caused by cost shifting, oligopolies, undue trade protectionism, in-work poverty etc. that arise if capitalism is allowed to evolve unchecked. All pro-capitalist arguments point to the extraordinary feats of innovation and productivity that result from private firms competing for market share, along with the real freedom of choice many enjoy in both labour and consumer markets.
5. Rephrased, Harvey meant that to arrive at *substantive* justice we must also institute *procedural* justice across all arenas where justice principles should apply.
6. One way to think about this is to say Harvey favours 'complex equality' in a future society, where 'unwanted differences', like extreme wealth and poverty, are eliminated but where equal rights to be different in other ways prevail. This implies a world where certain boundaries can be maintained between different arenas of social recognition, reward, regard and valuation. Without such boundaries, there is the risk that one or other arena may come to dominate, or squeeze-out, other ones over time, which then leads to new perceived injustices. The American social democratic philosopher Michael Walzer has made this argument about 'spheres of justice' for many years, though without Harvey's radical anti-capitalism. Similarly, the late Pierre Bourdieu's influential research into 'fields' and their specific forms of 'capital' offers a plural view of power and in/justice.
7. Whether Harvey is aware of it or not, this acknowledgement of how procedural justice deeply affects what counts, variously, as substantive justice among people and places echoes political philosopher John Rawls' famous elaboration of what he called the 'difference principle', according to which just distributions of wealth and income need not necessarily be equal 'but must be to everyone's advantage' (Rawls, 1971: 61). The principle can apply to non-economic phenomena, and for Rawls, the right of people to determine collective arrangements in a society always trumps rights attendant on the *outcomes* of those arrangements. Harvey cited Rawls here and there in *Social Justice and the City*, with Rawls' *A Theory of Justice* having appeared to great fanfare two years before the publication of the former, in 1971.

8. Environmental justice pertains to harms inflicted on people by virtue of their immediate environmental conditions, whereas ecological justice pertains to upholding the rights of non-human entities.
9. One useful way to conceptualise all this is in terms of *domains* and *scales* of justice. In a generic sense, domains are relatively well-defined and stable arenas where specific forms of justice are required to address specific sorts of power relations, risks of harm and so on. For instance, the private home is an arena, as is the institution of marriage or any number of work places. Justice may be dispensed formally or informally, depending on the arenas, and could involve everything from the police and courts to family interventions and religious decree. Domains can vary in their spatial scales and the temporal scales at which injustices arising within them need to be considered. For instance, private companies operating according to capitalist logics can be found everywhere, whereas, say, the Amish way of life is far more localised and sporadic. Likewise, the 'environmental externalities' created by capitalist firms are now very long term indeed, whereas the currently underpaid female Australian chief operating officer is suffering gender discrimination in need of immediate redress. Domains and scales can intersect in complicated and contradictory ways, creating a matrix of possibilities for the forms that injustice and its redress can take.
10. We might say that 'difference' and 'otherness' have three different, but related, normative functions in Harvey's thinking since *JNGD*: 'bad' difference is to be eliminated, other differences (e.g. one's sexuality) are the basis of justice claims but, in time, these differences might evolve to escape the oppressions that have shaped their content in the first place so as to 'freely flourish'. An atomised approach to injustice – treating each as a separate problem to be tackled – is, for Harvey, regressive and can only produce limited forms of justice (e.g. as with the recognition politics of what's sometimes called 'neoliberal multiculturalism').
11. Not everyone would agree on the need for some sort of humanism to ground a universal normative concept like rights or other general justice concepts like recognition and needs. For instance, in his celebrated work, Rawls sought after a meta-framework for determining the how and what of justice, rather than a universal justice principle that would somehow accommodate all others. Rawls was, like Harvey, a universalist in the normative sense but this was predicated on the recognition that the lives of otherwise different people are co-constituted and co-implicated. This fact, in Rawls' view, obliged societies to seek for ways to negotiate in an orderly fashion among diverse values and behaviours without allowing any one of them to dominate others. This, perhaps, is our global challenge today, whether in a reformist or more revolutionary cast. Nations must find ways to cooperate for all sorts of reasons, which requires shared procedural means to negotiate outcomes.
12. There's also the perennial problems of self-interest, ethnic hatred, apathy, greed, fanaticism, dogma etc., which threaten to derail even the most well-intended plans of neo-socialists.

13. A body of largely American socialist academics have advanced the 'real utopias' project over the last fifteen years, with the late Erik Wright the most prominent. See: www.realutopias.org/the-real-utopias-project/. This project seeks to unblock the elemental tension characterising all forms of radical analysis of the present. As Albena Azmanova nicely expressed it, there is 'a tension between political realism and normative stringency that haunts social critique. On the one hand, the higher we set our normative standards, the more we lose grip on political reality at the cost of our capacity to address the urgent issues of the day. If, however, on the other hand we weaken the stringency of our normative criteria, we enhance the political relevance of the model only at the expense of its critical potential' (2014: 357).
14. One could add that Harvey has said next to nothing about the practicalities and complexities of revolution either, glossing rapid and long revolutions, social and political revolutions, civic and military revolutions and so on.
15. Harvey employs exactly the same metaphor in his *Madness* book (2017a: 46) but, as noted above, doesn't give much attention to 'niches' and 'species' that might render capitalism more 'sane'. In his *Seventeen Contradictions* book, Harvey opts for the less suitable analogy of a ship, where capitalism is the 'engine' (2014a: 9) powering the propellers. Aside from the fact that Harvey pays scant attention to the various rooms and systems beyond the engine room, this analogy does not speak to how capitalism insinuates itself into *all* parts of the 'ship' (as opposed to simply moving those unchanging parts forward in space and time).
16. Looking ahead, it would also help mitigate the serious negative impacts of (i) climate change and (ii) technology-induced obsolescence of many current jobs.
17. Some version of the basic income idea has been around for a very long time. For instance, see the edited book by Philippe van Parijs (1982) *Arguing for Basic Income*. In post-apartheid South Africa, a country chock full of poverty, something like a UBI has been around for years and is explored in anthropologist James Ferguson's (2015) fine book *Give a Man a Fish*. Note that in terms of the normative meta-ideal of 'justice, justly arrived at', implementing a UBI proposal in many countries would require serious political reform to allow ordinary people greater political rights to have their views reflected in government. Indeed, we might say that the first aim of any political struggle against capitalism is to assert the 'primacy of the political', so that the economic logic and institutions of capitalism are rolled-back into a much smaller overall operating space. It is worth remembering that, currently, the majority of the world's people do not live in democracies, even though over 90 nations officially have 'democratic' political systems. Within 'real' democracies, therefore, a renewed Left has to sink its roots in civil society, forge a mass base to underpin effective political parties and gain control of state power. The sort of neo-socialism Marxists ought to strive for requires a democracy that's at once wide and deep. Political responsibility, justification and accountability thereby

come to saturate the body social. Without this, it would be well-nigh impossible to implement and sustain radical policies like tough anti-trust laws, sharp limits on private intellectual property, a move towards public infrastructure of all kinds, strict regulation of finance capital, limits on the production and consumption of 'frivolous' commodities that have negative environmental impacts, huge expansion of various 'commons' and so on.

18. Sayer's menu of questions, to be answered using clinical abstraction, thought experiments and counter-factuals are: (i) does capitalism necessarily cause the problems in question?; (ii) is it unique in that respect or would other systems generate the same problems?; (iii) can the problems conceivably be avoided?; and (iv) would resolving the problems create others equally as bad or worse? (1995: 37).

9

Marxism within and beyond the academy

Communicating critical thought in a 'post-public' era

Going public; The importance of speaking (out) in public; The idea of 'the public' and the realities of a 'post-public' era; The limits to Marxist reason and rhetoric; Conclusion

Since the turn of the century, David Harvey has undergone something of a 'public turn'. Much of his writing, and a fair bit of his speaking, has sought out wider audiences beyond the university realm where he made his name between the 1960s and 1990s. Today, Harvey might even be said to be a 'public intellectual' of sorts, and a global one too – albeit less well known than the likes of Noam Chomsky, Richard Dawkins, Naomi Klein or Steven Pinker. This is something of an achievement for a Marxist, especially in the United States of America (where Marxism has had little traction outside universities for decades). It's fitting that Harvey's public turn has occurred since his move from Baltimore to New York, a city once famous for its public intellectuals (though most of them, it must be said, anti-Marxist!). It's also fitting that Harvey has worked (since 2001) for one of the US' oldest public universities. Founded in 1847, the City University of New York (CUNY) seeks to offer the widest possible civic benefit through the teaching and research conducted by its academic staff.

In this final chapter, we assess the efficacy of Harvey's public turn. Like any Marxist studying the present, the changing empirical form of Harvey's object of interest (capitalism) has a very material bearing on the degree to which Marxism enjoys any sort of wider credibility beyond those already persuaded of its merits. That is, the object affects the conditions of reception

DOI: 10.4324/9780429028120-9

of the critique launched by Harvey and fellow Marxists – or, put differently, the degree to which a wider public audience feels aggrieved by capitalism at any given time affects its receptivity to a negative assessment of the system. We suggest that critics like Harvey today operate in a world that, paradoxically, makes them at once indispensable voices yet unlikely to be heard, let alone taken seriously, by more than a tiny minority of global humanity. This paradox does not make attempts to popularise Marxism – classical or otherwise – a waste of time. But it does (to use one of Harvey's favourite metaphors) place sharp limits on its ability to change thought and action in our extremely troubled world. At present, it seems to us that Harvey's attempt to keep the flame of Marxism alive outside the academy is both important, yet akin to holding a candle in a strong wind during a seemingly endless night. This reflects the extremely difficult historical-geographical conditions that Harvey and other Marxists find themselves operating in today. Since 2008, neoliberal capitalism has been remarkably resistant to the global financial crisis and other negative effects of endless accumulation. Like the proverbial cat, it seems to have at least nine lives (Plehwe, Slobodian and Mirowski, 2020).

Note that in this chapter we say a *lot* about the wider context in which Harvey's acts of public communication occur, in part because he has said relatively little about it – even though it has a significant bearing on the efficacy of his 'public turn'.

Going public

'Capitalism will never fall on its own. It will have to be pushed' – so wrote Harvey in *The Enigma of Capital and the Crises of Capitalism* (2010a: 260). He continued: 'The accumulation of capital will never cease. It will have to be stopped. The capitalist class will never willingly surrender its power. It will have to be dispossessed' (2010a: 260). This stark political message was, of course, more than rhetorical. It was, at some level, designed to inspire political practice. This is true of all Harvey's normative pronouncements over the years. But, as we noted in Chapter 8, political practice only occurs if there are social actors persuaded by certain arguments about the state of world, founded on credible evidence and resonant definitions of value-concepts (such as equality and justice) that align with the actors' experiences. And to reach such actors, anyone serious about translating analysis into practice needs access to various channels of social communication. As we noted towards the end of Chapter 2, Harvey has deliberately accessed certain of those channels since the turn of the millennium.

To recap: subsequent to the publication of *The New Imperialism* (2003a) Harvey has progressively shifted his focus away from academic audiences (i.e. other scholars and degree students). Through his website and his post-2009 books, in particular, he's sought to make Marxist thinking widely accessible, and relevant to the political-economic dramas of the new millennium. On the one hand, this has involved him bringing the nineteenth-century texts of Marx (who lived in an era of 'liberal capitalism') into the present era of neoliberal capitalism (via Harvey's online, recorded classes about *Capital* given at CUNY, via his regular podcasts[1] and via his 'Companions' to *Capital* published by Verso). On the other hand, it's involved Harvey using Marx and his own 'historical-geographical materialism' to write books (and give lectures, interviews etc.) about current affairs for the interested general reader (as with *Seventeen Contradictions and the End of Capitalism*, 2014a). By and large, these contributions involve Harvey communicating in fairly plain English, free from jargon and avoiding the arcane customs of academic speech and writing. At times, the writing borders on extempore. The contrast to earlier phases of Harvey's long career is pronounced. For instance, during the 1960s, 1970s, 1980s and 1990s – as we saw in Chapter 2 – Harvey was focussed on making original contributions to understanding that would interest fellow academic geographers and urbanists, his primary communicative vehicles being scholarly books, scholarly chapters and peer-reviewed journal articles.[2] In his twilight years, his view now is that 'academicism' is 'boring and irrelevant' (Harvey, 2018a: 1).

Today, then, Harvey is a tenured professor playing the role of a 'public intellectual' (though modest enough not to describe himself in these terms). An intellectual is someone who seeks to offer intelligent, well-informed analysis of 'big issues' (past or present). Intellectuals are not narrow specialists but, instead, seek to understand the metaphorical tapestry rather than one or other of the many threads. They do far more than provide information, or even 'knowledge': they interpret and make sense of things, usually adding a political inflection (see Figure 9.1). They need to make no pretence to 'neutrality' in a political sense. But they should observe high standards of evidential and logical rigour, thereby avoiding the charge that they are propagandists. By writing and speaking in ways that deliberately connect to major sections of national or global publics, many intellectuals (today and in the past) have sought to reach beyond a small circle of like-minded people. In Harvey's case – as with many public intellectuals today – a continuing university position has facilitated this effort to go public. It's given him the security, and the time, to do the things he's done since *The New Imperialism* was published. His Distinguished Professor title, and stellar academic track record, have also given him a degree of authority outside

Figure 9.1. Contemporary Left-wing public intellectuals. Harvey is today among the few Left-wing public intellectuals who enjoys an international profile, other examples (from left to right) being Naomi Klein, Vandana Shiva and George Monbiot.

the academic realm. This is not to say one now has to be a tenured academic to be a public intellectual (the examples of Rebecca Solnit in the United States of America, Arundhati Roy in India and George Monbiot in the United Kingdom prove otherwise).[3] But if one thinks of those people who, in various ways, now play the role of a public intellectual, most are university professors (such as Judith Butler, Clive Hamilton, Kimberlé Crenshaw, Paul Krugman, Michael Sandel and Slavoj Žižek, with even Naomi Klein recently seeking the security of a continuing academic position).[4]

Harvey deserves credit for his public turn. For decades, tenured academics in general, and 'tenured radicals', in particular, have been criticised for being far too inward-looking and far too 'Ivory Tower'. For instance, thirty years ago US sociologist Jon Huer, in his book *Tenure for Socrates* (1991), made this observation about US social scientists and humanities scholars:

> The professor has never been more secure economically or freer intellectually. Yet his [sic] voice in society is amplified only by its silence. With his livelihood secured by tenure, and his thought protected by academic freedom, he refuses to partake in the affairs of society. In the main, the average professor is neither seen nor heard in any meaningful way.
>
> (Huer, 1991: xiv)

Huer's assessment largely remains true, even if the word 'refusal' oversimplifies a more complex reality. Indeed, Raphael Sassower (2014) – like Huer focussing on the United States of America – has proposed that the federal government should spend a billion dollars to fund 10,000 public intellectual fellowships, giving each fellow a stipend of $100,000 a year for five years. In return, fellows would do monthly public engagements and at least four TV or radio broadcasts per year. Without such incentives, Sassower believes most academics will not make a sufficient public contribution.[5]

In this light, Harvey's voluntary decision to reach beyond the university places him in a distinct minority and would, no doubt, be strongly endorsed by Huer, Sassower and other critics of tenured academics. This decision has, perhaps unsurprisingly, occurred during a period of almost unprecedented economic crisis (triggered in 2007–2008) when the need to question capitalism has seemed especially important. This period has seen numerous street protests by citizens and activists in various parts of the world, as with the Occupy Wall Street movement in the United States of America and the Indignados in Spain. It is preferable that such protests are animated by strong critical arguments as well as slogans (useful though the latter can be e.g. 'We are not against the system, but the system is against us' or 'A world for the many, not for the few').

We should, though, note the particularity of Harvey's chosen channels of wider communication and engagement. First, he's relied heavily on traditional print media in the form of medium-to-long books. Since 2010, his two favoured publishers have been Profile Books (https://profilebooks.com/about-profile-books/) and Verso (https://www.versobooks.com/pg/about-verso).[6] The former is a relatively young independent publisher, with around 50 employees and publishing around 100 new books a year. So far, most of its books and authors lack the profile of, say, Joseph Stiglitz's *The Great Divide* (2015) or Elizabeth Kolbert's *Under a White Sky* (2021). The latter, Verso, is perhaps the Anglophone world's premier publisher of serious Left-wing thinking, with its books accessible, and of interest, to an international Left intelligentsia in the main. It also publishes around 100 new books per year.

Second, Harvey has his own website (plus plenty of audio-visual content on Facebook) and also posts on Twitter. This makes sense in an age of online communication and social media. But, of course, the colossal expansion of channels of electronic communication means it's ever harder for one person's voice to be heard in the cacophony. Indeed, the multiplication of websites, tweeters, influencers and so forth arguably fosters fragmentation of audiences as much as it encourages exposure of people to new and different information, arguments and ideas. Harvey has not had relatively regular access to the readerships of 'broad sheet' newspapers, like *The Guardian* or *The New York Times* (compare this with Jürgen Habermas, the highly distinguished German critical theorist or the late French sociologist Pierre Bourdieu, 1930–2002). Neither has he had a slot writing for 'intellectual' non-academic publications like *The New York Review of Books* or its London twin.

But even if he had, it's unclear how large or stable his public audience would be in an era where there's fierce competition to present 'content' to people on their smart televisions, laptops and other mobile devices. Questions also arise about people's attention spans and willingness to engage with 'difficult' or complex arguments. Compare this to a previous era where (national) public intellectuals like Bertrand Russell (1872–1970) in the United Kingdom or Simone de Beauvoir (1908–1986) in France could command the attention of a large, relatively stable and sociologically somewhat mixed audience over a period of time. A slice of this audience was well educated and, whether on the political Left or Right, saw itself as tasked with representing the interests of the wider society. Other slices were politically literate (or at least engaged) and enjoyed national representation so as to influence the political climate (e.g. through trade unions).

The importance of speaking (out) in public

We've just alluded to some of the challenges of being heard widely and accurately in the contemporary public domain. We will return to this important topic in the next section. But first, let us say something about the importance of what Harvey (like other public intellectuals) has tried, in his own way, to do in the last fifteen years or so (Figure 9.2).

Figure 9.2. David Harvey speaking to an audience in São Paolo, Brazil, in August 2019.

The capacity to shape people's thinking is a vitally important one. In dictatorial and autocratic states, this importance has long been recognised. To take one example, today the leadership of North Korea works hard to control the diet of information, arguments and value-propositions that its citizens consume. In political democracies, by contrast, along with countries suffering civil wars and the like, the diet is far more varied. Countries like Australia, Germany and Japan have citizens who are notionally free to think, speak and act (within certain limits). Such freedom is especially valued in the United States where Harvey resides. There, thinking is shaped within a relatively open environment, where schools, universities, the news media, the entertainment media, advertising, government agencies, the family, social media, churches, civic organisations and other entities converge, and sometimes collide, when seeking variously to inform, persuade, inspire, alarm, excite and motivate people.

The 'free flow' of information, opinion, advice and the like is taken to be part of the life-blood of democracies. In theory, it allows citizens to make informed choices about their own lives, and to make intelligent, non-coerced decisions about who will govern them locally and nationally. The shifting content of – and institutional-legal-economic 'boundary conditions' for – this 'free flow' defines what the critical cultural theorist Henry Giroux (2011) calls 'public pedagogy'. For Giroux, pedagogy – the formal and informal process of instructing and learning – extends far beyond educational institutions like CUNY, high schools or primary schools. Instead, it's a continuous, complex, society-wide process. Early in people's lives, the process shapes their sense of self (identity and personality). Later, the process has to reckon more with the 'solidifed' senses that people have of themselves, variously working with or against the grain to reinforce or alter perceptions of reality, values, norms, morals and so on. Anyone seeking to enact their vision of a better world needs somehow to both shape and harness the power of this complex, ongoing process.

As the history of Marxist thinking attests (along with many other bodies of critical thought), one of the useful, constitutive features of capitalist democracies is that they institutionalise and enable the ability to question and object to capitalism in its various historical-geographical incarnations. The tenure and academic freedom Harvey has enjoyed is part of that, as (among other things) is an independent news and journalism industry, free political elections and the right of people to associate with others in relatively unhindered ways. But, today, this capacity for critical thinking to flourish occurs against a background of great social pluralism (where very many identities, beliefs, wishes and desires clash, collide, compromise and sometimes synthesise). It occurs too against a background of acute economic inequality, where some have the monetary power to promote their preferred arguments, beliefs, norms and aspirations.

In this context, as the Marxist Antonio Gramsci famously noted a century ago, the reproduction of capitalism (so too things like patriarchy) occurs, in part, through hegemonic thinking. In any modern society, so argued Gramsci, there's an effort by powerful groups to normalise their preferred 'worldview' within 'civil society'. The challenge these groups face in democracies is to make their thinking hegemonic in the face of both moderate and more radical alternatives presented by various constituencies (such as religious fundamentalists or anarchists). After all, they cannot routinely resort to force in order to ensure civic compliance. Conversely, the challenge for those wishing to abolish or seriously reform capitalism is to win a long 'war of position'. It's not enough to seize hold of government and use executive power to transform a society. Such a move would lack legitimacy among the very people it is supposed to benefit. The war of position is a cognitive, cultural and symbolic war, or a 'soft war' if you will. It involves persuading citizens to embrace norms and goals that challenge those of elite groups. It requires organisations and spokespeople who enjoy autonomy from these dominant groups and who possess the longevity, resources, tactical nous and tenacity to forge a 'new consensus' in society. This new consensus, if or when achieved, requires a 'historic bloc' where various civil groups and organisations are brought together so as to bridge remaining ideological differences in the interests of a perceived 'better' society overall. Hegemony – be it of the Left or the Right – can never be complete and must always be worked at. It is thoroughly contingent.

Public intellectuals are part of any 'war of position' and can contribute more or less effectively to sustaining or challenging specific hegemonic arrangements in one or more countries.[7] The US sociologist Michael Burawoy (e.g. 2009) has argued that academics seeking to 'go public' can be 'traditional' or (after Gramsci) 'organic'. Traditional public intellectuals address a wide but possibly thin, fleeting and even inchoate constituency of readers and listeners. Organic public intellectuals, by contrast, are closely linked to specific societal groups and help to advance their political agendas. Then there are so-called policy intellectuals. These are, typically, academics with expertise in particular areas who make potentially actionable public claims about what governments ought to be doing. Many, today, are economists: prominent examples include the French-American economist Esther Duflo and the Italian-American economist Mariana Mazzucato. Unsurprisingly, some people are hybrid intellectuals, who blend the policy and public roles. One example is British sociologist Anthony Giddens who – in the 1990s and early 2000s – codified the principles and major political goals of the so-called Third Way (between socialism and liberalism). Giddens was, for a time, part

Table 9.1: Modalities of, and audiences for, knowledge work

	Academic audience	Extra-academic audience
Instrumental knowledge	*Professional*	*Policy practitioners*
Reflexive knowledge	*Critical-emancipatory*	*Publics*

Source: Adapted from Burawoy (2009: 192).

of the inner circle of the British (new) Labour Party. Another example is the former academic and elected politician Ioannis (Yanis) Varoufakis, a Left-leaning, Greek-Australian economist (see Table 9.1).

In his own contributions to 'public pedagogy', it seems that Harvey has been akin to an organic intellectual in terms of his cognitive and normative *messages* but a fairly traditional intellectual in a *practical* sense. Historically, Marxists have sought to speak for and with the labour movement (which, in the West, was strongly unionised for half of the twentieth century). The communist experiment in the USSR and elsewhere was driven by a Marxist desire for egalitarian, worker-controlled societies. Today, in a world chock-full of paid workers who must sell their labour power to live, there is no labour movement to speak of in most countries (including the United States of America), let alone transnationally. If there was, Marxists like Harvey would have some sort of solid organic base to speak to and with. In its absence, Harvey's public critique of capitalism is intended for anyone and everyone who cares to listen. As we've seen in Chapters 6–8 especially, this critique is relevant to *all* of us, not only the billions of people directly involved in the capitalist economy. In practice, in his many post-2010 talks and lectures (pre-pandemic, at least), Harvey often addressed a mixed Left-leaning constituency of social movement activists, community organisers and labour representatives. His books, one suspects, are largely read by a similar constituency, young and old. This points to the enduring importance, in many countries, of publics (or sub-publics) able to be convened and addressed about important issues. The question is to what degree do those publics today actually exist and is their character conducive to receiving the sort of reasoned messages someone like Harvey seeks to convey?

The idea of 'the public' and the realities of a 'post-public' era

In addressing this question, it's worth pondering the gap between ideals and realities. The classic depiction of the public sphere was offered over sixty years ago by Jürgen Habermas (published in English in 1989). Habermas traced the emergence of this sphere back to the slow demise of monarchical rule in Western Europe, taking Britain – the world's dominant capitalist economy for a century (from around 1820 onwards) – as a model case. This sphere was not so much a single physical space as an assortment of face-to-face and distantiated venues of local-to-national communication: for instance, coffee houses, salons, 'gentlemen's clubs', national newspapers and political magazines in early nineteenth-century England. The public sphere sat between the domains of elected government (including its executive and administrative arms), the economy and the private realm. Its emergence was coincident with the slow institution of representative democracy: that is, in ideal terms, 'rule by the people for the people' via elected spokespeople. Democracy offered a peaceful way to permit and manage political conflict. Habermas recognised that, in practice, the early public sphere was highly exclusive, being the domain of wealthy white men and thus thoroughly bourgeois. Over time, as voting rights were extended to more citizens, and as public schools and colleges were instituted, more and more people were able, in theory, to become members of a functioning public.[8]

Regardless of its sociological composition at any one historical moment, Habermas argued that for any public to exist in practice, the *idea* of the public needed (and still needs) to be baked into the societal cake. This idea signifies a set of reasoning individuals who, by virtue of (some or all of) a shared language, history and membership of a national territory, would have common concerns relevant to many or all. According to this idea, a public is not a homogenous or stable thing but a dynamic arena of argument and information-flow that crystallises into more – or less – coherent and consensual positions on key issues at different moments. Indeed, there may at times be 'sub-' or 'counter-publics' who emerge to challenge the majority public view. In Habermas's interpretation, an ideal public realm allows communicative power to be exerted by the people so as to influence actual and potential political leaders. As US sociologist Paul Starr recently expressed it,

> ... far from being a neutral analytic category, 'the public' has also been, and remains, a critical and aspirational idea. Unlike other terms for a collection of people (e.g. a 'population'), the noun 'public' bears normative freight. To speak of a public is plainly to dignify the people so grouped together. A public sits in judgment and acts like a tribunal: 'the court of public opinion'. Hence the fear, hope, and disappointment it often inspires. A public, as a long line of theorists have defined it, ideally consists of reasoning participants (in the political sphere, citizens) who recognise obligations beyond self-interest and are capable of rational discussion about the common good.
>
> (2021: 58–59)

Clearly, the idea of 'the public' is predicated on two key things. One is the ability and right of people to think and talk with relative freedom. The other are institutions, locations and media that enable communication among citizens about matters of shared concern (such as how tax revenue should be spent, the legal age of sex or whether a country should go to war). In an ideal world, a 'public' should not only be communicated to (e.g. by a public broadcaster such as the BBC) but should itself engage in reflective thought and communication. In turn, a well-informed public accustomed to intelligent debate, might hold political leaders to account effectively and make new, well-considered demands on them over time.[9] A functioning public is thereby central to ongoing problem-articulation and problem-solving in any society.

The idea of 'the public' has always been something of a high ideal. Habermas' vision of a power-free arena of open discussion involving mutual justification was scarcely ever a reality. Nearly a century ago, Walter Lippmann and John Dewey worried that, in practice, publics in the United States of America were mere shadows of the idea outlined above.[10] In the 1930s, for instance, some publics were in thrall to propaganda (e.g. in Germany and Italy) as right-wing populism and charismatic political leaders took hold in ways that seriously undermined democracy. After World War II (1939–1945), Habermas, in his 1962 book, expressed concern about the passivity of many citizens as a new era of affluence replaced the widespread austerity of the early 1950s. A decade later, US sociologist Richard Sennett – in *The Fall of Public Man* (1976) – argued that many citizens in representative democracies had withdrawn from their role as members of national publics. Work, family, consumerism and other things led, he argued, to an undue focus on the private and the personal. Democracy was increasingly reduced to (often poorly informed) periodic vote choices exercised during elections and referenda. Then, in the 1980s and once more in the United States, Neil Postman (1985) published *Amusing Ourselves to Death*. He famously conjectured that most citizens – when not working – were distracted by 'entertainment' (e.g. provided by Hollywood and, these days, Netflix) and fed a diet of limited information about serious issues at home and abroad.

Notwithstanding these declensionist analyses, we in no way need to idealise the past to recognise that, in many countries today, the gap between ideal publics and actual publics is probably as wide as it's been in the last 250 years. The public sphere is highly attenuated in much of the twenty-first-century world. Harvey, and many others seeking to seriously shape public thought, is having to operate to somehow bridge the unduly large gap. The challenges here are simply formidable. Five problems, it seems to us, warrant particular mention and have been widely discussed in recent years. Together, they suggest that the very idea of 'the public' is today under serious assault, never mind the fact its highly imperfect forms of material expression are a serious cause for concern.

The first problem is a virtual revolution in telecommunications media, the sharp rise of 'infotainment' and the relative decline of public-service communication compared to, say, the 1990s. Technologically, more people have access to ever more information, ideas, images, and much else besides, courtesy of the internet and affordable, compact smart devices. Much of the electronic material they receive – now almost a daily deluge – takes the form of soundbites, slogans, memes and other forms of shallow, decontextualised information. Much of it, delivered via global platforms like Twitter, Facebook and now TikTok, is designed to elicit a fleeting reaction rather than foster sustained thought. It's often focussed on lifestyle issues, aesthetics, commodity purchases, gossip, sensation, dramatic events and celebrities. 'Likes' and so-called virtue-signalling serially prevail over real discussion.

Relatively speaking, public-interest journalism, news and documentary making have been massively overshadowed by content from various alternative providers – in the United States of America, for instance, Fox News, Newsmax, One America News and Breitbart on the political right. Whatever the merits of having many more players in the news and entertainment industries, there's no doubt that their rise has allowed citizens worldwide to fracture into sub-publics and echo-chambers. Indeed, the use of algorithms, de-facto 'surveillance' and micro-monitoring by large digital platforms has actively promoted the formation of numerous 'tribes' of like-minded content-consumers. Meanwhile, partisan providers of news and current affairs material feed audiences a limited epistemic diet, where evidence and values fuse and alternative framings of reality are caricatured negatively or else ignored. In this context, as Starr (2021: 73) puts it,

> Many people with low levels of political interest opted-out of political news (e.g., abandoning old habits of buying the local paper or watching the evening news), while those with higher levels of political interest have self-sorted into ideologically differentiated news sources and devoted more time to them than before.

The second problem is the recent re-emergence of political populism in various parts of the globe, and an associated scepticism about the validity of what various 'experts' have to say about important issues of wide public relevance (e.g. anthropogenic climate change or vaccinations). The word 'populism' means many things. Here it designates a mindset that 'pits a [supposedly] virtuous and homogeneous people against a set of elites and dangerous "others" who are together depicted as depriving (or attempting to deprive) the sovereign people of their rights, values, prosperity, identity and voice' (Albertazzi and McDonnell, 2008: 1). Populism has grown since the global financial crisis of 2007–2008 and the austerity millions of people suffered in its aftermath. For instance, former President Donald Trump was a right-wing populist leader with a devoted electoral base which felt it had been ignored for too long by Washington's established politicians and bureaucrats. Usually, populism emerges more from anger and distress than reasoned debate about public problems and possible solutions. It's associated with scepticism about the honesty and integrity of established politicians and various experts who supply information about public issues (such as Anthony Fauci, the immunologist who dispensed health advice to the American people during the pandemic of 2020–2022). It's often also associated with an emotive politics channelled through charismatic, plain-speaking, 'strong' leaders who mock, discredit and simplify the messages conveyed by anti-populist voices.[11]

This brings us to a third problem. Any functional local, national or transnational public requires some stock of credible information on the basis of which it can construct arguments and views about various issues. However, in recent years, a virtual epidemic of doubt about the accuracy of putative 'facts' seems to have spread around the world. At the same time, the range of people who can 'credibly' make factual claims has multiplied, even when they comment on issues about which they have no expertise. This can serve as a conversation-stopper among potential interlocutors, who express strong scepticism about the evidence each side of an argument adduces. The terms 'post-truth', 'fake news' and 'alternative facts' have gained currency since 2016 as this scepticism has spread. Alarmingly, in this discursive climate even patently false claims manage to command public attention, at least for a time, and aren't easy to dismiss. Among the most egregious examples have been Donald Trump's claims about the 'record' number of supporters who attended his Presidential inauguration; his early 2020 claims about 'silver bullet' COVID-19 cures such as sunlight, bleach and the malaria drug hydroxychloroquine; and his incendiary late 2020 claims about the federal election he lost being 'stolen' through 'mail voter fraud'. Deliberate use of false and partial information has, it seems, become normalised around the world as advertising, spin, branding, conspiracy theories, science and political debate have threatened to collapse into each other.

Fourthly, in many countries worldwide, the ethos and institutions that served as a social glue to create fellow-feeling among citizens have been significantly weakened since the 1980s. There are many reasons for this, including heightened international migration, terrorist incidents (like the '9/11' attacks and the Manchester Arena bombing of 2017), the rise of 'identity politics' (as discussed in Chapters 7 and 8), the rise of single-issue politics and low trade union membership in older and younger capitalist countries. But a key reason, so argue many commentators (such as Wendy Brown, in her book *In the Ruins of Neoliberalism*, 2019), is the successful dissemination of ideas about personal 'freedom' and 'self-responsibility' since the mid-1980s (see Chapter 6). These ideas are central to a 'neoliberal rationality' that has become reality-saturating, according to students of the late Michel Foucault. People born since 1980 have been especially exposed to this 'common sense'. It's an open question how far these ideas create compliant 'neoliberal subjects' or whether they are hegemonised through discernible 'historic blocs' (on which see Watts, 2022). But there's little doubt that many national governments have actively used rhetorical, legal and administrative techniques to privatise and relinquish responsibility for all manner of important things (e.g. paying for university education, dental care, child care and old age care). This includes ostensibly Left governments like Tony Blair's New Labour going back to the 1990s. The resulting ethico-social interstices have, in part, been filled by religious and civil organisations that serve to segment national and international publics. Notions of a society-wide 'common good' now seem like quaint hangovers from a previous era. A valorisation of 'freedom' and 'liberty' has served as a sort of immune system to protect neoliberal societies from unmanageable levels of public protest about the maladies neoliberalism itself inflicts.

Finally, many critics suggest that we live in a 'post-political' era where, in both the leading democratic and more authoritarian states, alternative political futures are simply not up for discussion at all. According to Slavoj Žižek, Jacques Rancière, Henry Giroux and others, alternatives seem like utopian dreams – interesting but impractical. Oddly, the economic crisis erupting in 2007–2008 has not been matched by a crisis of mainstream political ideas. Post-neoliberalism has not come to pass, even though neoliberalism is an 'impure', hybrid, 'glocal' formation at this point (see Callison and Manfredi, 2020; see also the journal *Theory, Culture & Society*, volume 38, issue 6). In addition, other commentators note the rise of 'anti-politics'. Here, millions of citizens switch-off from the political process. They feel disillusioned or disenfranchised by their elected governments and dismayed at the undue power wielded by business elites and 'faceless bureaucrats'. They retreat to the private realm or civic enclaves in order to create a sense of meaning and agency in their lives.[12]

In this five-fold context, it might not be too much to say that we live in a 'post-public' epoch. In countries as varied as the United Kingdom, Brazil, Hungary, India, Turkey and the United States of America, polarisation has occurred within the public domain. In more autocratic states, like China and Russia, the public was never much of a thing in the first place. Even in established electoral democracies, the public's sense of itself *as* a public seems to be in serious doubt. At best, according to Mark Lilla (2017), we are left with 'pseudo politics'. This is ironic, as well as tragic. After all, we live in a supposed 'information age' where censorship is lower than in the past and knowledge far more abundant. We hear more voices and perspectives than ever before, as the formerly excluded are now included. People can endlessly post and react to written, audio and visual content. Yet the public domain – which is now more global than ever before – is 'wild', intolerant, rancorous and attenuated as much as it is lively, mind-expanding and inclusive. The term 'cancel culture' has gained currency to capture this. The political role of the public domain suffers as a result.

Consequential 'unknown unknowns' can proliferate in this context. It's even doubtful that publics' views count for much beyond the ballot box: since the early 2000s, for instance, numerous governments have evidently been unmoved by serious public protests (e.g. about embarking on wars in Iraq and Afghanistan in the early 2000s). Today we confront something approaching a sham or phantom public domain compared to Habermas' idealistic rendering, with social media enabling 'participatory propaganda' to become central to our lives as people navigate through an endless 'infodemic'. Sociologist William Davies (2021: 45) likens it to a 'combat zone' in which, he laments, 'freedom is only authentic if it means freedom to communicate anything to anyone, regardless of its epistemic, moral or aesthetic value'.[13] This produces a dialogue of the hard-of-hearing, if not the deaf.

The limits to Marxist reason and rhetoric

David Harvey is having to both operate in the context sketched above, while consciously using some of the resources afforded by it. As we've seen, he employs traditional print media (books), along with online communication tools (e.g. his podcasts – 'the Anti-Capitalist Chronicles' – are available on YouTube and Spotify, among other platforms). In key respects, the context to which he's adapted, and seeks to influence, is explicable by way of the Marxism he adumbrates. For instance, large digital platforms like Facebook and TikTok belong to large profit-seeking enterprises, while soaring economic inequality within (and between) nation states has created much of the social discontent that fuels populist politics of both the Left and Right. But is the 'discursive power' of that Marxism even noticed, let alone taken seriously, in what passes for today's public sphere? Is it even a blip on most people's hyper-stimulated radars?

By way of an answer we can only speculate. First, to our knowledge Harvey has not attracted too much criticism or opprobrium in the digital domain. If he had, especially in the United States of America, it would suggest that his thinking is being noticed by constituencies of a neoliberal and neo-conservative kind. We conjecture that Marxism, in general, is seen as such a limited threat to dominant modes of thinking that potential critics do not see it as worth attacking.[14] Indeed, some of Harvey's more recent books have enjoyed favourable reviews in high-profile broadsheets, such as *The Financial Times*, and he's been interviewed on the BBC.

Second, Harvey is very much an old-school 'rationalist' it seems to us. He believes in the efficacy of the better cognitive and normative argument, as if wedded to the venerable maxim that 'knowledge is power'. This places credible evidence (well marshalled) and logical rigour at the core of things. Harvey's faith no doubt works well when he's addressing people (like the present authors) who are already disposed to listen. But it arguably works less well in the inhospitable public domain of today where simplification, distortion and short attention-spans substitute for sophisticated, fair-minded and in-depth discussion of important, complex issues. Unfortunately, Harvey's preferred mode of argumentation does not lend itself to changing the thinking of those who are disposed to ignore Marxism. We say this because he rarely ever expounds (classical) Marxism by respectfully and systematically considering the strongest *non-Marxist* critiques of its core propositions. If he adopted a more dialogical or open form of reasoning, it might make his Marxism appear more robust to those who have presumed it to be dogma or some intellectual relic of a bygone era. Such a mode of argumentation is advantageous in the academy but might be even more so in the 'wild' post-public domain.[15]

We speculate, then, that outside a relatively self-selecting Left audience, historian Julian Zelizer's general assessment applies to Harvey. 'Public intellectuals', Zelizer writes, 'whose contributions rest on citizens' respecting and being able to perceive thoughtful and data-based analysis, find it difficult to convince the public as to the validity of their perspective' (2021: 2). However, even if we're right, one should not under-estimate the importance of Harvey seeking to keep Marxist ideas as part of the Left-lexicon outside universities. Preaching to the proverbial choir matters, especially if the choir is relatively small in global terms and is in danger of getting smaller in an era when neoliberalism, neo-conservatism and right-wing populism are (still) winning the political battle for hearts and minds. One might say that Marxism (or some differently labelled version of it) should appeal to more people than, seemingly, it does. But this is no reason for Harvey to throw in the towel or remain encased in the academy. One needs to light a flame before one can ignite a fire in the wider society.[16]

Here, there are lessons to be learned by Marxist intellectuals and Left thought-leaders of all persuasions from the tactics employed by the so-called neo-liberal thought collective. Since a revolution against capitalism seems to us to be out of the question, the lessons apply to the essential task of significantly reforming the system in its transnational, neoliberal mode. Such reform may seem like 'second best' for 'true Marxists', but it still matters a great deal since capitalism's concrete historical-geographical forms vary within a rather wide bandwidth. As we've noted at various points in this book, a neoliberalising capitalism has been remarkably resilient (though badly frayed), even after the largest economic crisis for decades. The seeds of this resilience were sown by a set of aspiring thought-leaders as far back as the 1950s. At that time, their arguments and aspirations seemed to be 'out of the question' in the same sense that Keynesianism and social democracy (never mind communism) are out of the question today in most parts of the world.

There are now many fine studies of the complex machinations of the 'neoliberal thought collective' after the Second World War (Peck, 2010; Mirowski and Plehwe, 2009; Slobodian, 2018; Stedman Jones, 2012). The key things to note in the context of this book are as follows. First, the likes of Friedrich von Hayek (1899–1992) – who went on to be a neoliberal thought leader – were deeply affected by the extended crisis of 'liberal capitalism' in the 1920s and 1930s. The alternatives of socialism and fascism were not to their liking. Second, they began to organise themselves at a time when they seemed to have lost the political and economic argument. The now (in)famous Mont Pèlerin Society (MPS) first met in 1948. Its members recognised that there were no guarantees they would discredit the emerging 'Keynesian compromise' in the West any time soon. Third, those in and around the MPS recognised early on that it was fruitless to win a battle for public opinion unless ready to seize governmental and legal power. In this sense, neoliberalism's founders were more interested in the 'long march through the institutions' than in winning a Gramscian 'war of position' in civil society – at least in the first instance. They set about training bright, articulate, highly skilled cadres in leading universities (such as Chicago and in Virginia) who would, they hoped, exert an influence by assuming positions in think tanks and foundations where they could preach the neoliberal gospel to the 'ruling class' in the United States of America, Britain, Switzerland, Austria and elsewhere.

Many of these neoliberals were academics who developed extensive 'vanguard networks' and, as time went on, developed public profiles. They were both public and policy intellectuals. A good example is Milton Friedman (1912–2006) in the United States of America, who, with his wife Rose, wrote manifestos for public consumption (such as *Free to Choose*, 1980) and used television to reach a mass audience. Friedman, like so many neoliberals, employed the social prestige accorded economics – his chosen discipline (he won the Nobel Prize for Economics in 1976) – to give neoliberal philosophy a technical expression that afforded it practical credibility. Legal philosophy, theory and practice were another preferred 'expert' means that neoliberals used to promote and enact their ideas. The key point here is that neoliberalism's advocates (a rather varied bunch) developed a formidable set of theoretical and practical tools well before they achieved any sort of hegemony. Confident, articulate and tenacious professionals, within and beyond academia, led the charge, building networks into the business world and attracting considerable funding in the process so as to elevate their profile over time.[17] On this basis, when circumstances provided an opening to enact their ideas, neoliberals took full advantage in Chile, the United States of America, the United Kingdom and elsewhere. Only later were neoliberal nostrums promoted widely through acts of 'public pedagogy' via Margaret Thatcher, Ronald Reagan and countless others. One reason neoliberalism has proven so durable is that it's now deeply and widely embedded in policy, administration and law globally, not only in many people's senses of self. This means that opponents of neoliberalism face a formidable, tedious, highly technical job of replacing hundreds of thousands of regulations, rules, laws and organisations that have, to use Quinn Slobodian's (2018) apt term, 'encased' it. Such opponents would need to fight long and hard to dismantle neoliberalism in the governmental and quasi-state realms, even were there to be broad enthusiasm for a new dispensation in civil societies around the world. The spectre of administrative-political gridlock thus hangs over aspirations to reform, never mind dismantle, neoliberal capitalism (see Madariaga, 2020).

Meanwhile, the other challenge for Harvey and like-minded radicals is to speak a language designed to capture the hearts and minds of people in diverse and fractious societies worldwide. There is a lot of discontent worldwide with 'zombie' neoliberalism as it staggers on, dead but dominant. What concepts and terms will expand people's sense of *shared* problems and *shared* goals? What stories and goals will motivate people to *act in concert*? We gained insight into Harvey's answer in Chapters 7 and 8. If our claims about a post-public era are not over-blown, it's more important than ever for critics like Harvey to craft a 'we language' that can build historic (and geographical) blocs in the Gramscian sense. This language must, somehow, connect to different people's lived experience but forge a sense of solidarity with, and empathy for, all manner of unlike others near and far. And it has to be motivating and aspirational, not merely critical and fault-finding. It might even, dare we say, need to be populist – recalling that not all populist discourse equates to propaganda (e.g. on which see Thomas Frank's excellent US-focused corrective *The People, No*, 2020).[18] To insinuate such a language throughout multiple civil societies, numerous national public domains and transnational versions of both, will require truly Herculean organisational efforts.

Conclusion

In this chapter, unlike the previous ones, we've focussed more on the wider context in which Harvey operates as a thinker, analyst, author and speaker than on the substance of his written and spoken words. We've done this because the context obviously has a significant bearing on whether and how Harvey's arguments and insights have any traction in a world he believes could (and should) be better. As we've seen, Harvey has used his secure professorial position as a foundation to reach beyond CUNY, thus avoiding the common academic habit of treating the university as an isolation chamber. His public activities have been serious and sustained, going beyond the 'usual' tokenistic acts of 'writing a piece for *The Nation*, showing up at a rally when time permits, or even throwing a rock at Israeli troops before going back to teach courses at [the university]' (Saccarelli, 2011: 774). Commendably, Harvey has resisted any urge to become a Left pundit, despite punditry suiting the demands of now ubiquitous platform media.

But as we've also seen, Harvey's public turn has occurred during an inauspicious period for Marxist thought (indeed, for *any* thought fundamentally critical of the present economic and political order). Marxism contains vital descriptive, explanatory and political messages, yet relatively few people alive today are likely to internalise these messages, let alone be in a position to act on them. Indeed, one of the extraordinary features of the last decade is that a largely neoliberal capitalist economic system has remained resilient despite generating all manner of problems and oppositional forces. There has been a crisis *of* neoliberal capitalism but not *for* it. Many of those badly affected by the global financial crisis and its aftermath remain unable, or unwilling, to think beyond the system. Yet that system is wide open to criticism, with Harvey one of its many dissenting voices. As he rightly observed fifty years ago: 'Revolutions in thought are ... possible and necessary without revolutions in social practice' (Harvey, 1973: 148).

In reaching this conclusion, we're not saying that Harvey has been deficient in his public-facing activities. Instead, in this chapter we've reflected on the huge challenges *any* radical thinker faces in trying to reach, let alone successfully influence, a wide and receptive audience. Using Harvey as a case study, we've asked 'how is it possible to make people listen?' And, more importantly, 'how is it possible to make people *want* to listen?' In an age when capitalism is more global and promiscuous than ever, and an age of post-national digital communication, it's ever harder to mount a sustained, widely visible and credible critique of capitalism in the (post-)public sphere.[19] Even so, it remains vital that those of us disenchanted with capitalism attempt to change thinking and sentiment in places where it matters.

It remains equally vital to do so by maintaining the highest standards of evidential and logical reasoning. As the post-1945 success of the neoliberal thought collective proves, university academics will be central to waging the long battle to end the stuttering rule of neoliberal capitalism.[20] The sociologist Max Weber once sagely observed that political change usually involves 'slow, steady drilling through hard boards' (1994: 369), with 'passion' and 'judgement' at the cutting edge. But to be effective change-agents, academics willing to get their hands dirty need to be properly organised, well-funded, resilient and have strategic goals in the short, medium and long term. They need to be both public and policy intellectuals. So far, the Left – Marxist and otherwise – has not been up to the job of taking us beyond neoliberalism in most parts of the world. Politically, it's thus experiencing its own sustained crisis at a time when the crisis of neoliberal capitalism should have been its signal opportunity to achieve wide appeal.

Further reading

Desch, M. (Ed.). (2016). *Public Intellectuals in the Global Arena*. University of Notre Dame Press, Parts II and III.

Drezner, D. (2017). *The Ideas Industry*. Oxford University Press, Chapters 1–3.

Notes

1. The podcasts are released with support from the non-profit organisation Democracy at Work (https://www.democracyatwork.info) and are crowdfunded via the platform Patreon.

2. One of the few pre-2000 videos of Harvey speaking to an audience can be found here: http://davidharvey.org/2014/06/video-history-present-condition-geography-historical-materialist-manifesto-1984/. It offers some insight into his more 'academic' mode of delivery and addressees prior to his more public turn in the 2000s.
3. Often, public intellectuals who are not academics are journalists, creative practitioners (e.g. novelists and poets) and, occasionally, religious leaders who speak beyond their constituency (e.g. the current Catholic Pope).
4. This said, not all publicly prominent academics are 'intellectuals'. Many are more like public educators, as with astrophysicist Brian Cox or ancient historian Mary Beard, both of whom regularly front television series. Likewise, not all publicly prominent people discussing serious issues are intellectuals. An example is the teen climate activist Greta Thunberg, who might best be regarded as a personified moral conscience of the younger generation.
5. During the final decade or so of his life, the English Marxist historian felt that academic life was not really compatible with making a real difference in the civic realm. He became virtually a full-time spokesperson and advocate for the Campaign for Nuclear Disarmament (CND) in the United Kingdom.
6. At the time of writing, he has also published one book – *The Anti-Capitalist Chronicles* – with established independent Left-wing publisher Pluto (Harvey, 2020a). Our understanding is that Harvey was attracted to Profile Books because his long-standing and favourite editor, the late John Davey, worked for Profile at the end of his career.
7. In more autocratic societies, such intellectuals are usually labelled as 'dissidents', a prime example being the former Czechoslovakia's Vaclav Havel, who went on to be the first President of the Czech Republic after Eastern Bloc communism ended dramatically after 1989.
8. Note that 'the public sphere' (or domain) is not synonymous with 'civil society'. Civil society is the network of relations and institutions that people create and sustain outside the home (or domestic realm) at different geographical scales. Civil society actions can occur without being 'public' (i.e. widely visible to others) and without involving 'public debate'. For instance, church congregations and local heritage groups are part of civil society. As such, civil society is a necessary but insufficient element of a functioning public.
9. In these senses, the idea of 'the public' is to be distinguished from the notions of 'the mob' and 'the mass', both of which imply citizens unthinkingly or passively acceding to majority opinion. It's worth noting that radical liberals question the idea of the public, thereby differing from social liberals and social democrats. For instance, 'There is no such entity as "the public," since the public is merely a number of individuals,' wrote Ayn Rand (1964: 88) in *The Virtues of Selfishness*. She thereby denied there's any such thing as the 'public interest' and more an aggregation of individual wills and preferences.

10. See Lippman (1965) and Dewey (1976). The two Americans debated whether, in large-scale societies, citizens could form well-reasoned positions on key issues of public concern and hold their political leaders to account. They noted numerous barriers, such as the complexity of many public issues and many citizens' inability to understand these issues.
11. Though right-wing populism is a worrying (if understandable) phenomenon of our times, we are not suggesting populism is always a malign political force. Chantal Mouffe has made the general case for a populism of the Left many times, while in the United States of America, Thomas Frank (2020) has made a specific case that social democracy needs to harness the power of populism. In practice, Left populism can, of course, be problematic, as Bolton and Pitts (2018) argued in relation to the British Labour Party in recent years. Ideally, Left populism should be anchored in a vibrant civil society, not in a fractious society whose members unthinkingly endorse a charismatic leader.
12. One key aspect of this anti-political and post-political drift is that politics now rarely if ever occurs in the economic domain. The relatively low levels of trade union membership globally, and the legal constraints now imposed on union action (e.g. strikes), compare unfavourably with a previous period when, in the Anglo-European sphere, politics occurred as much in the workplace as in civil society, the public sphere and the realms of the state.
13. Back in the 1980s and since then, the leading New Left theorists Ernesto Laclau (1935–2014) and Chantal Mouffe argued for an 'agonistic democracy' that would move beyond the contained democracy of the post-war capitalist states like Japan and the United States of America. These authors would surely not approve of the way the public domain today has become a 'free' space where conflict often involves people talking past each other rather than carefully considering each other's claims.
14. At best, in public discourse in the United States, Marxism is a boo word: if liberals or conservatives want to discredit a claim made by social democrats or Leftist new social movements, they often paint those claims as 'Marxist' or else 'socialist'.
15. It is no longer, if it ever was, credible for Marxists to talk about 'scientific socialism' as if it's the *only* desirable or likely future once capitalism's crisis tendencies are fully exploited by anti-capitalists. We discussed this near the end of Chapter 8. Once upon a time, some Marxists claimed that their 'scientific' analysis of capitalism showed that socialism was, if not inevitable, then the next 'logical' stage of world history. This collapsed the distance between the 'is' and the 'ought' in ways that ignored people's capacity to imagine all manner of progressive futures, of which socialism was but one. Related to this point, Harvey's early published critiques of 'status quo' and 'counter-revolutionary' theory (see Chapter 3) need updating. He would be well advised to offer precise, rigorous but respectful critiques of the 'best' versions of pro-capitalist reasoning (e.g. by economists, legal theorists and libertarian philosophers). These critiques would plumb the depths of debate about causes, effects, values, means and ends in the economic, governmental and other realms.

They would also be phrased in ways that inspire, as much as alarm, move or concern those exposed to these critiques. His *Marx, Capital and the Madness of Economic Reason* (2017a) book is perhaps the one that comes closest to the sort of dialogical mode of exposition that we are recommending here. But as we noted in Chapter 8, this is an exception that proves the rule.

16. And we should not assume that universities remain safe spaces from which to analyse problems in the wider world. The trends recounted in the previous section have directly impacted universities too. Indeed, there has been a great deal of angst expressed about the death of the idea of 'public universities', as successive governments have sought to privatise, commodify and render more competitive the processes of higher learning and producing research. Harvey has not written or said too much about this, though he is well aware of it.
17. For instance, as Harvey himself explains (2020a: 43–47), the exceedingly wealthy Koch brothers (Charles and David) have been long-term financiers of neoliberal think tanks (e.g. the Cato Institute), foundations and research projects (see also MacLean, 2017). Indeed, a number of entrepreneurs have been very active in setting-up a neoliberal knowledge and advocacy infrastructure, such as British chicken farmer Antony Fisher (1915–1988), who established the Institute of Economic Affairs and the Atlas Network, among other things.
18. In the realms of mainstream environmental politics, fifteen years ago Ted Nordhaus and Michael Shellenberger (2007) famously advocated a total reframing of green discourse in the United States of America. They argued that, to be politically effective today, the environmental movement needed to reset its linguistic compass, tapping into values and goals that would resonate with ordinary Americans. Analogously, we might ponder whether Marxists need to be prepared to keep the substance of their analysis but seriously alter its discursive presentation. Terms like 'class struggle' too easily raise hackles and perpetuate an 'us-them' mode of political encounter likely to change few minds.
19. Compare today's communicative environment for academic intellectuals with that of, say, the 1980s and 1990s. Stuart Hall, the influential British Marxist cultural studies professor, enjoyed a certain public profile courtesy of the BBC, Open University televised course materials, and Channel 4 (see Ang, 2016). If he were still alive, Hall would find it significantly harder to utilise the available 'techno-semiosphere'.
20. This is because – notwithstanding a previous footnote in this chapter – universities remain the pre-eminent site for cultivating in-depth independent thought, even though higher education has itself experienced the rigours of neoliberal reform and creeping managerialism since the late 1980s. As noted earlier in this book, universities are without doubt *the* place where Marxism and other bodies of radical thought today are able to still flourish, even as their fortunes remain very mixed in the wider world. If such thought were somehow to be extinguished in the universities, then the Left – broadly defined – would be in even worse trouble than it currently is in most parts of the world.

Conclusion 10

A Marxist for our time?

If you already knew something about David Harvey's Marxism, we hope that you now know an awful lot more having read this book. Equally, if you knew very little about him or his work at the start, we hope this book has enlightened rather than confused you. Harvey's body of published work is rather like the capitalist world he's spent more than fifty years analysing: it's large and complex yet possessed of considerable structure once one learns how to see the proverbial wood for the trees. The thematic approach we've adopted (Chapters 3–9) has sought to home-in on what makes Harvey's work both distinctive and broadly cohesive across seven decades.

As we've seen, since the early 1970s, Harvey's lodestar has been Karl Marx; in turn, Harvey has become a lodestar for thousands of others, while also introducing many new readers to Marx's nineteenth-century *oeuvre*. Harvey has been among the leading Marxist thinkers of the late twentieth and early twenty-first centuries. Like all Marxists, he asks the seemingly naïve, but for mainstream economists embarrassing, question: *what is an economy for and whose interests does it serve?* As we've shown in previous chapters, though, he's differed from other Marxist notables – such as Terry Eagleton, Angela Davis and the late Giovanni Arrighi, Ellen Meiksins Wood and Erik Olin Wright – in several ways.

First, he's made questions of geography (as much as temporality) central to the Marxist political economy at both a theoretical and empirical level (with only the likes of Rosa Luxemburg and Henri Lefebvre tackling those questions seriously after Marx's death, prior to Harvey and a few others). This is a very significant contribution to understanding, his answer serving to make (classical) Marxism a more complete account of capitalism, in both

DOI: 10.4324/9780429028120-10

descriptive-explanatory and political-normative terms.[1] As we've seen in this book, in Harvey's work 'geography' is much more than the local scale and far more than an inert expression of capitalist processes. Doreen Massey could have been summarising this work when she once memorably said that,

> The facts of distance, between-ness, unevenness, nucleation, co-presence, time-space distanciation, settings, mobility and differential mobility: *all* these affect how specified social relations work; they may even be necessary for their existence or prevent their operation ... [T]he fact of spatial variation itself, and of interdependence – of uneven development – has major implications. 'Geography matters' does not just mean 'locality matters' – it has much wider implications, greater claims to make, than this.
>
> (1991: 272, emphasis added)

Harvey insists that geographical knowledge must be threaded through *all* other forms of knowledge about the world (e.g. economics or sociology). This knowledge must somehow grasp the dynamics of absolute, relative and relational spaces to reveal, kaleidoscopically, a structured complexity.

Second, Harvey has developed something of a public profile in an era when Marxism is still (in the main) perceived negatively outside the social science and humanities arenas that his work has significantly influenced. To do this as a citizen of a famously anti-Marxist and arch-capitalist country – the United States of America – is a striking accomplishment (even if his Marxism has low public efficacy, as we argued in Chapter 9). A certain mix of confidence and bravery is required to be 'out there' in an often fractious public sphere.

The two projects are deeply connected, as we have shown. The 'geography matters' message is, for Harvey, not a mere means to promote the good name of Geography, the discipline. Instead, it's an attempt to make plain how geography ('space') – in all its complexity – shapes and is shaped by a constellation of relations, forces and pressures that are personally relevant to *all* of us (whoever we are, and wherever we happen to be). Despite the gaps in his theory (e.g. his thin conception of the state), Harvey's analytical outlook is holistic and encompassing: it alerts us to the simultaneity of multiple key factors in our capitalist, yet also more-than-capitalist, earthly universe. This ensemble of factors is intricate and largely invisible to people in their daily lives, yet very real and consequential in a range of registers. It comprises a moving totality of processes that do not so much unfold *across* time-space as fashion *their own* restless historical geography of matter and meaning.

Indeed, we might say that Harvey's grand intellectual ambition is a third thing that distinguishes his work from most other Marxists writing today. As we've seen, he tries to capture the exorbitant qualities of capitalism: that is, its insinuation into almost every nook and cranny of both the human and non-human worlds. This stereoscopic impulse is a strength but also, according to some of his critics, a weakness: it leads to a limited grasp of the 'more than capitalist' dimensions of life. We need a fully dimensioned account of our world, whereas Harvey can only gesture towards rather than deliver this.

Nonetheless, over fifty years since his initial, ebullient turn to Marxism, Harvey's critical energy and radical political beliefs remain undiminished, now on display in a far larger arena than academic Geography.

These three general observations having been made, in concluding our presentation and interpretation of Harvey's life's work, let us try to summarise its distinctiveness and value, as well as its weaknesses and blind spots, in more specific terms. There are eight points to make by way of a recapitulation of this book's principal insights, as follows:

1. Harvey has consistently accented the 'power of theory' (i.e. systematic conceptual abstraction) to shed light on complex and dynamic empirical events.
2. Harvey has long insisted that space (geography) and time (history) are constituted through processes and practices.
3. Relatedly, Harvey has further insisted that space-time has a material impact on the processes and practices that structure it at various scales.
4. Harvey, like most Marxists, has consistently depicted capitalism as thoroughly contradictory, his dialectical approach seeking to mirror in thought the elemental tensions of this mode of production. For him, the contradictions have serious consequences for people and the biophysical world, though can be ameliorated here and there with suitable management.
5. Harvey, again like most Marxists, has accented capitalism's exorbitant tendencies to pursue endless accumulation and to expand in spatial scope.
6. Harvey's work offers a rich depiction of how capitalism structures the everyday agency of billions of people as well as prospects for them exercising political agency.
7. Harvey's work has long presented justice as an animating normative concept, though has not fully explored how various forms of justice might somehow be achieved within a more-than-capitalist Left politics alive to multiple drivers of different sorts of injustices.
8. Since around 2007, Harvey is among the very few academic Marxists to develop a public profile of sorts, though his efficacy in this space is open to question.

Taking stock, in conclusion we can ask whether Harvey's total body of work makes him a Marxist *for* our time or, perhaps, merely *of* our time? It's a question we can ask of any living Marxist in the particular context of the early twenty-first century. Never has capitalism been so large (in scale and scope), and never has it generated so many significant problems on so wide a range of fronts. Yet, as we intimated in Chapter 9 and elsewhere, serious attempts to reform, never mind abolish, the system are almost nowhere to be seen. Harvey is one of those who has helped us understand how and why the problems arise. In that sense, he's a leading analyst of our troubled world. But to be an analyst *for* our time, Harvey would not only need to offer a more detailed sense of progressive political goals and possibilities (the focus of the last part of Chapter 8), he'd also, like other contemporary Marxists, need a live political movement (organised both outside and within the formal political sphere) that can channel the power of the people. In this sense, the circumstances of our historical geography are inauspicious for Marxists and other radical Leftists. The critique of capitalist political economy is necessary; but it lacks sufficient conditions to translate knowledge into progressive practice. Capitalism today is akin to a run-away train whose uber-wealthy drivers are enjoying the ride so much they are unwilling to apply the brakes; meanwhile, the reform- and revolution-minded Lefts are stuck in the passenger seats unable to reach the controls. Our historical geography seems less ours to make than we would want it to be. For many, the future times and spaces of our planetary condition look rather bleak.

Note

1. As noted at the end of Chapter 5, though, it's not clear that most of Harvey's many readers have grasped the full nature and importance of his arguments about 'space' (or geography).

Bibliography

Albertazzi, D. & McDonnell, D. (Eds.). (2008). *Twenty-First Century Populism: The Spectre of Western European Democracy*. Palgrave Macmillan.

Alonso, W. (1964). *Location and Land Use: Toward a General Theory of Land Rent*. Harvard University Press.

Anderson, P. (2019). Situationism à l'envers. *New Left Review*, 119, 47–93.

Ang, I. (2016). Stuart Hall and the tension between academic and intellectual work. *International Journal of Cultural Studies*, 19(1), 29–41.

Ashman, S. & Callinicos, A. (2006). Capital accumulation and the state system: Assessing David Harvey's *The New Imperialism*. *Historical Materialism*, 14(4), 107–131.

Azmanova, A. (2014). Crisis? Capitalism is doing very well. How is critical theory? *Constellations*, 21(3), 351–365.

Bivens, J., Gould, E., Mishel, L. & Shierholz, H. (2014). Raising America's pay: Why it's our central economic policy challenge. Briefing paper 378, Economic Policy Institute, 4 June.

Bolton, M. & Pitts, F. (2018). *Corbynism: A Critical Approach*. Emerald.

Bourdieu, P. (1977). *Outline of a Theory of Practice*. Cambridge University Press.

Bowman, A., et al. (2013). Central bank-led capitalism? *Seattle University Law Review*, 36(2), 455–487.

Brandmayr, F. (2021). Are theories politically flexible? *Sociological Theory*, 39(2), 103–125. https://doi.org/10.1177/07352751211016036

Brenner, N., Peck, J. & Theodore, N. (2010). Variegated neoliberalization: Geographies, modalities, pathways. *Global Networks*, 10(2), 182–222. https://doi.org/10.1111/j.1471-0374.2009.00277.x

Brown, W. (2019). *In the Ruins of Neoliberalism*. Columbia University Press.

Burawoy, M. (2009). Public sociology in the age of Obama. *Innovation: The European Journal of Social Science Research*, 22(2), 189–199. https://doi.org/10.1080/13511610903075837

Burnham, P. (2001). New Labour and the politics of depoliticisation. *British Journal of Politics and International Relations*, 3(2), 127–149.

Callison, W. & Manfredi, Z. (Eds.) (2020). *Mutant Neoliberalism*. Fordham University Press.

Castells, M. (1983). *The City and the Grassroots: A Cross-Cultural Theory of Urban Social Movements*. University of California Press.

Castree, N. (1996). Birds, mice and geography. *Transactions of the Institute of British Geographers*, 21(2), 342–362.

Castree, N. & Gregory, D. (Eds.) (2006). *David Harvey: A Critical Reader*. Blackwell.

Christophers, B. (2018). *The New Enclosure: The Appropriation of Public Land in Neoliberal Britain*. Verso.

Christophers, B. (2019). *Rentier Capitalism: Who Owns the Economy and Who Pays for It?* Verso.

Clarke, S. (1990). The Marxist theory of overaccumulation and crisis. *Science & Society*, 54(4), 442–467.

Cochrane, A. (1987). What a difference the place makes: The new structuralism of locality. *Antipode*, 19(3), 354–363.

Cooke, P. (1986). The changing urban and regional system in the United Kingdom. *Regional Studies*, 30(1), 243–251.

Cooke, P. (1987). Individuals, localities and postmodernism. *Environment and Planning D: Society & Space*, 5(4), 408–412.

Cox, K. & Mair, A. (1989). Levels of abstraction in locality studies. *Antipode*, 21(2), 121–132.

Crawford, N. C. & Lutz, C. (2021). Human cost of post-9/11 wars: Direct war deaths in major war zones. Costs of War Project, Brown University, 1 September.

Crawford, N. C. (2021). The US budgetary costs of the post-9/11 wars. Costs of War Project, Brown University, 1 September.

Crouch, C. (2011). *The Strange Non-Death of Neoliberalism*. Polity.

Dardot, P. & Laval, C. (2013). *The New Way of the World: On Neoliberal Society*. Verso.

Davies, W. (2016). Thoughts on the sociology of Brexit. Political Economy Research Centre, Goldsmith's University of London, 24 June. https://www.perc.org.uk/project_posts/thoughts-on-the-sociology-of-brexit/

Davies, W. (2021). Anti-equivalence: Pragmatics of post-liberal dispute. *European Journal of Social Theory*, 24(1), 44–64.

Deutsche, R. (1991). Boys town. *Environment and Planning D: Society and Space*, 9(1), 5–30.

Dewey, J. (1976). *The Middle Works of John Dewey, 1899–1924*. Southern Illinois University Press.

Diehl, S. (2022). Why immanent critique? *European Journal of Philosophy*, 30(2), 676–692.

Dohrn-van Rossum, G. (1996). *History of the Hour: Clocks and Modern Temporal Orders*. University of Chicago Press.

Dumenil, G. & Lévy, D. (2004). *Capital Resurgent: Roots of the Neoliberal Revolution*. Harvard University Press.

Duncan, J. & Ley, D. (1982). Structural Marxism and human geography: A critical assessment. *Annals of the Association of American Geographers*, 72(1), 30–59.

Eagleton, T. (1991). *Ideology: An Introduction*. Verso.

Eagleton, T. (2003). *After Theory*. Allen Lane.

Eagleton, T. (2005) Just my imagination. *The Nation*. 26 May. https://www.thenation.com/article/archive/just-my-imagination/

Elson, D. (1979). The value theory of labour. In D. Elson (Ed.), *Value: The Representation of Labour in Capitalism* (pp. 115–180). CSE Books.

Escobar, A. (2008). *Territories of Difference: Place, Movement, Life, Redes*. Duke University Press.

Federal Reserve. (2018). Report on the Economic Well-Being of US Households in 2017. Board of Governors of the Federal Reserve System. May.

Ferguson, J. (2015). *Give a Man a Fish: Reflections on the New Politics of Distribution*. Duke University Press.

Florida, R. (2002). *The Rise of the Creative Class*. Hachette Book Group.

Florida, R. (2004). *Cities and the Creative Class*. Routledge.

Foster, J. B. (1998). Hesitations before ecology: David Harvey's dilemma. *Capitalism, Nature, Socialism*, 9(3), 55–59.

Frank, T. (2020). *The People, No: A Brief History of Anti-Populism*. Metropolitan Books.

Fraser, N. (1997). *Justice Interruptus: Critical Reflections on the 'Post-Socialist' Condition*. Routledge.

Fraser, N. (2022). *Cannibal Capitalism: How Our System Is Devouring Democracy, Care, and the Planet – And What We Can Do About It*. Verso.

Friedman, M. & Friedman, R. (1980). *Free to Choose: A Personal Statement*. Harcourt & Brace.

Friedman, T. L. (2005). *The World Is Flat: The Globalized World in the Twenty-First Century*. Penguin.

Fukuyama, F. (1992). *The End of History and the Last Man*. Free Press.

Gamble, A. (1988). *The Free Economy and the Strong State: The Politics of Thatcherism*. Palgrave.

Giménez, M. E. (2019). *Marx, Women, and Capitalist Social Reproduction: Marxist-Feminist Essays*. Haymarket.

Giroux, H. A. (2011). *On Critical Pedagogy*. Bloomsbury Academic.

Goonewardena, K. (2022). Space. In B. Skeggs, *et al.* (Eds.), *The Sage Handbook of Marxism* (pp. 508–526). Sage.

Graham, J. & Gibson, K. (1996). *The End of Capitalism (As We Knew It)*. Blackwell.

Gregory, D. (2006). Troubling geographies. In N. Castree & D. Gregory (Eds.), *David Harvey: A Critical Reader* (pp. 1–25). Blackwell.

Habermas, J. (1989). *The Structural Transformation of the Public Sphere: An Inquiry into a Category of Bourgeois Society*. MIT Press.

Hahnel, R. E. (2021). Response to Moseley. *Review of Radical Political Economics*, 53(3), 525–534. https://doi.org/10.1177/04866134211003340

Hall, R. (2021). Largest debt amassed by student in England is £189,700. *Guardian*, 25 November. https://www.theguardian.com/education/2021/nov/25/largest-debt-amassed-by-student-in-england-is-189700

Hareven, T. K. (1982). *Family Time and Industrial Time: The Relationship between the Family and Work in a New England Industrial Community*. Cambridge University Press.

Hartung, W. D. (2021). Profits of war: Corporate beneficiaries of the post-9/11 pentagon spending surge. Costs of War Project, Brown University, 13 September.

Hayek, F. A. (1988). *The Fatal Conceit: The Errors of Socialism*. Chicago University Press.

Helleiner, E. (1993). When finance was the servant: International capital movements in the Bretton Woods order. In P. Cerny (Ed.), *Finance and World Politics: Markets, Regimes and States in the Post-Hegemonic Era* (pp. 20–48). Elgar.

Henderson, G. (2013). *Value in Marx: The Persistence of Value in a More-Than-Capitalist World*. University of Minnesota Press.

Herod, A. (1997). From a geography of labor to a labor geography: Labor's spatial fix and the geography of capitalism. *Antipode*, 29(1), 1–31. https://doi.org/10.1111/1467-8330.00033

Holgersen, S. (2022). The urban. In B. Skeggs, *et al.* (Eds.), *The Sage Handbook of Marxism* (pp. 1503–1524). Sage.

Honneth, A. (2017). *The Idea of Socialism: Towards a Renewal*. Polity Press.

Huer, J. (1991). *Tenure for Socrates: A Study in the Betrayal of the American Professor*. Bergin & Garvey.

Jameson, F. (1984). Postmodernism or, the cultural logic of late capitalism. *New Left Review*, I/146, 53–92.

Jameson, F. (1992). *Postmodernism or, the Cultural Logic of Late Capitalism*. Duke University Press.

Jessop, B. (2004). On the limits of *The Limits to Capital*. *Antipode*, 36(3), 480–496.

Katz, C. (2001). Vagabond capitalism and the necessity of social reproduction. *Antipode*, 33(4), 709–728.

Katz, C. (2006). Messing with 'the Project'. In N. Castree & D. Gregory (Eds.) *David Harvey: A Critical Reader* (pp. 234–246). Blackwell.

Katznelson, I. (2020). Is liberal socialism possible? Reflections on 'Real Utopias'. *Politics & Society*, 48(4), 525–538.

Kerr, E. & Wood, S. (2021). See 10 years of average total student loan debt. *US News*, 14 September. https://www.usnews.com/education/best-colleges/paying-for-college/articles/see-how-student-loan-borrowing-has-risen-in-10-years

Keynes, J. M. (2013). *Collected Writings: Volume 7*. Cambridge University Press.

Kolbert, E. (2021). *Under A White Sky*. Crown Books.

Laffer, A., Moore, S. & Tanous, P. (2008). *The End of Prosperity: How Higher Taxes Will Doom the Economy - If We Let It Happen*. Simon & Schuster.

Lanchester, J. (2016). Brexit blues. *London Review of Books*, 38(15), 28 July. https://www.lrb.co.uk/the-paper/v38/n15/john-lanchester/brexit-blues

Lapavitsas, C. (2013). The financialisation of capitalism: 'Profiting without producing'. *City*, 17(6), 792–805.

Latour, B. (2012). *An Inquiry into Modes of Existence: An Anthropology of the Moderns.* Harvard University Press.

Lefebvre, H. (1991). *The Production of Space.* Wiley-Blackwell.

Lefebvre, H. (1995). The right to the city. In E. Kofman & E. Lebas (Eds.), *Writings on Cities* (pp. 61–181). Blackwell.

Lilla, M. (2017). *The Once and Future Liberal: After Identity Politics.* Harper Collins.

Lippman, W. (1965). *Public Opinion.* Free Press.

Lucas, D. (2019). Measuring the cost of bailouts. *Annual Review of Financial Economics*, 11, 85–108. https://doi.org/10.1146/annurev-financial-110217-022532

Lucas, Jr., R. E. (2003). Macroeconomic priorities. *The American Economic Review*, March, 1–14.

MacLean, N. (2017). *Democracy in Chains: The Deep History of the Radical Right's Stealth Plan for America.* Scribe Books.

Madariaga, A. (2020). *Neoliberal Resilience: Lessons in Democracy and Development from Latin America and Eastern Europe.* Princeton University Press.

Maier, C. S. (1987). The politics of time: Changing paradigms of collective time and private time in the modern era. In C. S. Maier (Ed.), *Changing Boundaries of the Political: Essays on the Evolving Balance between the State and Society, Public and Private in Europe* (pp. 151–176). Cambridge University Press.

Marx, K. (1852). The Eighteenth Brumaire of Louis Bonaparte. https://www.marxists.org/archive/marx/works/1852/18th-brumaire/ch01.htm

Marx, M. (1973). *Grundrisse: Foundations of the Critique of Political Economy.* Pelican.

Massey, D. (1984). *Spatial Divisions of Labour Social Structures and the Geography of Production.* Macmillan.

Massey, D. (1991). The political place of locality studies. *Environment & Planning A*, 23(2), 267–281.

Mattick, P. (2008). Review: *The Limits to Capital*, David Harvey, London: Verso, 2006. *Historical Materialism*, 16, 205–232.

McKinsey Global Institute. (2021). *The Rise and Rise of the Global Balance Sheet: How Productively Are We Using Our Wealth?* McKinsey Global Institute.

Merrifield, A. (1993). The struggle over place: Redeveloping American can in southeast Baltimore. *Transactions of the Institute of British Geographers*, 18(1), 102–121.

Mirowski, P. & Plehwe, D. (Eds.) (2009). *The Road from Mont Pèlerin: The Making of the Neoliberal Thought Collective.* Harvard University Press.

Moseley, F. (2021). A Marxian reply to Hahnel: The relative explanatory power of Marx's theory and Sraffa's theory. *Review of Radical Political Economics*, 53(3), 511–524. https://doi.org/10.1177/0486613420957148

Moore, J. W. (2014). The end of cheap nature. Or how I learned to stop worrying about 'the' environment and love the crisis of capitalism. In C. Suter & C. Chase-Dunn (Eds.), *Structures of the World Economy and the Future of Global Conflict and Cooperation* (pp. 285–314). LIT.

Munn, N. D. (1986). *The Fame of Gawa: A Symbolic Study of Value Transformation in a Massim (Papua New Guinea) Society.* Duke University Press.

Nordhaus, T. & Shellenberger, M. (2007). *Break through: From the Death of Environmentalism to the Politics of Possibility*. Houghton Mifflin.
Ogle, V. (2015). *The Global Transformation of Time: 1870–1950*. Harvard University Press.
O'Neill, O. (1996). Introduction. In C. M. Korsgaard (Ed.), *The Sources of Normativity* (pp. xi–xv). Oxford University Press.
Orwell, G. (1937). *The Road to Wigan Pier*. Left Book Club.
Oxfam International. (2022). Inequality Kills: Methodology Note. January. https://oxfamilibrary.openrepository.com/bitstream/handle/10546/621341/tb-inequality-kills-methodology-note-170122-en.pdf.
Peake, L. & Jackson, P. (1998). 'The restless analyst': An interview with David Harvey. *Journal of Geography in Higher Education*, 12(1), 5–20. https://doi.org/10.1080/03098268808709021
Peck, J. (2010). *Constructions of Neoliberal Reason*. Oxford University Press.
Piketty, T. (2014). *Capital in the Twenty-First Century*. Harvard University Press.
Piketty, T. (2021). *Time for Socialism: Dispatches from a World on Fire, 2016–2021*. Yale University Press.
Pitts, F. H. (2021). *Value*. Polity.
Plehwe, D., Slobodian, Q. & Mirowski, P. (Eds.) (2020). *Nine Lives of Neo-Liberalism*. Verso.
Pollin, R. (2005). *Contours of Descent: US Economic Fractures and the Landscape of Global Austerity*. Verso.
Postman, N. (1985). *Amusing Ourselves to Death: Public Discourse in the Age of Show Business*. Viking Books.
Postone, M. (1993). *Time, Labor and Social Domination*. Cambridge University Press.
Primrose, D. (2013). Contesting capitalism in the light of the crisis: A conversation with David Harvey. *Journal of Australian Political Economy*, 71, 5–25.
Rand, A. (1964). *The Virtues of Selfishness*. New American Library.
Rawls, J. (1971). *A Theory of Justice*. Harvard University Press.
Resnick, S. A. & Wolff, R. D. (1987). *Knowledge and Class: A Marxian Critique of Political Economy*. University of Chicago Press.
Roediger, D. (2017). *Class, Race, and Marxism*. Verso.
Roitman, J. (2013). *Anti-Crisis*. Duke University Press.
Saccarelli, E. (2011). The intellectual in question. *Cultural Studies*, 25(6), 757–782.
Sassen, S. (1981). *The Global City: New York, London, Tokyo*. Princeton University Press.
Sassower, R. (2014). *The Price of Public Intellectuals*. Palgrave Macmillan.
Sayer, A. (1995). *Radical Political Economy: A Critique*. Blackwell.
Schiller, D. (1999). *Digital Capitalism: Networking the Global Market System*. MIT Press.
Schiller, D. (2014). *Digital Depression: Information Technology and Economic Crisis*. University of Illinois Press.
Sennett, R. (1976). *The Fall of Public Man*. Alfred Knopf.

Silver, L., et al. (2020). In US and UK, Globalisation Leaves Some Feeling 'Left Behind' or 'Swept Up'. Pew Research Center. 5 October. https://www.pewresearch.org/global/2020/10/05/in-u-s-and-uk-globalization-leaves-some-feeling-left-behind-or-swept-up/.

Skeggs, B. (2022). Class. In B. Skeggs *et al.* (Eds.), *The Sage Handbook of Marxism* (pp. 191–211). Sage.

Slobodian, Q. (2018). *Globalists: The End of Empire and the Birth of Neoliberalism*. Harvard University Press.

Smith, J. (2018). David Harvey denies imperialism. *Review of African Political Economy* (Blogpost), 10 January, http://roape.net/2018/01/10/david-harvey-denies-imperialism/

Smith, N. (1984). *Uneven Development: Nature, Capital and the Production of Space*. Blackwell.

Smith, N. (1987a). Dangers of the empirical turn. *Antipode*, 19(1), 59–68. https://doi.org/10.1111/j.1467-8330.1987.tb00149.x

Smith, N. (1987b). Gentrification and the rent gap. *Annals of the Association of American Geographers*, 77(3), 462–465

Soederberg, S. (2014). *Debtfare States and the Poverty Industry: Money, Discipline and the Surplus Population*. Routledge.

Soja, E. W. (1980). The socio-spatial dialectic. *Annals of the Association of American Geographers*. 70(2), 207–225. https://doi.org/10.1111/j.1467-8306.1980.tb01308.x

Springer, S. (2014). Why a radical geography must be anarchist. *Dialogues in Human Geography*, 4(3), 249–270.

Starr, P. (2021). The relational public. *Sociological Theory*, 39(2), 57–80. https://doi.org/10.1177/07352751211004660

Stedman Jones, D. (2012). *Masters of the Universe: Hayek, Friedman and the Birth of Neoliberal Politics*. Princeton University Press.

Steinbeck, J. (1939). *The Grapes of Wrath*. The Viking Press.

Stiglitz, J. (2015). *The Great Divide: Unequal Societies and What We Can Do About Them*. Penguin.

Swyngedouw, E. (1997). Neither global nor local: 'glocalisation' and the politics of scale. In K. Cox (Ed.), *Spaces of Globalisation: Reasserting the Power of the Local* (pp. 137–166). Guilford.

Tett, G. (2009). *Fool's Gold: How Unrestrained Greed Corrupted a Dream, Shattered Global Markets and Unleashed a Catastrophe*. Abacus.

Thompson, E. P. (1967). Time, work discipline and industrial capitalism. *Past & Present*, 38, 56–97.

Thompson, E. P. (1978). *The Poverty of Theory*. Merlin Press.

Thrift, N. J. (1987). No perfect symmetry: A response to David Harvey. *Environment and Planning D: Society and Space*, 5, 400–407.

Tooze, A. (2018). *Crashed: How a Decade of Financial Crises Changed the World*. Allen Lane.

Tricontinental. (2019). The rate of exploitation (the case of the iPhone). Notebook 2. Tricontinental: Institute for Social Research. https://thetricontinental.org/the-rate-of-exploitation-the-case-of-the-iphone/

United Nations. (2020). *World Social Report 2020: Inequality in a Rapidly Changing World*. United Nations.

US Census Bureau. (2021). Income and Poverty in the United States: 2020. Current Populations Reports, P60-273. US Government Publishing Office. September.

Van Parijs, P. (Ed.) (1992). *Arguing for Basic Income*. Verso.

Walker, R. A. (1981). A theory of suburbanization: Capitalism and the construction of urban space in the United States. In M. Dear & A. J. Scott (Eds.), *Urbanization and Urban Planning in Capitalist Society* (pp. 383–429). Routledge.

Watts, G. (2022). Are you a neoliberal subject? On the uses and abuses of a concept. *European Journal of Social Theory*, 25(3), 458–476. https://doi.org/10.1177/13684310211037205

Webber, M. J. & Rigby, D. L. (1996). *The Golden Age Illusion: Rethinking Postwar Capitalism*. Guildford Press.

Weber, M. (1994). The profession and vocation of politics. In P. Lassman, & R. Speir (Eds.), *Weber: Political Writings* (pp. 309–369). Cambridge University Press.

Wilson, J. & Swyngedouw, E. (2014). Seeds of Dystopia: Post-Politics and the Return of the Political. In J. Wilson & E. Swyngedouw (Eds.), *The Post-Political and Its Discontents: Spaces of Depoliticisation, Spectres of Radical Politics* (pp. 1–22). Edinburgh University Press.

World Bank. (2020). *Breaking Out of Fragility: A Country Economic Memorandum for Diversification and Growth in Iraq*. World Bank.

Wright, E. O. (1985). *Classes*. Verso.

Wright, E. O. (2010). *Envisioning Real Utopias*. Verso.

Wright, E. O. (2019). *How to Be an Anti-Capitalist in the Twenty-First Century*. Verso.

Wright, M. (2006). Differences that matter. In N. Castree & D. Gregory (Eds.), *David Harvey: A Critical Reader* (pp. 80–101). Blackwell.

Wyly, E. K., Atia, M. & Hammel, D. J. (2004). Has mortgage capital found an inner-city spatial fix? *Housing Policy Debate*, 15(3), 623–685. https://doi.org/10.1080/10511482.2004.9521516

Young, I. M. (1990). *Justice and the Politics of Difference*. Princeton University Press.

Young, I. M. (1998). Harvey's complaint with race and gender struggles: A critical response. *Antipode*, 30(1), 36–42.

Zelizer, J. E. (2021). The public intellectual in the age of Twitter. *Law, Culture and the Humanities*. https://doi.org/10.1177/17438721211035462

Žižek, S. (2002). A plea for Leninist intolerance. *Critical Inquiry*, 28(2), 542–566.

Appendix 1: David Harvey: List of publications

Single-authored publications

(2022a). Reflections on an academic life. *Human Geography*, 15(1), 14–24. https://doi.org/10.1177/19427786211046291

(2022b). The double consciousness of capital. In G. Albo, L. Panitch & C. Leys (Eds.), *Socialist Register 2022: New Polarizations, Old Contradictions – The Crisis of Centrism* (pp. 281–298). Merlin Press.

(2021a). Rate and mass: Perspectives from the *Grundrisse*. *New Left Review*, 130, 73–98.

(2021b). Once more on rate and mass: Reply to Dylan Riley. *New Left Review*, 132, 99–106.

(2020a). *The Anti-Capitalist Chronicles*. Pluto.

(2020b). Value in motion. *New Left Review*, 126, 99–116.

(2020c). We need a collective response to the collective dilemma of coronavirus. *Jacobin*, 2 April.

(2020d). Socialists must be champions of freedom. *Jacobin*, 22 October.

(2020e). Capitalism is not the solution to urban America's problems: Capitalism itself is the problem. *Jacobin*, 2 June.

(2020f). Anti-capitalist politics in the time of COVID. *Jacobin*, 20 March.

(2019a). Foreword. In R. Rolnik (Ed.), *Urban Warfare: Housing under the Empire of Finance*. Verso.

(2019b). Realization crises and the transformation of daily life. *Space and Culture*, 22(2), 126–141.

(2019c). Karl Marx is useful for our time, not just his. *Jacobin*, 8 July.

(2018a). *A Companion to Marx's Capital: The Complete Edition*. Verso.

(2018b). *The Misunderstandings of Michael Roberts*. https://thenextrecession.wordpress.com/2018/04/02/marxs-law-of-value-a-debate-between-david-harvey-and-michael-roberts/

(2018c). Universal alienation. *Journal for Cultural Research*, 22(2), 137–150.
(2018d). Realities on the ground: David Harvey replies to John Smith. *Review of African Political Economy* (Blogpost), 5 February. https://roape.net/2018/02/05/realities-ground-david-harvey-replies-john-smith/
(2018e). Universal alienation and the real subsumption of daily life under capitalism: A response to Hardt and Negri. *Triple C: Communication, Capitalism and Critique*, 16(2), 449–453.
(2018f). Why Marx's *Capital* still matters. *Jacobin*, 12 July.
(2017a). *Marx, Capital and the Madness of Economic Reason*. Profile Books.
(2017b). A commentary on *A Theory of Imperialism* by David Harvey. In U. Patnaik & P. Patnaik (Eds.), *A Theory of Imperialism* (pp. 154–172). Columbia University Press.
(2017c). Listen, anarchist! A personal response to Simon Springer's: Why a radical geography must be anarchist. *Dialogues in Human Geography*, 7(3), 233–250.
(2016a). *The Ways of the World*. Profile Books.
(2016b). *Abstract from the Concrete*. Harvard University Graduate School of Design and Sternberg Press.
(2016c). Neoliberalism is a political project. *Jacobin*, 23 July.
(2016d). Crisis theory and the falling rate of profit. In T. Subasat (Ed.), *The Great Financial Meltdown: Systemic, Conjunctural or Policy Created* (pp. 37–54). Edward Elgar.
(2014a). *Seventeen Contradictions and the End of Capitalism*. Profile Books.
(2014b). The crisis of planetary urbanization. In P. Gadanho (Ed.), *Tactical Urbanisms for Expanding Megacities* (pp. 26–31). Museum of Modern Art.
(2014c). Alienation and urban life. In J. K. Brekke, D. Dalakoglu, C. Filippidis & A. Vradis (Eds.), *Crisis-Scrapes: Athens and Beyond* (pp. 195–204). crisis-scape.net.
(2014d). Afterthoughts on Piketty's *Capital in the Twenty-First Century*. *Challenge*, 57(5), 81–86.
(2013). *A Companion to Marx's Capital: Volume Two*. Verso.
(2012a). *Rebel Cities: From the Right to the City to the Urban Revolution*. Verso.
(2012b). The urban roots of financial crises: Reclaiming the city for anti-capitalist struggle. In L. Panitch, G. Albo & V. Chibber (Eds.), *Socialist Register 2012: The Crisis and the Left* (pp. 1–35). Merlin Press.
(2012c). History versus theory: A commentary on Marx's method in *Capital*. *Historical Materialism*, 20(2), 3–38.
(2012d). La geografía como oportunidad política de resistencia y construcción de alternativas. *Revista De Geografía Espacios*, 2(4), 9–26.
(2011a). Nice day for a revolution. *The Independent*, 29th April.
(2011b). The enigma of capital and the crisis this time. In C. Calhoun & G. Derlugian (Eds.), *Business as Usual: The Roots of the Global Financial Meltdown* (pp. 89–112). New York University Press.
(2011c). Roepke Lecture in Economic Geography: Crises, geographic disruptions and the uneven development of political responses. *Economic Geography*, 87(1), 1–22.

(2011d). The future of the commons. *Radical History Review*, 109, 101–107.
(2010a). *The Enigma of Capital and the Crises of Capitalism*. Profile Books.
(2010b). *A Companion to Marx's Capital*. Verso.
(2010c). Organizing for the anti-capitalist transition. *Human Geography*, 3(1), 1–17.
(2010d). A financial Katrina? Geographical aspects of the financial crisis. In *World Social Science Report, 2010: Knowledge Divides* (pp. 21–23). UNESCO.
(2009a). *Cosmopolitanism and the Geographies of Freedom*. Colombia University Press.
(2009b). The crisis and the consolidation of class power. *Red Pepper*, February–March.
(2009c). Reshaping economic geography: The *World Development Report 2009*. *Development and Change*, 40(6), 1269–1277.
(2009d). Commonwealth: An exchange. *ArtForum*, November.
(2008a). Introduction. In K. Marx & F. Engels (Ed.), *The Communist Manifesto*. Pluto Press.
(2008b). The right to the city. *New Left Review*, 53, 23–40.
(2008c). The dialectics of spacetime. In B. Ollman & T. Smith (Eds.), *Dialectics for the New Century* (pp. 98–117). Palgrave Macmillan.
(2007a). The Kantian roots of Foucault's dilemmas. In J. Crampton & S. Elden (Eds.), *Space, Knowledge and Power: Foucault and Geography* (pp. 41–48). Ashgate.
(2007b). The geography of accumulation: An interview with David Harvey, by J. J. Williams. *Minnesota Review*, 69, 115–138.
(2007c). The freedom of the city. In M. Swenarton, I. Troiani & H. Webster (Eds.), *The Politics of Making* (pp. 15–24). Routledge.
(2007d). Reflections: David Harvey interviewed by Alberto Toscano. *Development and Change*, 38(6), 1127–1135.
(2007e). Neoliberalism as creative destruction. *The ANNALS of the American Academy of Political and Social Science*, 610(1), 21–44.
(2006a). Space as a keyword. In N. Castree & D. Gregory (Eds.), *David Harvey: A Critical Reader* (pp. 270–293). Blackwell.
(2006b). The right to the city. In R. Scholar (Ed.), *Divided Cities: The Oxford Amnesty Lectures 2003* (pp. 83–103). Oxford University Press.
(2006c). Neo-liberalism as creative destruction. *Geografiska Annaler: Series B, Human Geography*, 88(2), 145–158.
(2006d). Editorial: The geographies of critical geography. *Transactions of the Institute of British Geographers*, 31, 409–412.
(2005a). *A Brief History of Neoliberalism*. Oxford University Press.
(2005b). *Spaces of Neoliberalization: Towards a Theory of Uneven Geographical Development*. Franz Steiner Verlag.
(2005c). The sociological and geographical imaginations. *International Journal of Politics, Culture and Society*, 18(3–4), 211–256.
(2005d). The political economy of public space. In S. Low & N. Smith (Eds.), *The Politics of Public Space* (pp. 17–34). Routledge.
(2005e). El futuro de la ciudad contenido en el pasado de la ciudad. In M. Guttman (Ed.), *Construir Bicentenarios: Argentina* (pp. 137–141). Observatorio Argentina.
(2005f). 'For a ruthless criticism of everything existing': Jim Blaut's Contribution to Geographical Knowledge. *Antipode*, 37(5), 927–935.

(2004c). Geographical knowledges/political powers. *Proceedings of the British Academy*, 122, 87–115.
(2004a). The new imperialism: Accumulation by dispossession. In L. Panitch & C. Leys (Eds.), *Socialist Register 2004: The New Imperial Challenge* (pp. 63–87). Merlin Press.
(2004b). Retrospect on *The Limits to Capital*. *Antipode*, 36(3), 544–549.
(2003a). *The New Imperialism*. Oxford University Press.
(2003b). *Paris, Capital of Modernity*. Routledge.
(2003c). The fetish of technology: Causes and consequences. Macalaster International, 13, article 7. https://digitalcommons.macalester.edu/macintl/vol13/iss1/7/
(2003d). The city as a body politic. In J. Schneider & I. Susser (Eds.), *Wounded Cities: Destruction and Reconstruction in a Globalized World* (pp. 25–46). Berg.
(2003e). City and justice: Social movements in the city. In L. Girard, B. Forte, M. Cerreta, P. De Toro & F. Forte (Eds.), *The Human Sustainable City* (pp. 235–254). Ashgate.
(2003f). The right to the city. *International Journal of Urban and Regional Research*, 27(4), 939–941.
(2003g). City future contained in city past: Balzac in Paris. In J. Ramon (Ed.), *After-Images of the City* (pp. 23–48). Cornell University Press.
(2002a). Memories and desires. In P. Gould & F. Pitts (Eds.), *Geographical Voices: Fourteen Autobiographical Records* (pp. 149–188). Syracuse University Press.
(2002b). The art of rent: Globalization, monopoly and cultural production. In L. Panitch & C. Leys (Eds.), *Socialist Register 2002: A World of Contradictions* (pp. 93–110). Merlin Press.
(2002c). Cracks in the edifice of the Empire State. In M. Sorkin & S. Zukin (Eds.), *After the World Trade Center* (pp. 57–68). Routledge.
(2001a). Globalization and the 'spatial fix'. *Geographische Revue*, 2, 23–30.
(2001b). *Spaces of Capital: Towards a Critical Geography*. Routledge.
(2001c). The cartographic imagination: Balzac in Paris. In V. Dharwadker (Ed.), *Cosmopolitan Geographies* (pp. 63–87). Routledge.
(2001d). The spaces of utopia. In D. Goldberg, M. Mushenyo & L. Bower (Eds.), *Between Law and Culture: Relocating Legal Studies* (pp. 95–121). University of Minnesota Press.
(2000a). *Spaces of Hope*. Edinburgh University Press.
(2000b). Reinventing geography (interviewer P. Anderson). *New Left Review*, 4, 75–97.
(2000c). The work of postmodernity: The labouring body in global space. In J. E. Davis (Ed.), *Identity and Social Change* (pp. 27–52). Transactions Press.
(2000d). Cosmopolitanism and the banality of geographical evils. *Public Culture*, 12(2), 529–564.
(1999a). The Humboldt connection. *Annals of the Association of American Geographers*, 88(4), 723–730.
(1999b). The body as referent. *The Hedgehog Review*, 1, 41–46.
(1999c). Social movements and the city: A theoretical positioning. In O. G. Ling (Ed.), *Urban Best Practices*, Vol. 2 (pp. 104–115). Urban Redevelopment Authority and the Institute of Policy Studies.

(1999d). On fatal flaws and fatal distractions. *Progress in Human Geography*, 23(4), 557–566.

(1999e). Frontiers of insurgent planning. *Plurimondi*, 2, 269–286.

(1999f). Considerations on the environment of justice. In N. Low (Ed.), *Global Ethics and Environment* (pp. 109–130). Routledge.

(1998a). An anniversary of consequence and relevance. *Environment and Planning D: Society and Space*, 16, 379–385.

(1998b). The body as an accumulation strategy. *Environment and Planning D: Society and Space*, 16(4), 401–421.

(1998c). What's green and makes the environment go round? In F. Jameson & M. Miyoshi (Eds.), *The Cultures of Globalization* (pp. 327–355). Duke University Press.

(1998d). The geography of class power. In L. Panitch & C. Leys (Eds.), *Socialist Register 1998: The Communist Manifesto Now* (pp. 49–74). Merlin Press.

(1998e). Spaces of insurgency. In J. Beverly, P. Cohen & D. Harvey (Eds.), *Subculture and Homogenization*. Fundació Antoni Tàpies.

(1998f). Retrospective on postmodernism. In *Architecture and the Public Sphere* (pp. 38–51). Architectural Review at the University of Virginia.

(1998g). Perspectives urbanes per el segle XXI. *La Ciutat: Visiones. Analisis i* Reptes. Ajuntament de Girona.

(1998h). Marxism, metaphors, and ecological politics. *Monthly Review*, 49(11), 17–31.

(1998i). David Harvey: The politics of social justice. Interview with R. Baruffalo, E. McCann & C. Staddon. *Disclosure: A Journal of Social Theory*, 6, 125–43.

(1997). The new urbanization and the communitarian trap. *Harvard Design Magazine*, Winter/Spring, 68–69.

(1996a). *Justice, Nature, and the Geography of Difference*. Basil Blackwell.

(1996b). The environment of justice. In A. Merrifield & E. Swyngedouw (Eds.), *The Urbanization of Injustice* (pp. 65–99). New York University Press.

(1996c). Poverty and greed in American cities. In W. Saunders (Ed.), *Reflections on Architectural Practices in the Nineties* (pp. 104–112). Princeton Architectural Press.

(1996d). On architects, bees and possible urban worlds. In C. Davidson (Ed.), *Anywise*. MIT Press.

(1996e). Globalization in question. *Rethinking Marxism*, 8(4), 1–17.

(1996f). Entrevista: David Harvey. *Geographikos: Una Revista De Geographia*, 6, 55–66.

(1995a). A geographer's guide to dialectical reasoning. In N. Thrift & A. Cliff (Eds.), *Diffusing Geography* (pp. 3–21). Blackwell.

(1995b). Militant particularism and global ambition: The conceptual politics of place, space and environment in the work of Raymond Williams. *Social Text*, 42, 69–98.

(1995c). Nature, politics and possibilities: A debate with David Harvey and Donna Haraway. *Environment and Planning D: Society and Space*, 13, 507–527.

(1995d). Cities or urbanization? *City*, 1/2, 38–61.

(1994). The invisible political economy of architectural production. In O. Bouman & R. van Torn (Eds.), *The Invisible in Architecture* (pp. 420–427). Academy Editions.

(1993a). Class relations, social justice and the politics of difference. In J. Squires (Ed.), *Principled Positions: Postmodernism and the Rediscovery of Value* (pp. 85–120). Lawrence and Wishart.

(1993b). Towards reclaiming our cities: Experience and analysis, an Interview with David Harvey. *Regenerating Cities*, 1(5), 4–10 & 1(6), 3–9.

(1993c). The nature of environment: The dialectics of social and environmental change. In R. Miliband & L. Panitch (Eds.), *Socialist Register 1993: Real Problems, False Solutions* (pp. 1–51). Merlin Press.

(1993d). From space to place and back again: Reflections on the condition of post-modernity. In J. Bird, B. Curtis, T. Putnam, G. Robertson & L. Tickner (Eds.), *Mapping the Futures: Local Cultures, Global Change* (pp. 3–29). Routledge.

(1992a). The view from Federal Hill. In E. Fee, L. Shopes & L. Zeidman (Eds.), *The Baltimore Book: New Views on Local History* (pp. 227–249). Temple University Press.

(1992b). Social justice, postmodernism and the city. *International Journal of Urban and Regional Research*, 16(4), 588–601.

(1992c). Postmodern morality plays. *Antipode*, 24(3), 300–326.

(1992d). Capitalism: The factory of fragmentation. *New Perspectives Quarterly*, 9, 42–45.

(1991a). Flexibility: Threat or opportunity? *Socialist Review*, 21, 65–78.

(1991b). The urban face of capitalism. In J. F. Hart (Ed.), *Our Changing Cities* (pp. 227–249). The Johns Hopkins University Press.

(1990a). Between space and time: Reflections on the geographical imagination. *Annals of the Association of American Geographers*, 80, 418–434.

(1990b). Looking backwards on postmodernism. In A. C. Papadakis (Ed.), *Architectural Design Profile* (pp. 10–12). Academy Editions.

(1989a). *The Condition of Postmodernity*. Basil Blackwell.

(1989b). *The Urban Experience*. Basil Blackwell.

(1989c). From managerialism to entrepreneurialism: The transformation of urban governance in late capitalism. *Geografiska Annaler*, 71B, 3–17.

(1989d). From models to Marx. In W. Macmillan (Ed.), *Re-modelling Geography* (pp. 211–216), Basil Blackwell.

(1988a). Urban places in the 'global village': Reflections on the urban condition in late twentieth century capitalism. In L. Mazza (Ed.), *World Cities and the Future of the Metropoles* (pp. 21–31). Electa.

(1988b). The production of value in historical geography. *Journal of Historical Geography*, 14, 305–306.

(1988c). The geographical and geopolitical consequences of the transition from Fordist to flexible accumulation. In G. Sternlieb & J. Hughes (Eds.), *America's New Market Geography* (pp. 101–134). Rutgers Center for Urban Studies.

(1988d). Foreword. In S. Zukin (Ed.), *Loft Living*. Radius Editions.

(1987a). Three myths in search of a reality in urban studies. *Environment and Planning D: Society and Space*, 5, 367–386.

(1987b). The world systems trap. *Studies in Comparative International Development*, 22, 42–47.

(1987c). The representation of urban life. *Journal of Historical Geography*, 13(3), 317–321.
(1987d). Flexible accumulation through urbanisation: Reflections on postmodernism in the American city. *Antipode*, 19(3), 260–286.
(1987e). Urban housing. Entry in *New Palgrave Dictionary*.
(1986). The essential and vernacular landscapes of J. B. Jackson. *Design Book Review*, Fall, 12–17.
(1985a). *The Urbanization of Capital*. Basil Blackwell.
(1985b). *Consciousness and the Urban Experience*. Basil Blackwell.
(1985c). The geopolitics of capitalism. In D. Gregory & J. Urry (Eds.), *Social Relations and Spatial Structures* (pp. 128–163). Macmillan.
(1984a). On the history and present condition of geography: An historical materialist manifesto. *The Professional Geographer*, 36, 1–11.
(1984b). Geography & urbanisation. Entries in T. Bottomore (Ed.), *Dictionary of Marxist Thought*. Blackwell.
(1983). Owen Lattimore: A memoire. *Antipode*, 15(3), 3–11.
(1982a). *The Limits to Capital*. Basil Blackwell.
(1982b). The space-economy of capitalist production: A Marxian interpretation. In International Geographical Union. Latin American Regional Conference. Symposia and Round Tables, 2.
(1982c). Marxist geography & Mode of production. *Entries in Dictionary of Human Geography*. Blackwell.
(1981a). The spatial fix: Hegel, von Thunen and Marx. *Antipode*, 13(3), 1–12.
(1981b). Rent control and a fair return. In J. Gilderbloom (Ed.), *Rent Control: A Source Book*. Foundation for National Progress.
(1979). Monument and myth. *Annals of the Association of American Geographers*, 69(3), 362–381.
(1978a). The urban process under capitalism: A framework for analysis. *International Journal of Urban and Regional Research*, 2(1–3), 101–131.
(1978b). On planning and the ideology of planning. In J. Burchall (Ed.), *Planning for the '80s: Challenge and Response*. Rutgers University Press.
(1978c). On countering the Marxian myth – Chicago style. *Comparative Urban Research*, 6(1), 28–45.
(1977a). Labor, capital and class struggle around the built environment. *Politics and Society*, 7(2), 265–295.
(1977b). Government policies, financial institutions and neighborhood change in U.S. cities. In M. Harloe (Ed.), *Captive Cities* (pp. 123–139). John Wiley.
(1976). The Marxian theory of the state. *Antipode*, 8(2), 80–89.
(1975a). The geography of capitalist accumulation: A reconstruction of the Marxian theory. *Antipode*, 7(2), 9–21.
(1975b). The political economy of urbanism in advanced capitalist societies: The case of the United States. *Urban Affairs Annual*, 9, 119–163.
(1975c). Some remarks on the political economy of urbanism. *Antipode*, 7(1), 54–61.

(1975d). Class structure and the theory of residential differentiation. In M. Chisholm & R. Peel (Eds.), *Bristol Essays in Geography*. Heinemann Press.
(1974a). Population, resources and the ideology of science. *Economic Geography*, 50, 256–257.
(1974b). What kind of geography for what kind of public policy? *Transactions of the Institute of British Geographers*, 63, 18–24.
(1974c). Discussion with Brian Berry. *Antipode*, 6(2), 145–149.
(1974d). Class-monopoly rent, finance capital and the urban revolution. *Regional Studies*, 8(1–3), 239–255.
(1973). *Social Justice and the City*. Johns Hopkins University Press.
(1972b). Revolutionary and counter-revolutionary theory. *Antipode*, 4(2), 1–25.
(1972c). Social processes, spatial form, and the redistribution of real income in an urban system. In M. Chisholm (Ed.), *Regional Forecasting* (pp. 267–300). Butterworth Scientific Publications.
(1972d). Social justice in spatial systems. In R. Peet (Ed.), *Geographical Perspectives on Poverty and Social Well Being* (pp. 12–25). Clark University Geography Department.
(1972e). A Commentary on the comments. *Antipode*, 4(2), 36–41.
(1972f). Revolutionary and counter-revolutionary theory in geography and the problem of ghetto formation. In *Perspectives in Geography*, Vol. 2, Northern Illinois University Press.
(1972g). On obfuscation in geography: A comment on Gale's heterodoxy. *Geographical Analysis*, 41(3), 323–330.
(1972h). The role of theory. In N. Graves (Ed.), *New Movements in the Study and Teaching of Geography* (pp. 29–41). Temple Smith.
(1970a). Social processes and spatial form: An analysis of the conceptual problems of urban planning. *Papers of the Regional Science Association*, 25, 47–69.
(1970b). Behavioural postulates and the construction of theory in human geography. *Geografica Polonica*, 18, 27–45.
(1969a). *Explanation in Geography*. Edward Arnold and St Martin's Press.
(1969b). Conceptual and measurement problems in the cognitive behavioural approach to location theory. In K. Cox & R. Golledge (Eds.), *Behavioural Problems in Geography: A Symposium* (pp. 16–28). Northwestern University Press.
(1968a). Some methodological problems in the use of the Neyman type A and negative binomial probability distributions for the analysis of spatial point patterns. *Transactions of the Institute of British Geographers*, 44, 85–95.
(1968b). Pattern, process and the scale problem in geographical research. *Transactions of the Institute of British Geographers*, 45, 1–8.
(1968c). Geographical processes and the analysis of point patterns: Testing models of diffusion by quadrat sampling. *Transactions of the Institute of British Geographers*, 44, 85–95.
(1967a). The problem of theory construction in geography. *Journal of Regional Science*, 7(2), 1–6.

(1967b). Models of the evolution of spatial patterns in human geography. In R. J. Chorley & P. Haggett (Eds.), *Models in Geography* (pp. 549–608). Methuen.
(1966). Theoretical concepts and the analysis of agricultural land use patterns. *Annals of the Association of American Geographers*, 56, 361–374.
(1965). Monte Carlo simulation models. *Forskningsrapporter Kultu Rgeografiska Insitutionen*. Uppsala University.
(1964). Fruit growing in Kent in the nineteenth century. *Archaeologia Cantiana*, 79, 95–108.
(1963). Locational change in the Kentish hop industry and the analysis of land use patterns. *Transactions of the Institute of British Geographers*, 33, 123–140.
(1962). Aspects of agricultural and rural change in Kent, 1815–1900. PhD Thesis, Cambridge University.

Co-authored and co-edited publications

With Robles-Durán, M. (2011). The neoliberal city: Investment, development and crisis. In T. Kaminer, M. Robles-Durán & H. Sohn (Eds.), *Urban Asymmetries: Studies and Projects on Neoliberal Urbanization* (pp. 34–45). 010 Publishers.
With Potter, C. (2009). The right to the just city. In P. Marcuse, J. Connolly, J. Novy, I. Olivo, C. Potter & J. Steil (Eds.), *Searching for the Just City: Debates in Urban Theory and Practice* (pp. 40–51). Routledge.
With Asad, T., Katz, C., Smith, N. & Susser, I. (2001). Local horror/global response. *International Journal of Urban and Regional Research*, 25(4), 901.
With Hayter, T. (Eds.). (1993). *The Factory in the City*. Mansell.
With Swyngedouw, E. (1993). Industrial restructuring, community disempowerment and grass-roots resistance. In T. Hayter & D. Harvey (Eds.), *The Factory in the City* (pp. 11–25). Mansell.
With Scott, A. (1989). The practice of human geography: Theory and empirical specificity in the transition from Fordism to flexible accumulation. In W. Macmillan (Ed.), *Re-Modelling Geography* (pp. 217–219). Basil Blackwell.
With Smith, N. (1984). Geography: From capitals to capital. In B. Ollman & F. Vermelya (Eds.), *The Left Academy*, Vol. 2 (pp. 99–121). Praeger.
With Chatterjee, L. (1974). Absolute rent and the structuring of space by governmental and financial institutions. *Antipode*, 6(1), 22–36.
With Chatterjee, L. & Klugman, L. (1974). *PHA Policies and the Baltimore City Housing Market*. The Urban Observatory Inc.
With Chatterjee, L., Wolman, M. & Newman, J. (1972). *The Housing Market and Code Enforcement in Baltimore*. The Baltimore Observatory.

Appendix 2: David Harvey's books

- *Explanation in Geography*, Edward Arnold and St Martin's Press, 1969 (translated into Portuguese, Spanish, Russian, Chinese, Japanese); reprinted by Rawat Publications, New Delhi, India, 2003.

  Harvey's first book, this made his name in Anglophone Geography overnight. It offered a sophisticated examination of the philosophy and practice of a scientific approach to geographical research. The book became a key reference point for a generation of 'spatial scientists'.

- *Social Justice and the City*, Edward Arnold and The Johns Hopkins University Press, 1973 (translated into Japanese; Spanish; Italian; Korean); reissued with an introduction by Ira Katznelson, Basil Blackwell, 1992; revised edition re-published by Georgia University Press, 2009.

  This book examined the relationships between social relations and processes, on the one hand, and their spatial form on the other, with a focus on the internal geography of cities as well as cities' overall role in different modes of economic production. Unlike the proclaimed 'neutrality' of the scientific approach advocated in Explanation in Geography, Social Justice adopted an avowedly normative approach. Harvey embraced Marxism in part II of the book, arguing that social and geographical justice in metropolitan areas ultimately required capitalist society to tackle to power relations that underpinned systematic inequality.

- *The Limits to Capital*, Basil Blackwell (Oxford) and University of Chicago Press, 1982; reissued in 1999 with a new introduction by Verso, London; new Verso edition with a new introduction in 2006; Verso Reprint Edition 2019 (translated into Japanese, Portuguese, Spanish; Korean, Chinese).

  This magisterial book took almost a decade to prepare and write. It offered a synoptic and systematic exploration of how infrastructures of various kinds (factories, houses, transportation networks etc.) are integral elements of the capitalist mode of production. The book uses Karl Marx's concepts, particularly those developed in his post-1850 works. It uses dialectical reasoning to illuminate the totality of capitalism as a complex socio-geographic phenomenon.

- *Consciousness and the Urban Experience*, Basil Blackwell (Oxford) and Johns Hopkins University Press, 1985.

  One of two books that collected Harvey's various post-1973 writings about capitalist cities. The writings are more consistently Marxist than the early essays assembled in Social Justice. The book's chapters offer a set of insights into the relationships between capitalist class relationships and urban form, with a particular focus on the nineteenth-century Paris. The book foregrounds human agency, operating within tightly defined social relations of production.

- *The Urbanization of Capital*, Basil Blackwell (Oxford) and Johns Hopkins University Press, 1985 (translated into Japanese).

  This book complimented Consciousness and the Urban Experience, *having a more 'structural' focus on the processes driving urban growth and restructuring in capitalist societies. One of its central claims is that cities are integral to sustaining capitalism's punctuated patterns of accumulation.*

- *The Urban Experience*, Basil Blackwell (Oxford) and Johns Hopkins University Press, 1989 (translated into Italian, Japanese, Chinese, Portuguese, Spanish).

  This book was Harvey's first 'greatest hits' collection of essays. It assembled writings about the capitalist city written between the early 1970s and late 1980s.

- *The Condition of Postmodernity*, Basil Blackwell (Oxford and Cambridge, Mass), 1989 (translated into Italian, Portuguese, Korean, Japanese, Turkish, Chinese, Spanish, Arabic).

  This book brought Harvey to wider attention in the social sciences and humanities. It offered a critical explanation of the rise of post-modern cultural practices in art, literature, architecture and film, as well as in the realms of academic thought. Harvey audaciously argued that post-modernism was the 'cultural clothing' worm by a restructuring and globalising late twentieth-century capitalist system. The book made a strong pitch for the ongoing relevance of Marxist analysis and politics. It sold thousands of copies and has been translated into many languages.

- *The Factory in the City: The Story of the Cowley Automobile Workers in Oxford* (edited with Teresa Hayter), Mansell (Brighton), 1993.

  This book assembled essays about the context for and details of a dispute between car workers living near Oxford and their employer. The book was edited against the background of an ascendant Thatcherism in British life which sowed the seeds of long-term neoliberalism in England, Wales, Scotland and Northern Ireland.

- *Justice, Nature and the Geography of Difference*, Basil Blackwell (Oxford), 1996 (translated into Spanish, Portuguese, Chinese).

One of Harvey's largest books, but with a less cohesive structure than The Limits to Capital. The book offers a broad defence of Marxism's analytical and normative tool kit, including its relevance to geographical issues of space, place, region and the natural world. This defence takes account of the positive elements of post-modern, post-structural and post-foundational thought in the social sciences and the humanities.

- *Spaces of Hope*, Edinburgh University Press, Edinburgh; University of California Press, Berkeley, CA, 2000 (translated into Korean, Spanish, Italian, Portuguese, Turkish and Chinese).

  A collection of essays about political options and necessities for the Left at a time when Marxism's appeal was waning but when globalisation was proceeding apace and neo-liberalism was ascendant. This book explored anti-capitalist politics bridging between the 'old' and 'new' Left.

- *Megacities Lecture 4: Possible Urban Worlds*, Twynstra Gudde Management Consultants, Amersfoort, The Netherlands, 2000.

  This book draws together several of the threads from JNGD and Spaces of Hope into one extended lecture.

- *Spaces of Capital: Towards a Critical Geography*. Edinburgh University Press, Edinburgh; Routledge North America, 2001 (translated into Spanish, Portuguese and Chinese).

  A second 'greatest hits' collection of Harvey's essays encompassing more than a quarter century of Marxist writing.

- *The New Imperialism*, Oxford University Press, Oxford, 2003; reissued in 2005 with an Afterword (translated into Spanish, Italian, German, Japanese, Korean, Norwegian, Portuguese, Turkish, Rumanian, French, Greek, Chinese and Arabic).

  A big picture analysis of the links between a globalising capitalist economic system and the related reconfiguration of political power on the world stage. The book focusses on the decline of US hegemony and the US-led invasion of Iraq, positing a contradiction between 'molecular' (economic) power and 'territorial' (political) power. This book was based on a series of lectures delivered at Oxford University, where Harvey had worked. It was the first book to give Harvey something of a public profile.

- *Paris, Capital of Modernity*, New York, Routledge, 2003 (translated into Spanish, French, Korean, Turkish, Portuguese, Chinese, Taiwanese and Japanese).

  This book assembles a set of mostly published writings by Harvey about Paris, which he uses as a laboratory to comment on the wider dynamics of capitalist urbanisation since the nineteenth century.

- *A Brief History of Neoliberalism*, Oxford, Oxford University Press, 2005 (translations into Spanish, Russian, Japanese, German, Romanian, Finnish, Norwegian, Greek, Turkish, Italian, Portuguese, Korean, Polish, Croatian, Chinese).

Following on from the big picture, current affairs focus of The New Imperialism, this readable book explores how and why neoliberalism rose to ascendancy as the preferred modality of modern capitalism since 1973. It helped to garner a readership for Harvey among sections of the 'educated public' and Left political activists.

- *Spaces of Neoliberalization: Towards a Theory of Uneven Geographical Development* (2004 Hettner Lectures, Department of Geography, Heidelberg), Weisbaden: Franz Steiner Verlag, 2005; reprinted as *Spaces of Globalization: A Theory of Uneven Geographical Development*, London, Verso, 2006 (translated into Japanese, Chinese, Korean and German).

  Based on a set of lectures given at the University of Heidelberg, this short book is somewhat eclectic, with chapters about the rise of neoliberalism globally, about uneven geographical development, and about the nature of terrestrial 'space'.

- *Cosmopolitanism and the Geographies of Freedom* (the Wellek Lectures); New York, Columbia University Press, 2009 (translated into Spanish, Portuguese, Korean, Chinese).

  Based on a set of invited lectures, this book explores the links between global capitalism, socio-cultural plurality, people's 'right to geographical difference', and the geographical grounding of all human life. The book is highly interdisciplinary in its reference points, advancing the Marxist cause in generous and non-strident terms.

- *A Companion to Marx's* Capital, *Volume One*, New York, Verso, 2010 (translated into German, Chinese, Japanese, Korean, Portuguese, Turkish, Spanish).

  The first of several books that introduce readers to key texts in Karl Marx's oeuvre, in this case volume one of Capital. Harvey walks readers through each chapter of Marx's classic text. Harvey has been among a very few Marxists in recent years seeking to popularise Marx's writings among a younger generation of university students and activists.

- *The Enigma of Capital: And the Crises of Capitalism*, London, Profile Press; New York, Oxford University Press 2010 (translated into Spanish, Japanese, Portuguese, Chinese, Spanish, Turkish).

  Arguably the first fully 'public' book Harvey wrote, this accessible text offers a critical analysis of capitalism's enduring features and its recent dynamics, culminating in the global financial crisis of 2007–2008.

- *Rebel Cities: From the Right to the City to the Urban Revolution*, London, Verso, 2012 (translated into Portuguese, Spanish, Italian, Japanese, Korean, Chinese, French, Turkish, Greek, German).

  Another accessible, essayistic book about why much civic protest is urban based, about the importance of people's 'right to the city' and about the urban focus required of any anti-capitalist politics.

- *A Companion to Marx's Capital, Volume Two*, London, Verso, 2013 (translated into Portuguese, Japanese, German, Chinese).

Continuing Harvey's project to popularise Marx's key texts among a younger generation, this book focusses on Harvey's lesser read volume two of Capital.

- *Seventeen Contradictions and the End of Capitalism*, London, Profile Books; New York, Oxford University Press, 2014 (translated into Spanish, Portuguese, Turkish, Chinese, Japanese, Korean).

  This accessible book examines the totality of capitalism today through the lens of contradiction and dialectical change. It is addressed to the general reader.

- *Ways of the World*, London, Profile Books; New York, Oxford University Press, 2015; paperback version 2017 (translated into Chinese, Greek, Korean, Turkish).

  Yet another 'greatest hits' collection of Harvey's writings, with commentaries on each piece written by the author.

- *Abstract from the Concrete*, Harvard University Graduate School of Design, Sternberg Press, 2016.

  This short book comprises the complete transcript of a lecture Harvey gave at the Harvard University Graduate School of Design in March 2016, focussing on the rise and transformation of China for the most part. The back of the book contains a brief interview with Harvey by two architects based at Harvard.

- *Marx, Capital and the Madness of Economic Reason*, London, Profile Books; New York, Oxford University Press, 2017; paperback versions 2019 (translations scheduled in Chinese, Taiwanese, Japanese, Korean, Spanish, Turkish, Portuguese, Italian).

  Another book by Harvey that offers a Marxist interpretation of capitalism and its core characteristics. It is accessible and synoptic, mixing abstract analysis with references to contemporary economic and political affairs.

- *A Companion to Marx's Capital: The Complete Edition*, London, Verso, 2019.

  This large book covers all three volumes of Marx's Capital, introducing the texts to readers unfamiliar with them, while also making reference to Marx's notebooks from 1857 to 1861, first published as The Grundrisse in English in 1973.

- *The Anti-Capitalist Chronicles, London,* Pluto Press, 2021.

  This is a collection of edited transcripts of Harvey's video and podcast series of the same name. Conversational in style, Harvey covers many of Marx and Harvey's own key ideas but he attempts to show how these connect with current affairs, from the election of Trump, to Black Lives Matter, to the COVID-19 pandemic.

- *A Companion to Marx's* Grundrisse, London, Verso, forthcoming.

  Building on Harvey's companions to the three volumes of Capital, this book introduces readers to Marx's important preparatory notes from 1857 to 1861.

Appendix 3: A timeline of events of significance in David Harvey's lifetime

Wall Street crash; start of Great Depression	1929	
New Deal programme begins in the USA	1933	
	1935	David Harvey born in Gillingham, Kent, England
Second World War begins	1939	
	1943	Harvey is evacuated from Gillingham to escape bombing raids
Bretton Woods conference establishes new international monetary system	1944	
Second World War ends	1945	
National Health Service founded in the UK	1948	

Communist Party takes control of China	1949	
	1957	Harvey awarded degree, Cambridge University
	1960	Harvey spends one year as a postdoctoral researcher in Uppsala, Sweden
	1961	Harvey awarded PhD, Cambridge University; takes up Lectureship at Bristol University
Martin Luther King Jr. is assassinated in Memphis; rioting in US cities	1968	
	1969	Harvey moves to Johns Hopkins University, Baltimore; publishes *Explanation in Geography*
	1970	Harvey reads Marx for the first time
	1971	Harvey begins teaching Marx's *Capital*
Bretton Woods system is abandoned; General Pinochet takes power in Chile	1973	Harvey becomes full professor at Johns Hopkins; publishes *Social Justice and the City*
Threat of bankruptcy of New York City	1975	Harvey takes sabbatical leave in Paris

'Winter of Discontent' in the UK; China begins to open its economy	1978	
M. Thatcher becomes UK Prime Minister	1979	
R. Reagan becomes US President	1980	
Debt crisis in Latin America	1982	Harvey publishes *The Limits to Capital*
Miners' strike in the UK	1984	
	1985	Harvey publishes *The Urbanization of Capital* and *Consciousness and the Urban Experience*
Deregulation of the London Stock Exchange	1986	
	1987	Harvey becomes Halford Mackinder Professor of Geography at Oxford University
The fall of the Berlin Wall; democratic revolutions across Central and Eastern Europe	1989	Harvey publishes *The Condition of Postmodernity* and *The Urban Experience*
End of the USSR; deadly fire in Hamlet, North Carolina	1991	
Maastricht Treaty establishes the EU	1993	Harvey returns to Baltimore full-time; publishes *The Factory & the City*
NAFTA is ratified; Zapatista uprising	1994	
Commercial internet launched; WTO founded	1995	
	1996	Harvey has a major heart surgery; publishes *Justice, Nature and the Geography of Difference*
First New Labour government in the UK; Southeast Asian financial crisis erupts	1997	
'Battle of Seattle' protests against the WTO; G20 created	1999	
	2000	Harvey publishes *Spaces of Hope*
9/11 attacks on New York City and the Pentagon; US-led invasion of Afghanistan	2001	Harvey moves to CUNY; publishes *Spaces of Capital* collection

US-led invasion of Iraq	2003	Harvey publishes *The New Imperialism* and *Paris, Capital of Modernity*
	2005	Harvey publishes *A Brief History of Neoliberalism*
	2006	Harvey publishes *Spaces of Global Capitalism*
	2007	Harvey launches his website
Lehman Brothers collapse; start of GFC	2008	
World recession	2009	Harvey publishes *Cosmopolitanism and the Geographies of Freedom*
	2010	Harvey publishes *The Enigma of Capital* and *Companion to Marx's* Capital *vol. one*
Occupy Wall Street protests	2011	
	2012	Harvey publishes *Rebel Cities*
	2013	Harvey publishes *Companion to Marx's* Capital *vol. two*
	2014	Harvey publishes *Seventeen Contradictions*
	2015	Harvey publishes *Ways of the World*
Brexit vote in UK; D Trump becomes US President	2016	Harvey publishes *Abstract from the Concrete*
	2017	Harvey publishes *Marx, Capital and the Madness of Economic Reason*
COVID-19 lockdowns across the world	2020	Harvey publishes *Anti-Capitalist Chronicles*
Russia invades Ukraine; spike in energy prices, rising inflation across the world	2022	Harvey publishes *Companion to Marx's Grundrisse*

Index

Note: Page references in *italics* denote figures, in **bold** tables and with "n" endnotes.

Taylor & Francis Group
an informa business

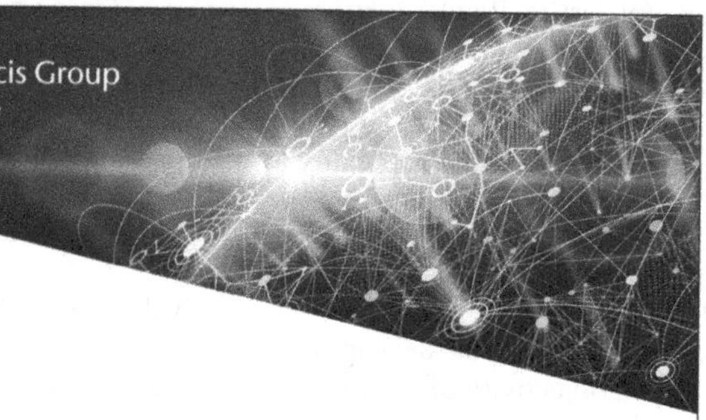

Taylor & Francis eBooks

www.taylorfrancis.com

A single destination for eBooks from Taylor & Francis with increased functionality and an improved user experience to meet the needs of our customers.

90,000+ eBooks of award-winning academic content in Humanities, Social Science, Science, Technology, Engineering, and Medical written by a global network of editors and authors.

TAYLOR & FRANCIS EBOOKS OFFERS:

- A streamlined experience for our library customers
- A single point of discovery for all of our eBook content
- Improved search and discovery of content at both book and chapter level

REQUEST A FREE TRIAL

support@taylorfrancis.com

Routledge
Taylor & Francis Group

CRC Press
Taylor & Francis Group